"If you are in the market for a historically informed guide to Trappist beer and each community's unique spirituality, Tomszak has brewed up the perfect recipe. He crafts his tales with vividness and ease, demonstrating that monastic life and its liquid gifts have more to offer us than we might expect. This insider's account of the finest Belgian beers is also a theological argument on radical alternatives to our hyper-capitalist ailments. It's a delightful book—drink up!"

—Colby Dickinson
Professor of Theology, Loyola University Chicago

"Marty Tomszak brings a unique perspective to his research, combining a passion for monastic spirituality with the connoisseurship of a true devotee of Trappist beers, presented as an enthusiastic journal of a pilgrimage. Silence, separation from the world, and care for creation are contemplated beside the time and space a brewery provides for fermentation, revealing the transformative power of both, encouraging encounter, conversation, and appreciation of the truly beautiful."

—Sr. Joanna Dunham
OCSO

"With this contemplative offering, Marty Tomszak deftly explains how, why, and where the rhythm of monastic life and the rhythm of brewing beer intersect. And when he talks to monks about 'listening with your heart' the need to read this book with your own heart becomes obvious."

—Stan Hieronymus
Author of *Brewing Local: American-Grown Beer*

"An insightful portrait of Trappist brewing, where quality, humility, and stewardship come together and can be tasted in the glass. A welcome companion for readers seeking more than tasting notes—seeking the Benedictine spirit behind them."

—Manu Pauwels
Head of Marketing, Brouwerij der Trappisten van Westmalle

"A novel and important work, Dr. Marty Tomszak is in a unique position to bridge the gap between the secular and religious worlds where these beers, breweries, and monks reside. More than a simple history or compilation of tasting notes, *Time, Silence, and the Yeast* gives us insight into who the monks are, the life they have chosen, and how their beers are both a product and reflection of these tenets and communities."

—John Laffler
Founder, Off Color Brewing

Time, Silence, and Yeast

Time, Silence, and Yeast

*A Song of Appreciation
for Trappist Communities
and Their Beer*

MARTY TOMSZAK

CASCADE *Books* • Eugene, Oregon

TIME, SILENCE, AND YEAST
A Song of Appreciation for Trappist Communities and Their Beer

Copyright © 2026 Marty Tomszak. All rights reserved. Except for brief quotations in critical publications or reviews, no part of this book may be reproduced in any manner without prior written permission from the publisher. Write: Permissions, Wipf and Stock Publishers, 199 W. 8th Ave., Suite 3, Eugene, OR 97401.

Cascade Books
An Imprint of Wipf and Stock Publishers
199 W. 8th Ave., Suite 3
Eugene, OR 97401

www.wipfandstock.com

PAPERBACK ISBN: 979-8-3852-3735-7
HARDCOVER ISBN: 979-8-3852-3736-4
EBOOK ISBN: 979-8-3852-3737-1

Cataloguing-in-Publication data:

Names: Tomszak, Marty, author.

Title: Time, silence, and yeast : a song of appreciation for Trappist communities and their beer / Marty Tomszak.

Description: Eugene, OR : Cascade Books, 2026 | Includes bibliographical references and index.

Identifiers: ISBN 979-8-3852-3735-7 (paperback) | ISBN 979-8-3852-3736-4 (hardcover) | ISBN 979-8-3852-3737-1 (ebook)

Subjects: LCSH: Trappists. | Breweries—Guidebooks. | Beer—Guidebooks. | Alcohol Religious aspects—Christianity.

Classification: TP577 .T66 2026 (paperback) | TP577 .T66 (ebook)

VERSION NUMBER 011326

To the Trappist monks that welcomed me with open arms and shine as a beacon of hope in the darkness, may contemplative vocations grow in perpetuity. You truly are leaving the world in a better place than you found it.

"I drink beer whenever I can get my hands on any. I love beer, and by that very fact, the world."

—Thomas Merton

Contents

Acknowledgments | ix
Introduction: Ancient Answers to Modern Conundrums | xiii

Chapter 1
Vibrant Community, Benedict of Nursia, Bernard of Clairvaux, and Armand-Jean de Rancé | 1

Chapter 2
Silence, Listen Carefully with the Ear of Your Heart | 22

Chapter 3
Abdij van Onze Lieve Vrouw van het Heilig Hart van Westmalle | 36

Chapter 4
Abbaye Notre-Dame de Scourmont | 57

Chapter 5
Abdij Maria Toevlucht | 77

Chapter 6
Abbaye Notre-Dame de Saint Rémy | 94

Chapter 7
Sint-Sixtusabdij Westvleteren | 105

Chapter 8
Abbaye Notre-Dame d'Orval | 123

Chapter 9
Abdij Onze Lieve Vrouw van Koningshoeven | 139

Conclusion: Only the Beginning of Perfection: A Word of Hope | 154

Bibliography | 159
Index | 163

Acknowledgments

THE LIST OF PEOPLE that deserve thanks for their hospitality, assistance, inspiration, commiseration, or simply their presence in my life as I worked could fill a book on its own. The nature of this project was communal from its very inception as the possibility of pursuing such a wild idea could never have been an individual undertaking. I am forever indebted to everyone listed below and if in my absentmindedness I have forgotten to mention someone, know that I thank you in the silence of my heart.

To begin with, my gratitude goes out to my loving wife, Betsy Tomszak. Her patience, support, and encouragement over the eighteen months that it took this project to move from the planning stages to its final submission were nothing short of saintly. Few partners would find it in their hearts to allow for a nearly four-month absence for beer drinking, monastic retreat, and research, much less push for it. In times when my imagination and will fell short, she gave me strength. Additional thanks go to our loving dogs, Birdie, Bobo, and Stasiu, who despite not understanding their role in providing joy during this process were ecstatic about doing so. To my brothers, Jacob Tomszak and Mike Tomszak, both of whom accompanied me on various parts of the journey at home and abroad; their growth as beer connoisseurs has already shown the infectiousness of these Trappist beers. Never-ending thanks are also due to Carolyn Latshaw who not only patiently and painstakingly proofread drafts of this manuscript, gave joyous feedback, and echoed its potential, but who pushed me to make the history and theology here vivid and lively. To Kamil Szpara, whose constant pushing of the boundaries of possibility and encouragement of my gifts are partially responsible for this idea in the first place. To my father Jarek Tomszak, whose introduction to Chimay started this all and whose own passion for writing I inherited. To my mother-in-law Mary Hopper Welander, who made the trek to visit me in Leuven and serves as an inspiration in blending

Acknowledgments

passion with vocation. To Stephen Hogberg, who housed me for the beginning portion of my European excursion and, more importantly, provided friendship throughout the journey. To David Andrew Schultz for challenging me to see the beer world differently. To Dan Martin whose support in navigating vocational struggles was invaluable during this project. Thanks also go to Whitney Harper and Magnolia for their companionship while I lived in Leuven, bringing a sense of normalcy to my life as I wrote. To Max Dennis whose early feedback set the tone for engaging with multiple audiences. To Renaud Gueret, whose constant curiosity about this project and nostalgia about his own Belgian roots proved motivational. To John Laffler, who never once hesitated to answer my industry-related questions but also served as an incredible partner for tastings, writing beer descriptions, and entertaining my overall silliness. Your role as a friend and mentor goes beyond what I can articulate. In a similar vein, thanks must extend to Colby Dickinson who not only read early drafts of this manuscript but whose role as my advisor and academic mentor directly led to my work here. I am thankful for such a loving community.

With regards to acknowledging those that came before me and served as inspiration for my work here, I must start with Stan Hieronymus whose prowess as *the* modern beer writer goes without saying. For him to take the time to meet with me in person on a trip to Chicago and offer not just encouragement and advice, but to express genuine interest in the project, was surreal. My indebtedness knows no bounds. To Caroline Wallace, Sarah Wood, and Jessica Deahl, though we have never met, your work on Trappist beer around the globe showed me where a passion project can lead and how to navigate the logistical intricacies of such an undertaking. Joy and quality exude from every word you write, and I cannot thank you enough. Similarly, to Jef van den Steen whose whimsical explorations of Belgian beer in his work helped me navigate the cultural intricacies I faced during my sojourn. To the great Michael Jackson, whose career blazed a trail for English speaking writers to enter the Belgian beer sphere generally and these abbeys specifically. We all follow in your footsteps. To the late Terrence G. Kardong, OSB, your commentaries on the Rule really made it a living document and showed its continued potential. A true evangelist for monastic vocations. To Carl McColman for your work on silence and its place in the modern Church, an important lesson that I hope to echo here. To Fr. Philip Timko, OSB, I am grateful for you instilling love for the ascetic tradition in me; my trajectory would have been so much different without you.

I would also like to thank those that made this book logistically possible. To my managing editor, Matthew Wimer and the rest of the Wipf and Stock/Cascade staff, your patience in entertaining my vision can never be repaid. To Lisa Driver, Carrie Miller, and the CAS Dean's office at Valparaiso University, your professional development funds and travel grants made this work possible. To Richard Klee, who first said "You should write a book about it." To Judith Gruber and the Katholieke Universiteit Leuven visiting researcher program, you gave me the space to pursue this project from a place of comfort. To the staff at Beer Temple, Hopleaf, Map Room, Dovetail, and especially Off Color Mousetrap, you provided not only places to work but opportunities for tasting, reflection, and contemplation as I wrote. Your feedback, commiseration, and guidance were constant reminders of how joyful beer spaces can be.

Lastly, to the brothers at Abbaye Notre-Dame de Scourmont, Abbaye d'Orval, Abbaye Notre-Dame de Saint-Remy, Sint-Sixtusabdij, Abdij van de Trappisten van Westmalle, Abdij Onze Lieve Vrouw van Koningshoeven, and Abdij Maria Toevlucht, I cannot put into words what I owe you. I will never be the same person again, for the better. I hope that gratitude exudes from these pages as more people come to value your labor, participate in your prayer, and grow to love you. Thank you, thank you, thank you.

Introduction

Ancient Answers to Modern Conundrums

Psssshhht! I will never forget the first time I opened a bottle of Trappist beer and poured it into the appropriate glass that came in the four-pack gift set given to me by my father on my twenty-first birthday. Chimay, he explained, was one of the best beers in the world—not only that but it was made by monks! This was to be of special interest to me as a student at Benedictine University double majoring in history and theology where some of my professors walked across from the Abbey to teach between breaks in the Liturgy of the Hours. My father reminisced about special occasions on which he had shared the beer with friends and now he was sharing it with me; it was marked as somewhat a rite of passage that I did not fully understand at that moment.

At the time, I was a burgeoning craft beer connoisseur working at a local bar that was riding the wave of the early 2010s craft expansion in the United States. The likes of Sierra Nevada, New Belgium, Goose Island, Dogfish Head, Stone, Bells, Two Brothers, and Firestone were well established brands that I was eagerly sampling after shifts, while Half Acre, Revolution, and Metropolitan were the new kids on the block in Chicago. I had an expanding palate (or so I thought) and an interest in the world's favorite beverage that went beyond college parties with kegs of whichever macro brand was cheapest that day. Beer reps visiting the bar along with friends working at breweries gave me access to a wide portfolio and I began pursuing the Cicerone certificates that were available to me at the time. I was spoiled by a diversity of riches and eager to learn. But trying that Chimay Bleu was something else entirely.

Everyone remembers moments that redefine what we thought we knew. Whether it is a life-changing novel, an album that shifts the direction of your discography, a theologian that alters the way one understands the Divine, a meal that shapes your tastes, or a palate defining beer, there are paradigmatic shifts in life, and this was one of those moments for me. Now, having worked in various capacities in the beer industry for over fifteen years including bartending, managing taprooms, staff education, brewing, and curating tastings, I can tell you all about Chimay Bleu. It is a Belgian strong dark ale stylistically (sometimes confused as a Quad) that pours a medium-heavy amber in color, 30–31 SRM (the fancy color chart that beer nerds use!), but with a creamy head; comes in at 9 percent ABV; is refermented with a second douse of yeast in the bottle leading to a higher carbonation level and making it highly quaffable; has notes of roasted malt, prunes, dates, raisins, and candied sugar on the body with a slight warm boozy finish; aromatics of stone fruit/peach are found on the nose from the distinct yeast profile; and a pleasantly crisp hop bitterness in its fresh iterations. Back then, I knew none of those things, but what I could articulate was "Wow."

The aroma, the taste, the texture, were like nothing I had ever had before, and it set me off on a course of trying every Trappist made beer I could get my hands on. Luckily for me, Chimay's entire catalogue and Orval were readily available to me in the States and my newfound appreciation for Belgian yeast expanded beyond just the Trappist made variants or even the Belgian oriented breweries themselves. I learned but was not surprised in the least bit by the fact that the likes of New Belgium and Goose Island had themselves been inspired by these styles and even had beers in their portfolios that were odes to these classics. Goose's Matilda was a clone of the glasses of Orval that founder John Hall consumed on a life-changing trip to Belgium, and New Belgium's Abbey Beer was a nod to the monk-made elixirs that quenched the thirst of Kim Jordan and Jeff Lebesch as they biked across the country and dreamed of an American brewery of their own. Those formative years in the industry followed a similar trajectory for me as Trappist beers became a gold standard for quality, opportunities for dialogue/the expansion of customer palates, and a staple presence on the beer lists that I had opportunities to influence.

Simultaneously, I was expanding in understanding the undergirding ethos of the Trappist beers I was enjoying so much. Working in those spaces was largely a means to an end as I pursued not just the aforementioned degree, but continued down an academic trajectory in theology. I completed my MA in early church history at Wheaton College and sat with

Introduction

the texts of early monastics in the process. Athanasius's *Life of St. Antony*, Basil of Caesarea's sermons blending communal living with Christian ethical imperatives, Gregory of Nazianzus's *Orations*, Gregory the Great's hagiography of St. Benedict, and St. Benedict's Rule itself all lined my shelves next to the likes of Michael Jackson's *Great Beers of Belgium* and Randy Mosher's *Tasting Beer*.

My first academic posting was at my alma mater where I taught required courses on the Benedictine tradition—a move that ensured all students leaving the school understood its monastic roots and appreciated the values associated with the Rule. After several years I began a PhD program in Theology at Loyola University Chicago and took a job in Metropolitan Brewing's taproom shortly after it opened as a way of supplementing my stipend. My dissertation focused on the radical community founded by Dorothy Day and Peter Maurin—the Catholic Worker—itself influenced by the monastic tradition generally and Dorothy Day's position as an Oblate at St. Procopius Abbey specifically (the very one located on Benedictine University's campus). Beer and monasticism, these two threads continued to weave between the intricacies of my life.

The two have been more definitive for me than I had originally thought, a revelation that occurred when friends, colleagues, and taproom guests started asking me not just to talk about the beers and communities that brewed them but when they began encouraging me to write about the intersection of two topics that I am passionate about. The following project is a synthesis of that knowledge made available to me by my training in the two fields. It is the product of several questions that I do not seek to answer but rather begin a conversation on. Mainly, why are some of the best beers in the world made by a group of persons who tie its production, at least partially, to divine inspiration? Why are those communities leading the charge in not just quality but also sustainability, eco-friendliness, and rejecting greedy consumerist models of growth? What do monastic communities based on the observance of St. Benedict's Rule have to teach us about the hectic and overwhelming ethos of contemporary society? How can the virtues of hospitality, silence, manual labor, and humility find their resurgence in that same sphere? Why might a 1500-year-old document and way of life have such an appealing hook for a spiritually decaying era? How could the communities and rhythmic liturgy that influenced me so much help others? And perhaps most importantly, may I have another glass?

Introduction

Naturally, these questions are not rhetorical, and conversations cannot happen in a vacuum. So, in conjunction with my place as a professor of theology in the American landscape, I was able to secure a visiting researcher grant at the Katholieke Universiteit Leuven in Belgium during the summer of 2024. In doing so, I began a journey of asking these questions and starting the conversation with the people best situated for such an endeavor, the monks themselves. Over the course of three months, I visited the seven active Trappist breweries in Belgium and the Netherlands. Stays at each community for several days at a time were accompanied by full participation in the liturgy of the hours; interviews with monks and lay brewing staff; retreat in meditative silence; in-depth historical research of each community; and a few surprises along the way.

Abbaye Notre-Dame de Scourmont (Chimay); Abbaye d'Orval (Orval); Abbaye Notre-Dame de Saint-Remy (Rochefort); Sint-Sixtusabdij (Westvleteren); Abdij van de Trappisten van Westmalle (Westmalle); Abdij Onze Lieve Vrouw van Koningshoeven (La Trappe); Abdij Maria Toevlucht (Zundert); and an apartment on campus at KU Leuven were my home for the summer. I will be forever grateful for the hospitality shown to me by each abbey and for their patience in entertaining my project. In the pages below, I hope to share not just the theological, historical, and beer-oriented knowledge I garnered over the course of three months, but also the deeply human renewal possible for all who visit these vibrant and loving communities.

With that being said, the fundamental purpose of this monograph is to re-visit the intricacies of the monastic vocation within the realm of Trappist communities that choose the production of beer as their source of livelihood. I aim to make that narrative accessible to the various publics that might be most impacted by this exploration. Academic theologians, lay persons interested in the uniqueness of religious orders, members of those orders themselves, students discerning their own vocations amidst a changing spiritual landscape, beer lovers enamored with Trappist beverages, brewers in awe of the technical aspects associated with these communities, countercultural brewery marketing teams, and those persons that traverse these groups in differing ways will hopefully be edified by the outcomes of this trip.

As a brief note, in undertaking this project, a central point of intersection between the processes present in the brewhouse and the processes present in the sanctuary undergirded my initial assumptions of how I

Introduction

would approach the aforementioned questions and audiences. While most religiously oriented pilgrims to these communities might enjoy the beer, they most often have little appreciation for those specifics of the monastic vocation that lead to its production or to the technical aspects of brewing itself. Conversely, those a-religious persons that congregate outside of the Abbey gates in anticipation of the impeccable liquid seldom care to understand how or why the beer in their glass is different from that of any other they have poured at their local establishments outside of its rarity, assumed technical excellence, and mystique.

Though I will address these questions in the body of this work, they were of far less importance than what I came to learn on this journey. Mainly, although the beer unequivocally sustains the work that these communities do, and perhaps it helped drive conversation at times, the beer became of secondary importance to relationships I built with and lessons I learned from those responsible for its production. There were tiny flames of both beer hunting and religious pilgrimage initially associated with the project that were quickly extinguished and replaced with a far deeper, more beautiful, and loving understanding of these communities.

To facilitate this ongoing conversation, the organization of the book itself will be structured in such a way that the themes and points of interest for each distinct audience can be opportunities for entry, but I hope the work is read and dissected in its entirety. Chapter 1 will begin by providing an overview of St. Benedict and the formation of his Rule, the Cistercian reforms of the twelfth century under St. Bernard of Clairvaux, and a brief summary of the Trappist reform under Armand-Jean Le Bouthillier de Rancé. This is a recap for those unfamiliar with the intricacies of monastic living and also highlights the distinct aspects of the Trappist tradition. Such contextualization is necessary for discussing the current contours of these communities and their ability to speak to the audiences highlighted above. Moreover, the unique trajectory of each Abbey bears explication as varying interpretations of mission creates the plethora of approaches present under the Trappist umbrella.

Chapter 2 will begin to ask questions and spark conversation about the lessons on offer from the Trappist communities via a discussion of the centrality of silence to the Cistercian Order, an element of human life starkly absent from our contemporary societal models. Beyond just discussing the contours of silence in the Rule of St. Benedict, allowing the monks themselves to highlight the importance of silence and allowing room for reflection, listening to others, and opening ourselves up to the divine in the everyday will take precedence. Where appropriate, my own reflections on the contemplative life experienced over the course of the three months spent in community will be added as I seek to connect the wisdom on offer from the brothers to some of the struggles I see within my own communities (the classroom, the beer industry, and our world generally). This conversation continues by exploring the ways in which the Trappist virtue of hospitality comes to the fore in these communities. Each abbey operates a guesthouse and makes hosting others a focal point of their vocation. However, the mere presence of quarters for retreat or refuge does not begin to cover the depth with which hospitality is ingrained into Trappist communities. In a world where we do not know our neighbors, much less care for their well-being, this segment of the monograph aims to revitalize fundamental aspects of human care.

The remaining chapters elevate the distinctions present in each abbey based on individual interpretations of Benedict's insistence on *Labora* (work) and their approaches to sustaining their community by the production of beer. Though each abbey shares similarities, no two are the same with regards to style, method, scale, marketing, or any other aspects of production. The trajectory of these chapters aims to not just satiate questions regarding the day-to-day operations of these communities across the beer enthusiast and religious person spectrum, but to allow them to shine in their own understanding of St. Benedict's model of proper living. Though I hope each of the chapters is given its own fair reading, these latter chapters will likely be a point of interest for beer nerds and religiously curious readers alike.

They include histories, an analysis of the contemporary facets of each abbey and brewery, along with interview transcripts that shed light on the beers and prayers alike. I also hope to begin a more nuanced conversation with regards to how each community interacts with a socio-economic and political world that is drastically at odds with the central ethos of both Christianity generally and the Cistercian understanding of contemplative praxis specifically. Discussions of sustainability, anti-profit models of production, care for creation, mutual aid orientation, and impact simplicity as guiding factors for subsistence will come to the fore here. By way of summary through a phrase I heard repeatedly from the brothers I met, these profiles will help to understand the importance of "leaving the world in a better place than we found it." This lesson is vital as both the secular and religious realms face an uphill battle against the destruction of the natural world we have seemingly forgotten that we are a part of and are actively killing.

It is my simple hope that through this project I may inspire readers not just to enjoy the beers created by these Trappist breweries, which everyone rightfully should, but that they may come to appreciate the persons, communities, and tenets responsible for creating them. Not a surface level nod to decaying ancient sensibilities, but an authentic engagement with forward thinking and lively people committed to serving the world and others. A quiet and subtle message with profound impacts on anyone who takes the time to listen is on offer here, I invite you to sit down with a glass or two of a Trappist beverage and tune in with the ear of your heart.

Chapter 1

Vibrant Community, Benedict of Nursia, Bernard of Clairvaux, and Armand-Jean de Rancé

WHILE THE BULK OF this project will focus on contemporary communities and the conversation I had with the brothers at each abbey, no examination would be complete without a distinct understanding of the guidelines adhered to by each community and their 1,500-year-old legacy. Three central figures shape the Cistercian tradition, and what follows is a brief introduction to them, as well as a basic primer to the daily activities, central beliefs, and vocational goals of the order.

Benedict of Nursia revolutionized Western Christianity as we know it, so much so that he is venerated as the patron saint of Europe and called the father of Western monasticism. His Rule (guidebook) serves as the bedrock for most Catholic monastic orders that follow a contemplative cenobitic lifestyle. For those new to monastic terms, this just means that these monks live in community with one another behind the walls of a cloister and focus on self-reflection, a rigorous prayer schedule, and the spiritual growth of their community as a whole.

Other religious orders, though devoted to prayer, can be labeled as "active" or "apostolic," meaning that they also turn outwards towards the world around them—though this book will show that Benedictine-influenced communities still serve others in their own way. Though all religious communities have a great respect for St. Benedict and his sixth-century monastic formulations, it is only the contemplative orders that strictly adhere to his Rule. My discussion of silence, humility, hospitality, labor, and prayer in the remaining chapters would not be possible without the guiding document authored by St. Benedict.

The second figure, twelfth-century monastic reformer Bernard of Clairvaux, was key in reinvigorating a stricter observance of St. Benedict's original Rule during a time when adherence to it had become lax. Leaving behind humility, simplicity, contemplation, and manual labor, the monks of Bernard's context held lavish land tracts, became involved in worldly affairs, and held political, economic, and church power far above anything Benedict could have imagined or wanted.

Bernard joined like-minded monks at the abbey in the French town of Citeaux that had spent the past century attempting to take a literal approach to Benedict's Rule and were granted official status and formed their own constitution in his lifetime. Under his leadership, a new community was formed in Clairvaux, and the movement grew to new heights. Communities proliferated across Europe in a wave of renewal, and Bernard's work can be directly tied to the continued success of the order today. Each of the abbeys visited on my trip owes its spiritual and geographic foundations to Bernard.

Lastly, Armand-Jean Le Bouthillier de Rancé is the third figure of importance. He served as Abbot of La Trappe in the seventeenth century and was key in reforming the Cistercian Order of the Strict Observance after another period of laxity. Taking steps beyond what Bernard had originally envisioned, penitential practices, silence, rededications to poverty, strictness in fasting, and even a cap on the pursual of education defined de Rancé's form of piety. Though often mentioned less than his two predecessors, his influence is distinctly felt throughout each Trappist community.

Benedict of Nursia: The Founder of Western Monasticism

St. Benedict was born c. 480 CE in Nursia, Italy, to a wealthy family that included his twin sister Scholastica (herself a founder of an adjacent community for women). In his early twenties, Benedict became disillusioned with the moral decay of the pagan world around him as he saw his peers at university plagued by vice, greed, and selfishness. He retreated into seclusion where he sought to outline a way of living that was drastically different from that of society and focused on simplicity, humility, contemplation, and spiritual growth. As his guide he had the examples of the Eastern monastic tradition (Alexandrian communities of the second century and the monastic Rule authored by Basil of Caesarea) as well as a burgeoning movement in the hills outside of Rome attempting to reinvigorate the ascetic tradition. The development of such a lifestyle led to his foundation of a new monastic community which served as refuge for like-minded seekers.

This is largely where the generally verifiable historical information we have on Benedict of Nursia stops because there are only two written sources that corroborate information about his life. First, the Rule that Benedict authored for himself and his communities to follow. This gives us insight into how he lived rather than being a collection of biographical details. The bulk of my reflection on contemporary communities will reference this document as it continues to be vital for the day-to-day operations of monastic life.

The second and most prominent document, Pope Gregory the Great's account of Benedict's life in his *Dialogues*, is a collection of stories about the pious lives of Italian saints.[1] Authored in the late sixth century, Gregory was uplifting these figures to provide hope to an Italian peninsula ravaged by famine, plague, and a series of tribal invasions in the wake of the fall of Rome. Their miraculous works, communal living, virtuous examples, and unshakable faith were to serve as inspiration for people who thought they had been abandoned by God as their world was collapsing around them.

Though insightful, Gregory's account is categorized as hagiography. This means the purpose of the literature is not to provide an unbiased historical accounting of someone's life but to emphasize and elevate their holiness for the purpose of veneration. Moreover, poetic exaggerations and a focus on miracles take center stage to reiterate the saint's ability to serve as a model for spiritual edification and pious emulation.

This is not to say that Pope Gregory's account of Benedict's life was entirely fictitious. Gregory attests to the fact that he was given the biographical details by four monks that knew Benedict well. Three of these were abbots of various communities founded by Benedict including Honoratus, the abbot of Montecasino. For contemporary readers, it seems strange that word of mouth would be a trusted source, but for cultures largely reliant on oral histories, this was not a problem. Though Pope Gregory's *Dialogues* are readily available in their entirety, I will attempt to briefly summarize some key events in Benedict's life.

---

1. Kadong, *Life of St. Benedict by Gregory the Great.*

Pope Gregory begins his account by alluding to Benedict's virtue, humility, and longing for solitude being present at an early age, going as far as to tell readers that even as a young boy Benedict had the heart of an old man and was wise beyond his years. It is also made clear that he came from a wealthy, deeply religious, and well-respected family, which also meant that he had access to the precious resource of education. He left Nursia to study in Rome, but he was not alone as his status allowed him to be accompanied by a nurse (a mix of chaperon and servant). There, he pursued what we today might call a degree in humanities. Like most students, he was faced with questions of purpose, vocation, the meaning of life, and how to avoid the vice of the world at odds with his own burgeoning desire to live a more virtuous life pleasing to God.

While trying to party less, deciding that college isn't for you, or having a religious conversion are timeless occurrences on university campuses, the path that Benedict chose instead was truly unique. He left behind his family's wealth (except for his nurse who refused to leave him) and departed for a semi-monastic community attached to St. Peter's Church in the Affile neighborhood of Rome. His time here was spent in deep prayer and devotion that planted the seeds of ascetic life that would define him.

This was also the site of Benedict's first miracle, according to Gregory, where a wheat sieve borrowed from a neighbor by his nurse broke, leaving her distraught. Benedict too was moved to tears seeing her in anguish and upon praying over it, the sieve was repaired and returned whole. The community was in awe of the holiness of the then-still-young Benedict and praised him relentlessly.

Following this episode, Benedict sought further seclusion and fashioned a home for himself out of a remote cave in Subiaco where for three years he engaged in prayer, contemplation, and rigorous fasting. The only person who knew his whereabouts was a monk, Romanus, from a monastic community near the hills that occasionally brought Benedict loaves of bread that he would stow away from meals at the abbey. The sojourn in Subiaco was a time full of temptation and hardship for Benedict as he grew in his spiritual journey (a motif that is supposed to mirror Jesus of Nazareth's forty days in the desert). This is also where Benedict's affinity for reciting the Psalms grew as they provided consistency, refuge, and a schedule that would make their way into his Rule.

He was eventually interrupted by shepherds following their flock and coming across his dwelling (sometimes interpreted as another reflection of Jesus's own life). Gregory shares that this encounter was followed not just by their conversion to virtuous living but through word-of-mouth, crowds of people visited Benedict to hear him preach and proclaim the joys of ascetic living.[2] His newfound fame came with the usual hallmarks of deflecting praise and wishing only for solitude. This was not to be, as the local monastic community asked Benedict to replace their abbot in the wake of his passing.

Reluctantly, Benedict agreed but only after a distinct warning that his own understanding of spiritual rigor might be at odds with their lifestyle. By this point of his monastic career, he had developed an understanding that each day should be divided into equal parts of prayer, work, and sleep with little room for deviation. It was only a matter of time before Benedict's initial weariness was justified as the community began grumbling about the rigidity of their new schedule.

Determined to remedy their mistake, the monks plotted to kill Benedict and return to their laxity. Having poisoned the glass of wine that was customary to have with dinner, they awaited his death. However, upon praying over it to give thanks, the glass miraculously shattered. Benedict humbly told the community there was no need for such drastic measures and that they should go find an abbot more to their liking. He returned into solitude where the hagiography recounts him "growing in virtues and miracles" for many years.

There came a time when Benedict's vocation turned outwards, and he was called to teach others the virtuous life. Gregory recounts the formation of the twelve monastic communities founded by Benedict as he sought to make the "secrets" of his spiritual living available to everyone who chose to pursue such a path. Under his guidance, the communities thrived as word spread of something special happening in the hills of Subiaco. So much so that even the most well-off and politically connected families sought to have their children raised in the Benedictine monastic communities.

As clamor grew, so did envy. Gregory shares another attempt on Benedict's life from a jealous priest and a poisoned loaf of bread (this time carried away by a friendly crow that Benedict fed and preached to). To escape further plots, Benedict selected a group of monks to start a singular large mother house far away from the original communities. In 529 CE, they settled in a mountainous region eighty miles southeast of Rome. The cloister at Montecasino was constructed on the site of a former temple to

---

2 Kadong, *Life of St. Benedict by Gregory the Great*, Book II, Ch. 1.

Apollo—the alter of which Benedict destroyed as he built a Christian chapel in its place. Montecasino reflected the ardent dedication to manual labor present in Benedict's communities as the *Dialogues* extensively portray its construction. Fashioning every aspect of their home by hand would set a trend that continued for centuries.

The Benedictine value of stability was certainly formulated in the wake of Benedict's own tumultuous life up until this point. Montecasino would be his home for the duration of his life and is the site of his tomb, which is a pilgrimage destination for thousands each year. Gregory tells us that Benedict prepared his burial place on his own as he wanted to ensure he was buried within the walls of the cloister. This aspect of eternal membership is beautifully reflected even today with each of the Trappist abbeys boasting well-manicured cemeteries for all the brothers who have passed (often next to the sanctuary that is the center of the monastic day).

It is also here that Benedict codified all of his teachings and authored his Rule to govern over the communities that came to call him Father. Gregory does not dwell on its authorship or content—because it is attached in its entirety to the *Dialogues*—but importantly notes that it is a vital resource to understanding Benedict "for the holy man could not possibly teach otherwise than he lived."[3] Though it will be outlined extensively below, it is important to note here that the Rule's authorship was not undertaken as a rigid and immovable doctrinal document but as guidebook and incremental outline for those joining the growing order. It was a blueprint born out of Benedict's own experience and spiritual journey.

The remainder of the account in *Dialogues* outlines miracles performed by Benedict, highlights the curbing of temptation by his community, catalogues the expansion of the Benedictine order to numerous daughter monasteries in his own lifetime, shows Benedict navigating the tumultuous political sphere with tact, and emotionally portrays his death and burial at Montecasino in 547 CE.

Thematically, many of the miracles continue to mirror occurrences from the Gospel narratives themselves—the multiplication of bread to feed the monastery, the healing of a leper, raising a boy from the dead, and various exorcisms—as the connection between the holiness of Benedict and the figure of Jesus are made clear. Benedictine abbots are the representatives of Christ within their respective communities in the wake of this example. Again, whether we accept the occurrences as factual or not is beyond the

---

3. Kadong, *Life of St. Benedict by Gregory the Great*, ch. 37.

scope of this work and is found within the realm of faith for each reader. However, the aura of inspiration from the humble figure of Benedict is something I hope everyone can take away from these attestations.

In Benedict, we have someone that was appalled by the ways of the world around him—its greed, wastefulness, spiritual stagnation, selfishness, and chaos—choosing instead a life of solitude, simplicity, and contemplation in service of God. So revolutionary was his turn to the labor of his own hands, prayer, fasting, and service to others that those similarly disillusioned with society flocked to him. I now turn to the guidebook that led them.

The Rule of St. Benedict: A Little Guide for Beginners

In order to navigate the multiplicity of audiences for this book, this introduction to the Rule is not meant to be exhaustive nor theologically overwhelming. This is meant to be an overview that is both approachable and curiosity inspiring. Yes, the Rule has been predominantly utilized to outline the daily living of those that have taken religious vows, but Benedict also reminds us in the prologue that his words of guidance are aimed at all who undertake journeys of spirituality. Therefore, the Rule has also been utilized by parishes, schools, individual seekers, and curious skeptics to answer questions about virtuous living, communal formation, discipline, compassionate leadership, and interpersonal relationships.

Nothing illustrates this better than the confluence of people I encountered in my summer of abbey visits. I shared meals, prayer services, and conversations with visitors that included practicing Catholics (from conservative skeptics of the then Pope Francis to a queer professor whose various ministries were supported by the Trappists), Presbyterians, a Baptist minister, agnostics, atheists, and even a Buddhist monk that had an affinity for the Trappist life because of Thomas Merton's writing. Obviously, these visitors were not adhering to the Rule in its entirety, but their involvement in these communities via retreat points to the widespread influence that this ancient document has had and continues to have for all sorts of persons beyond the walls of cloisters.

So, what exactly is a Rule? Translated from the Latin *regula*, it literally referred to a ruler or a straight edge used for measurement. Within the religious sphere, it refers to documents that emerged in the late third and early fourth centuries as ascetic communities attempted to find uniformity in guidance, organization, and spiritual practice. This helped to focus the ascetic life in a way that was less scattered and rooted in accountability.

The most famous Rules before Benedict authored his were Pachomius's Rule (traditionally seen as the first written *regula*), St. Basil's *Asketikon*, and the lengthy *Rule of the Master* (written anonymously). All three heavily influenced the *Rule of St. Benedict* with parts being borrowed verbatim from all three documents—a common practice as these were guidebooks for living, not theological treatises or personal literary projects. What Benedict was attempting to do with his own Rule was to concisely summarize the lengthier anonymous rule while also adding his own wisdom.

Structurally, the Rule is divided into seventy-three chapters preceded by a prologue. The "chapters" themselves are fairly short with some only being a few sentences and the document totals less than ninety pages. Benedict was aware of how daunting the previous iterations of rules were, and he wanted to provide a starter guide for those pursuing virtuous living. The final chapter reiterates this approach and recommends in-depth analysis of Scripture and the writings of the early church for those who are ready. It is no surprise that this text became the standard for Western monasticism as it is easily accessible and yet packed full of insight.

Thematically, it deals with just about everything one can think of with regards to monastic living. It provides the practical outline for how the day is to flow; including what times to pray and how (outlining services coinciding with Psalms); the types of work to be done around the monastery; the schedule of meals, how much is to be eaten and drunk, what is to be read to the monks as they contemplate in silence over their food; and even how the rooms are to be organized for sleeping. Such rigid structures were not just a remedy for the laxity that Benedict had seen throughout his career, but a reflection of the balance necessary between work, prayer, and rest for monks to grow in the way he had.

This focus on cohesion and moderation naturally prioritizes prayer—monks are to drop whatever it is they are doing when the bells chime for the seven daily liturgical services—but Benedict was very much trying to avoid a life of pure piety devoid of personal and communal responsibility. He warned against the types of monks that wandered lost without the guidance of a rule or a commitment to work, detesting the ways in which they were guided by individual whims and appetites.

Work was the great equalizer within Benedict's communities as those monks with impoverished backgrounds and those offered up by the extremely rich, those with education and those without, all labored side by side. Pope Gregory recounts in the *Dialogues* that even the sons of senators were handed agricultural tools upon entering the communities, a drastic difference from both the secular realm of the time and other monastic communities that were more leisurely. This was because Benedict saw structured labor as spiritually forming. Not in the same way as prayer was, but just as important.

Although the phrase most associated with the Benedictine tradition—*Ora et Labora* (work and prayer)—was never actually uttered by Benedict, he did coin such gems as "idleness is the enemy of the soul" and "those that live by the labor of their hands are truly monks." The thirty-first chapter of the Rule even tells us that the mundane tools of labor—kitchen utensils, garden tools, even the clothes that the monks wear—are to be regarded with the same honor as the sacred vessels on the altar. Self-sustainability became a hallmark of Benedictine communities and is the facet most responsible for our ability to share the wonderful beers that will be covered later in this book.

This labor-centric ethos was also reflected in the way that Benedict approached the prayer life of his communities. There was no secret passcode, no euphoric outpouring of nirvana, or magic snapping of the fingers to reach spiritual breakthrough. Rather, Benedict was pragmatic in his understanding of growth. Repetition, consistency, and communal accountability were his chosen tools of prayer as he laid out his program for advancing along the path of loving and serving God.

The Divine Office, sometimes known simply as the Liturgy of the Hours, is the schedule that governs the day for each monastic community. It consists of seven designated communal prayer times spread throughout the day, including Night Office (4:00 a.m.), Lauds (7:00 a.m.), Terce (10:30 a.m.), Sext (noon), None (2:00 p.m.), Vespers (5:00 p.m.), and Compline (7:30 p.m.), one of which also serves as a service with Eucharist (usually Sext). Monks are expected to be at each of these unless there is need for an exception, which although rare, did occur throughout my time at the abbeys. Visitors, whether on a retreat or from the local parish, are of course welcome to attend any of these and I cannot recommend full participation in the liturgy enough.

The format for these services revolves around the singing of the Psalms, the inclusion of other Scripture readings in congruence with the schedule of the Catholic Liturgy of the Word, and the recitation of the Lord's

Prayer. St. Benedict focused on the Psalms explicitly because of their ability to be easily repeatable (many of the brothers have the Psalter memorized), the praise-oriented nature of the passages, and the general feel of calling for God's presence. The spiritual transformation achieved through such a cyclical recitation is evident even in just a few days spent at an abbey and one quickly gains an appreciation for the liturgical life of the Benedictine tradition.

In addition to the public prayer life of the monasteries, the Rule also calls for personal growth via *Lectio Divina*, a unique way of prayerfully reading Scripture that can be done individually or in a group. Initially developed by Gregory of Nyssa in the fourth century, it was extensively implemented by Benedict. Literally translated as "divine reading," the practice calls for full immersion into contemplative reflection on short passages from the Bible. The goal is not to gain theological insight or to parse the passages via biblical criticism (historical context, authorship details, linguistics, etc.) but to be present with God. It is a meditative approach done in silence with the goal of spiritually listening to what God is saying to individuals.[4]

Divided into four steps—*lectio* (read), *meditatio* (meditation), *oratio* (prayer), *contemplatio* (contemplation)—the process revolves around a repetitive reading of the same passage at least four times alongside each of the steps. After a period of silence, the first read is done with an eye on any words, images, or associations that stick out to the individual. The second read is meant to spark a conversation with God, meditation here means listening to where the Holy Spirit is guiding us. Meaning is assigned to the passage from the outside rather than evoked by the individual themselves. Upon a third reading, we are called to respond to what God is saying to us. This prayer can be done in various ways. Some people prefer journaling during this time, others pray silently, or if it is being done in a group, a prayer leader might speak on behalf of the group before giving time for individual response. The fourth and final read through is followed by a time of complete silence where the individual is meant to just sit in the presence of God and be guided to a final reflection on what the chosen passage might mean for their life.

Again, the process in its entirety is ultimately about fostering a relationship with God rather than being an instance of biblical study. Its implementation throughout the day is not limited to the cloister, each guest room also has a Bible and basic instructions for *Lectio Divina*. Whether someone

---

4. For more, see Linman, "Lectio Divina and Holy Conversation."

is religious or not, the meditative practice and rhythmic silence can be calming and centering, so I encourage all visitors to give it a try. It became a point of commonality among my fellow guests as everyone, regardless of background, felt that they were growing in community together.

Beyond its structural aspects, the Rule also provides instruction on developing virtues like humility, hospitality, obedience, stability, silence, moderation, and stewardship not just internally but with regards to the entire community and facing outwardly towards the World beyond the cloister as well. Roughly a quarter of its length is devoted to growth in these areas of spirituality and personhood which are interconnected with the more mundane aspects of daily living. The wholistic shaping of both the spirit and the body is reflective of the overarching dual-natured reality present in the Catholic understanding of humanity.

The *imago Dei* of each person (the reality of being made in the image of God) is reflected in creativity, intellect, spirit, responsibility, and labor simultaneously. Benedict's guidelines allow for the flourishing of humanity in each of these categories. The later chapters of this work follow some of these virtues as I came to appreciate and understand them in my time with the Cistercians and which I hope might provide answers to some of the burning questions of our era. I will attempt to tie them together via the reflections offered by the monks themselves in our interviews together, but it is important to note now that human progress is at the heart of how Benedict understood his faith.

Benedict also extensively discusses what type of person and leader the abbot should be. Mirroring Christ, they run the community with both ultimate authority and a deep sense of humility where they lead by example and through compassion. Exceptions to the Rule are encouraged where necessary—such as for the elderly, the sick, or those struggling with a particular aspect of monastic life. The Rule extends such discretion to readmitting monks that may have abandoned their vocation or left the community and reconciling with brothers that have seriously violated the Rule. The abbot is responsible for making decisions specific to their community as he guides them along both spiritually and in the labor aspects so vital for each monastery.

Ultimately, St. Benedict's Rule came to be the benchmark for Western monasticism. Though Montecasino was overrun by Lombardian raiders in 577 CE, the first community founded by Benedict was able to seek refuge in Rome and continue its way of life there. An initial growth spurt was largely aided by Pope Gregory the Great as he himself spent his early clerical career in a monastery and encouraged the vocation for others.

The *Dialogues* made the remnants of the Western Empire aware not just of the Rule but of the virtuous life of Benedict as well (I often make the comparison for my students that reading through the lives of the Saints was like scrolling through Instagram for sixth-century persons). As communities spread in the centuries that followed, Benedict's guidelines for monastic life became the official format for all monasteries in Western Europe in 816 CE. This plan of conformity codified what was already common practice, and the lineage of Benedict was further enshrined into the Western Church. His Rule continues to be the bedrock of monasticism even in its modern forms.

By way of summary, the Rule in its entirety is a guide for divesting from one's own earthly desires and selfish will in order to grow both individually and communally in the presence of God. It would go on to be a guidebook for thousands of communities across centuries as they pursued a life that was self-sustaining, fulfilling, and focused on obedience to Christ, the abbot, and to the Other. It is vital to us not just historically but as the central reason for the hospitality shown to me throughout my summer sojourn in Belgium and the Netherlands. In a sense, it is truly a living document that we may experience both in the vibrant communities born from it and in the individual contemplative growth taught in its pages.

Bernard of Clairvaux: Guide, Orator, and Doctor of the Church

Though there are active Benedictine communities today, it is the Trappists that concern me here. So, I must briefly describe how it is we got from a discussion of St. Benedict and his Rule to a different Order. To do so, I must present Bernard of Clairvaux, a semi-controversial figure, but one largely responsible for the spread of the communities deeply revered for the fruits of their manual labor. Much like with Benedict, without Bernard the beer you are holding as you read this might never have been brewed.

In a pattern quite familiar to monasticism throughout Christian history, ebbs and flows between sincerity and laxity are common and came to the fore in the late tenth and early eleventh centuries. With regards to the Benedictine tradition, the property holdings, political influence, and financial wealth acquired from donors seeking to be involved in the Order had drastically altered the day-to-day operations within monasteries. The separation between the world and the cloister had been impacted as growing responsibilities to both society and the institutionalized church became the norm and allowed for frequent exceptions to the Rule.

Dissatisfaction with a looser interpretation of Benedictine guidelines came to a head in 1098 at the Benedictine Abbey of Molesme, a daughter house of the famous Cluny Abbey in France. Abbot Robert believed that the order had strayed too far from the ideals of voluntary poverty, simplicity, humility, intertwined community, and manual labor. In response, he and twenty-one of his monks decided to start a new community in Citeaux with an eye on a stricter interpretation of Benedict's guidelines. It is important to note that at this moment they did not break from the Benedictine tradition but rather saw themselves as living more faithfully to the vows they had taken.

As some of the community of Molesme remained behind, Robert was recalled to the motherhouse while Abbot Alberic took over at Citeaux and Brother Harding (later to succeed Alberic) began outlining chartering documents for what would become the Cistercian Order. Abbot Harding's *Carta Caritatis* (literally the Charter of Charitable Love) was revolutionary as a founding document.[5] When it was finally accepted as a Dogmatic Constitution by Pope Calixtus II in 1119, the Cistercians became the first ever official Catholic monastic order in the way that we understand them now.

The charter itself aimed to reform the way that individual abbeys were run, especially via uniformity across communities; required visitation of each community by abbots of other houses; a required General Chapter meeting; expanded and clarified processes for taking vows; and a streamlining of the way in which new communities could be founded and sustained without the interference of benefactors or other outside influences. In a sense, it took the spirit of both the Rule and Benedict's life, codified them, and looked to avoid the shortcomings that had become apparent in Western monasticism. The structure for the Cistercian Order was clear, and Bernard of Clairvaux was the perfect person to spark an unprecedented period of growth.

Unlike with St. Benedict, Bernard's story comes to us from a multitude of sources and extensive historical corroboration. Similarly, the texts available to us authored by Bernard himself far outnumber the singular Rule offered by Benedict. With regards to the most comprehensive account of

5. Gregg, "Beginning with the *Carta Caritas.*"

Bernard, we have the *Vita Prima*, authored by his friend, companion, and unofficial secretary, William of Saint Thierry, while Bernard was still alive.[6]

The *Vita Prima* in its final form of six parts was edited and further expanded by both Arnold of Bonneval and Geoffrey of Auxerre in the decades following Bernard's death as part of the process of his canonization. It importantly traces not just the traditional aspects present in biographies but gives readers an extensive look into the spiritual progression that Bernard underwent throughout his life, including extensive struggles with his own piety and participation in monastic community. These reflections would go on to serve as sources of humility for generations of monks to come and gave raw access to a monastic figurehead in a way that is unique for a figure of his historical importance.

Beyond just the *Vita Prima*, the sheer number of publications available to us authored by Bernard himself also help situate the Trappist orders of today in terms of organization and theological trajectory. Correspondences with religious leaders (including a direct line of communication with his former monk Pope Eugenius III) and secular leaders alike allowed him to "network" as the movement grew. His biblical commentaries, sermons, meditations, theological treatises, and prayer compilations are equally impressive, bolstering his contributions to Christianity. All of these documents together offer us a look into Bernard's most formative moments.

Born in 1090 to Burgundian parents who by modern terms might be considered upper class, Bernard lived a comfortable life that included an education in the humanities that prepared him for the intense rhetorical prowess and high level of biblical interpretation he would become famous for. His family's land holdings were supported by the various knights in his father's charge. Though the knight's vocation was shared by some of Bernard's brothers, Bernard himself would never take up the sword (at least not literally).

In various historical texts available to us, he recounts both the military campaigns his father supported as well as times he and his brothers played knights growing up. This ingrained a sense of rigidity and order as well as an affinity for military-like organization in Bernard's life that would serve him well in his more spiritually oriented life. It also helps to explain how and why Bernard would later come to help found the Knights Templar and advocate for a Crusade to reclaim the Holy Land.

---

6. William of Saint-Thierry, *Vita Prima of Bernard of Clairvaux*.

Shortly after his schooling in the humanities, somewhere around 1111, Bernard began an informal monastic-like community within the bounds of his property at Chatillon. Likely sparked by the recent death of his mother (the source of Bernard's vigorous faith), this initial entrance into the ascetic life lasted for several months and was a foreshadowing of the influence that Bernard would have in the future. Through his strong personality, full of charisma and charm, as well as his advanced literary skills, he was able to convince over two dozen family members and close friends to join him in his ascetic foray.

This time was largely shaped by a sense of rigor that would come to dominate Bernard's monastic approach. Intense fasting, unceasing prayer, an extreme dedication to scriptural commentary, and a focus on emulating Christ's sojourn in the desert were the central facets of Bernard's ascetic model. This experimental period was formalized into a permanent vocation as Bernard convinced his early followers to join him in committing fully to this lifestyle within the walls of Citeaux in 1112. His entrance into the burgeoning Cistercian community would radically alter his life's trajectory, and the Order itself would never be the same again.

Upon arriving in Citeaux, Bernard and his followers immediately began an intensive lifestyle that revolved around not just the spiritual aspects of the monastic vocation but focused on the revival of manual labor undertaken by Citeaux's then abbot, Stephen Harding. When the time came to pursue Harding's vision of communal expansion via daughter houses, Bernard was selected to become abbot of a new monastery in Clairvaux just three years into his sojourn at Citeaux.

The hagiographical account in the *Vita Prima* points to a lack of basic resources plaguing the new monastery as they approached their first winter in 1115. Disaster was averted by Bernard miraculously healing a man whose wife in turn enthusiastically donated supplies to the monks. This occurrence was followed up with a plethora of healings attested to in the *Vita* and helped garner even more attention to the new Cistercian house. Bernard's fame grew far and wide, through which the Cistercian Order came to have connections and correspondences with people throughout the region.

Unfortunately, it also became clear that Bernard's dedication to the extremes of monastic life was not just causing a growth in curiosity or spiritual fervor but that his own well-being was severely impacted. Bouts of illness and prolonged inability to perform manual labor were common as his malnutrition, sleep deprivation, and what today we might call anxiety or depression ran rampant. Not only did it impact his day-to-day functioning as an abbot, but Bernard was ill throughout the General Chapter meeting of 1119 that formally created the Cistercian Order.

The year following the monumental General Chapter meeting was significant for Bernard in that he spent time in seclusion from the monks at Clairvaux to regain his health. Frequent vomiting from his eating disorder had reached the point of becoming disruptive to the community. Although he would suffer from such illnesses for the rest of his life, this initial attempt at separation and accommodation was fruitful for Bernard. His seclusion saw the publication of his first official works, which included *De Gradibus Superbiae et Humilitatis*—a treatise expanding on St. Benedict's guide for humility—and a collection of homilies entitled *De Laudibus Mariae*—all dealing with a revitalization of praising the Virgin Mary. The former would become foundational in Cistercian spiritual formation as monks grew into their vocation and the latter reemphasized the association that the burgeoning Order had to the Mother of God.

Even to this day, the commentary on the "Steps of Humility" is among the first texts that someone entering the novitiate (a monastic trial period) begins studying. For Bernard, focusing on the realization of our human shortcomings (pride, selfishness, arrogance, laziness, etc.) opens the door for the humble trifold remedy of loving God, loving ourselves, and loving others. In many aspects, this is the true purpose of monastic community. This timeless text became the foundation for exploring whether the vocation is right for each individual and ultimately reveals just how well Bernard understood the inner struggles faced by the faithful. A reorganization of priorities, dedication to the service of others, and a commitment to pursuing virtue has helped countless monks to follow in his footsteps as they begin their ascetic life in this reflection on humility. Ultimately, Bernard was able to articulate the depths of the human condition in a way that was simple, approachable, and yet deeply profound and soul stirring.

With regards to the homilies on Mary, each abbey is dedicated to her and their names reference some theological title of Christ's Mother. The reflections on the Virgin Mary also led Bernard down a path of frequently incorporating the theological theme of abbot as mother when discussing the type of leadership that was to be present in Cistercian Abbeys. The maternal imagery present in the homilies and other treatises is not only reserved for Mary but also includes references to God as Mother; Christ as Mother of the church; other biblical figures as maternal; and most importantly Bernard/any Cistercian abbot as mother of the community. I share this here not only because it offers insight into the commonality of feminine portrayals of the Divine in previous centuries but because it also points to the continued ability of Cistercian communities to explore biblical themes in a way that might seem countercultural to the rest of the institutional church.

A more extensive look at the theological development of Bernard's career is not necessary here. For those that are interested in the vast collection of his correspondences with various high-profile church figures as well as the plethora of treatises, sermons, and prayers that he compiled I would suggest both *Sancti Bernardi Opera* edited by Jean Leclerq (*the* Bernard scholar) and *The Letters of St. Bernard of Clairvaux* gathered and translated by Bruno Scott James. What is important to note is that this initial year of writing would not be an anomaly for Bernard, and his eventual title of "Doctor of the Church" was well deserved for the Cistercian giant. This prestigious designation is officially bestowed by the Catholic Church on those that have made significant contributions to doctrine, theology, and the growth of understanding among the faithful and is not a common occurrence (only thirty-seven such titles have been given in almost two thousand years of Catholic history).

Over 500 letters, almost 300 sermons, and two-dozen treatises made up his impressive bibliography that has been a source of awe from theologians, Cistercian monks, and every day lay persons since their authorship. Moreover, a defense of Catholic Trinitarian Orthodoxy during a famous dispute with Peter Abelard added to the merit of his title and is where Bernard's name appears most commonly in theology courses.

In just the first three years after the founding charter, Bernard adopted three more monasteries at Tres-Fontaines, Fontenay, and Foigny. The fervor associated with the Order increased beyond what was initially thought to be possible as Bernard was responsible for the founding of sixty-eight daughter houses in his lifetime. The total number of Cistercian monasteries influenced by him reached around one hundred and seventy. Beyond this tangible growth, Bernard has always been referred to as the Order's "spiritual father" and at times Cistercians have been referred to as "Bernardines."

Even before his passing in 1153, this magnanimous figure had become one of the most influential persons of the twelfth century, whose legacy in the monastic realm is unmatched save perhaps by St. Benedict himself. The shaping of Cistercian spirituality, the Order's organization, the proliferation of its monasteries, an unwavering commitment to communication and accountability between houses, a homiletic approach of care and contemplation, responsibility to the outside world, and practices of sustainability through labor are just a few of Bernard's influences.

Armand-Jean le Bouthillier de Rancé: Strict Observance and Pivotal Reform

This brings me to the third and final figure responsible for the Trappist tradition as we know it today, Armand-Jean le Bouthillier de Rancé. Born into a prestigious Parisian family on January 9, 1626, de Rancé would inherit a life of wealth, power, and controversy. Named after his godfather Cardinal Armand-Jean de Richelieu, a magnanimous figure that rose to prominence in both the Cathlic hierarchy and the French State, de Rancé's fate was seemingly preordained. Aunts, uncles, cousins, and brothers all held positions of abbots, abbesses, foreign dignitaries, military officials, bishops, and the like. Naturally, the private tutoring followed by the university education that he received only elevated de Rancé's status as he prepared to do great things.

Ordained in 1651, he was bestowed with several official and honorary titles soon after (chaplain to the royal family, secular "abbot" and clerk of La Trappe, archdeacon of Tours, Canon of Notre Dame, and various positions among other monasteries that provided ample income) and seemed to be well on his way to following in the footsteps of his name sake. In 1652, with the passing of his father, de Rancé inherited unimaginable amounts of wealth, which fueled a lifestyle that did not mirror the ecclesial positions he had been bequeathed.[7]

By 1657 de Rancé's worldly positions and holdings were not enough, and a distinct shift in his spiritual life began. For him, there was something missing even amidst his ecclesial affiliations, and he sought to fill it through a renouncing of his possessions and titles. Many point to a wrestling with his former transgressions as a catalyst for this turn. Years of wealth extraction via his noble standing and ecclesial power without fulfilling the leadership responsibilities associated with them left him riddled with guilt—a fact attested to in private letters and diary entries. The fragility of life along with questioning its ultimate purpose came to the fore and he found himself at a crossroads in life.

7. Krailsheimer, "Armand-Jean de Rance."

Whether described as a reawakening or even a conversion, de Rancé spent the next several years reading heavily, praying even more heavily, and adhering to a strict asceticism/interpretation of the Rule. He shifted to a meager diet, practiced self-affliction, dedicated himself to poverty and simplicity, and fully participated in the Liturgy of the Hours. This coincided with a dispersal of his vast wealth among many of the monasteries that he and his family had ties to, including La Trappe in Soligny, France.

Previously interested in the wealth it could generate, de Rancé now wanted the buildings and community to physically and spiritually mirror the worldly prestige that he held. He joined the Cistercian Order officially after a short novitiate and transitioned from an honorary abbot to an actual one in 1664, bringing with him an air of rigor, reform, and renewal at La Trappe. A return to the need for manual labor, self-sustainability, serving the surrounding poor, mandatory *Lectio Divina*, and diligence in observation of the liturgy were just starting points for de Rancé.[8]

The harshest observers said that he was building something more akin to a prison than a monastery, sparking written feuds with theologians and other abbots alike. Extreme "silence" (speech limited to one communal session per week), the abolition of all animal-derived food and instilling a diet that bordered on malnourishment, corporal punishment, declaring that it was the Holy Spirit (God Godself) that authored the Rule rather than Benedict, and allusions to the fact that other interpretations of the Rule starkly missed the point were the most contentious subjects. Additionally, restrictions on what texts the brothers could read during their contemplative studies, the banning of visits from the monks' former family members, harsh penitential practices, acts of humility that bordered on humiliation of individual monks, and a strange aversion to celebrating the feast days of saints caused further doubt about de Rancé's approach. Two big controversies stemmed from these theological interpretations.

First, a very protracted and heated public row with Benedictine abbot Dom Jean Mabillon about the role of education within monasteries centered differences between higher learning and spiritual formation. For de Rancé, the latter was far more important and avoided entrapment in various sins like certainty, over-curiosity, vanity, etc. while Mabillon thought scholarly pursuits within the cloister were a fundamental part of the monastic vocation. The pair reconciled amicably, though de Rancé's strict observance still outlawed scientific and philosophical pursuit in favor of biblical studies.

---

8. Bell, "'Holy Familiarity.'"

This aversion is no longer present in Trappist communities (quite the opposite in fact) and has been reinterpreted by many scholars not as a hatred of learning but a comment on the true meaning of contemplative life as outlined by the Rule.[9]

Second, due in part to the extensive influence that St. Augustine had on him, de Rancé was caught up in the Jansenism controversy of his context. Without delving too deeply into complicated theological positions, the Jansenist movement was a genuine attempt at reconciling various Papal assertions on the presence and role of free will within theological anthropology and the overwhelming grace offered by God. Bishop Cornelius Jansen of Ypres argued that the entrance of sin into the world—the original Fall—negated human capacity for choosing goodness freely. Only divine intervention (the grace of God) could shift the tide of human choice. Additionally, this divine grace is irresistible and not offered to all. Ultimately, Jansen's rejection of free will in accepting God's grace was deemed heretical and in the time of de Rancé, even loose affiliations with his conclusions were seen as problematic. Despite signing an official condemnation of the Jansenist position, de Rancé's strict observance of the Rule was due in part to his negative assumptions about human nature and an individual's capacity for good.

In response to detractors, de Rancé went on to author several treatises along with several lengthier tracts and books cataloguing his interpretations of the Rule. Among them, *Vies de plusieurs solitaires de La Trappe, Le Traité de la Sainteté et des Devoirs de la vie Monastique,* and *La Règle de S. Benoît, Traduite et Expliqué Selon son Véritable Esprit.*

In the end, his dedication to pursuing what he saw as St. Benedict's original intent of the Rule led to irreconcilable differences with the General Chapter of the Order followed by official Papal approval recognizing his stricter observance in 1678. His legacy was picked up again in the mid-nineteenth century as much of the controversy surrounding his reforms had dissipated and the Trappist observance was made a distinctly separate Order by Pope Leo XIII in 1892 as more and more Cistercian communities accepted the rigor of La Trappe.

Ultimately, the imprint of all three men—Benedict, Bernard, and de Rancé—is felt throughout any stay at a Trappist Abbey today, and arguably their presence can be found in the delectable products that concern me here. This extensive focus on contextualizing each figure is a reminder that the

---

9. Bell, "On a Rough Road, Drive Fast."

contemplative way of life, its various interpretations, and a constant thread of pursuing perfection ultimately influence every aspect of the Trappist vocation, including each community's chosen path of self-sustainability.

Chapter 2

Silence, Listen Carefully with the Ear of Your Heart

Listen carefully, my child, to your teacher's precepts, and incline the ear of your heart. Receive willingly and carry out effectively your loving Father's advice, that by the labor of obedience you may return to Him from whom you had departed by the sloth of disobedience.

—The Rule of St. Benedict, Prologue

SWEATING, I PAUSE FOR a drink of water and to wipe my brow on my already soaked T-shirt. I had just walked 5.5 km from the town of Zundert in Southern Holland to what the wooden sign told me was the final turn to Abdij Maria Toevlucht—the Abbey of Mary Our Refuge. The journey was anything but serene given that the bus from Breda was running on an "at will" basis rather than any sort of schedule, delaying my arrival by two hours already. A humid day full of scattered showers provided the backdrop for my first excursion to a Trappist monastery outside of the US. Adding to the stress, the abbey at Zundert was one of only two communities that I could not get firm details from about my stay. The journey was made in hope and had been hectic, loud, and anxiety-ridden. In many ways, it was the exact opposite of the experience that was to follow.

Turning onto the paved road that led seemingly nowhere, I forced myself to take a moment to breathe. This is what I had been building towards for the last several months. All of the grant proposals, the preliminary research, gathering my ideas for a rough manuscript outline, re-reading the Rule of St. Benedict fervently and frequently, and attempting to make sure I didn't look like a fool with regards to beer knowledge, historical understanding, or theological grounding all built up into a whirlwind of thought and emotion. To be honest, it was difficult to take in and manage in that moment. That is until I looked up and took in the sheer beauty of my surroundings.

A row of trees lined either side of the road, stretching their branches out towards one another to make for a uniform canopy above the path. It was almost as if they were there to welcome any visitors, a reassurance that this was indeed the right place. Nature's very own greeting committee. In the distance on either side were also pastures filled with grazing cows and the only sound to be heard outside of the occasional semi-truck passing by behind me was the distinct chatter of Cuckoo birds above and a Woodpecker drumming away in search of lunch.

The reason I share this here is not to provide the beginnings of a memoir, but to set up the contrast between the baggage I brought with me from the outside world and the fundamentally different way of living offered by the communities I would call home for the summer. This was the first moment in which I was able to begin to experience Benedict's words not on the printed pages of my worn-down copy of the Rule, but in the way that I think he meant for them to be experienced—in moments of contemplation and lived reality. In this spirit, I begin with a reflection on the opening verse of the Prologue that I have provided above.

Obsculta! The very first word of the Rule is a Latin imperative, a command to listen. However, this is not just an instruction to hear the words coming from Benedict but rather an exhortation to conform one's whole being to what he says. This is further emphasized by Benedict choosing the flowery and metaphorical language of *aurem cordis tui* (the ear of your heart), an approach that the straightforward abbot was not usually inclined to—behooving extra attention. In utilizing this language, Benedict is also quoting the book of Proverbs, an appropriate nod to the wisdom that is to follow.[1]

These two phrases together reflect the type of synergy between contemplation, active listening, and the implementation of commands within the realm of lived experience that encapsulated Benedict's blueprint for

---

1. For more on the implications of *Obsculta*, see Kardong, *Benedict's Rule*.

monastic life. They also introduce the themes of silence and reserved speech. Ultimately, the oscillation between reflection and praxis impacts our internal relationship with ourselves, our relationships with others, and our relationship with the Divine. All of this is predicated on something that seems so strange to us: silence.

Silence is perhaps the Cistercian theme to begin with here not just because of chronology in the Rule but because it is one of the most difficult to grasp. In a world of constant noise, stimulation, instant gratification, and sensory overload, silence is a distant concept for most of us. Whether it is earbuds pumping our favorite playlists and latest podcast episodes into our brains, the constant conversation available to us at the push of a button or at the mere stroke of a key, the never-ending barrage of binging shows broken up only by commercials for the latest products, or the ebb and flow of sounds coming from scrolling through our social media feeds of choice, the noise of our daily lives varies between a constant hum and a concentration shattering audio bludgeon.

By way of anecdote, our over-reliance on such auditory stimulation and our complete lack of comfort in being present in the moment is further evidenced by the groans and shocked faces of my students when I announce that my classrooms are technology-free zones on syllabus day. The fear of being present with our own thoughts and the thoughts of others is on full display as our young scholars come to grips with the fact that for at least an hour (a whole long arduous hour) they will be subject to such a backwards existence. This is exacerbated when our first reflection prompt is on an excerpt from Howard Thurman's *Meditations of the Heart* focusing on silence, centering down, and forming an "Island of Peace" in our souls where they are asked to set aside a block of time on the weekend to also go technology free and sit in silence.

The contemporary person not only cannot fathom silence, they dread the very possibility of it. We take solace in knowing that escape from reality is just an app away, we construct our worldview upon a constant flow of information that is predicated on absorption rather than contemplation, and we allow our interactions with ourselves and others to be dictated by incessant noise—most clearly evidenced by modern notions of "listening" being most aptly described as merely waiting for our own turn to talk.

Conversations within the classroom are slow in developing over the first few weeks as students are both traversing new subject matter and also being asked to reflect their own understandings of a particular text, pinpoint what the author is saying, and respond to the opinions of others in their classroom community. In many ways, our inability to be fully present in the moment can be seen as an all-too-human spiritual flaw that has only been exacerbated by our current context.

We feel uncomfortable with ourselves and with others precisely because we have not spent time reflecting on either. Discernment, formation, contemplation, such processes are seen as backwards and ancient when we add the instant gratification associated with every part of our lives. Fast food, fast cars, fast fashion, fast internet, fast, fast, fast. We cannot fathom that things might take time, that we might have to wait, that our progress in any facet of life is not meant to be as instant as our oatmeal.

Such a mentality seeps into the way many of us even think about intellectual growth and comes to the fore when we face such process-oriented subjects like theology, philosophy, literature, music, the study of language, etc. The biggest stumbling block for my students (after the lack of technology) is that humanities courses are based in subjectivity and concerned with intellectual growth through dialogue. Many just want to know what the right answer is, or whether a particular question will be on the exam rather than cultivate curiosity.

I certainly don't blame them for such attitudes when their business, information sciences, and economics courses that they need for their majors are designed in such a way. This comes to the fore tangibly when I tell students that using AI bots to answer prompts is plagiarism while those other courses encourage it as a tool of efficiency. Universities themselves are diving headfirst into adopting such cultural norms that are averse to personal formation. Our fear of silence and contemplation is stark indeed.

These observations are only compounded when I add my experience working in the beer industry. Bartending in some of the busiest taprooms in Chicago has given me a unique perspective into these phenomena of the fear of silence, the aversion to listening, and a general discomfort with reflection. I am not just talking about the noisiness of a bar setting with regards to chatter, music, the clinking of glasses, the reverberations of chairs screeching across the floor, the interjection of notifications from computers or phones, and the other auditory ebbs and flows inherent in serving beer, but the noisiness of the anxiety, restlessness, and inability to concentrate evident in such settings.

This takes on a wider-reaching character in much the same way that my students' initial aversions to silence and contemplation do. Metropolitan

Brewing was, until its closing in late 2023, *the* lager house not only in Chicago but I would say in the country. Nearly fifteen years of existence perfected a core portfolio of German-inspired lagers that drew praise from US industry leaders and world travelers alike. And yet, so many of the visitors to the taproom were completely oblivious of just what was in their glass.

There were those that would take a photo of their beer for Instagram before even trying it, those that checked our various offerings in Untappd without stopping to appreciate their choice if they had even made one of their own volition rather than based on popularity, or those that were appalled that we did not offer flights of beer (a terrible vehicle for truly appreciating a brewery's offerings).

It also refers to those that would approach the bar to order a Miller Lite or "whatever your favorite IPA is," without the slightest clue that both were antithetical to the mission of Metropolitan. Yes, this allowed our staff to shine and explain what we were all about, but it is also a metacommentary for how oblivious persons are of their surroundings and how rampant the ethos of self-gratification is in our culture. Taking the time to learn, to contemplate where our palates are in a certain moment of our life, or simply to rest and enjoy outside the realm of pure consumption is drastically missing from our taprooms—even those that try to make such things a part of their identity.

That is not to say that brewery taprooms cannot be seen as places of refuge. I am fully aware of the potential for silence and reflection within these spaces as well. These, however, are exceptions and not the norm. Overall, the hustle and bustle of the outside world is reflected in the places where we drink. In the end, we have forgotten the positive physical, spiritual, and emotional connotations of silence and contemplation.

I think this is exactly where Cistercian spiritually can offer insight. The quote above provides an entry point into not just listening but the contemplation and moral formation that follows in its wake. Benedict further expands upon this understanding both when he outlines the role of listening in chapter 6 of the Rule, "On the Spirit of Silence," and in the seventh chapter, "On Humility," where the ninth step is described as "controlling your tongue." The former explicitly outlines that speaking must only follow in the wake of permission being granted from the abbot as a way of avoiding both frivolity and demeaning language while also opening up the monks for their true purpose. The latter takes this a step further to clarify that aimless talk opens the door for sin and instability.

It is important to remember that Benedict's approach to the Rule was founded on care and guidance rather than rigidity or strictness for their own sake. The focus on virtuous silence was not a punishment for persons but rather allowed for monks to truly focus on their relationship with God, their internal relationship with themselves, and also the needs of those around them. Yes, sin might make itself manifest in things like sloth, selfishness, greed, etc. and its avoidance is a good thing, but the virtuous cultivation of relationships and obedience to others are the true goal. In this way, silence was, is, and will continue to be integral for the communities that follow in Benedict's footsteps.

Though a common misconception, Trappists do not actually take vows of silence within the monastery, but the practice of silence is accentuated as a virtue in the wake of both Benedict's Rule and Bernard of Clairvaux's reflections that it served as a pathway towards "greater things." Rather than simply being categorized as a lack of speech, silence for both was seen as a placeholder for the contemplative cycle and served as the ideal environment for learning. In a beautiful encapsulation of what is on offer from silence, Bernard's letter to the Abbot of St. Denis in 1127 states that "He who in the present [silence] gathers the fruits of a good conscience, feels in himself a desire for future good works."[2] An oscillation between thought and labor lends itself to the ideal human condition and it is with an ear towards reflection on silence that I started my conversations with the monks.

Each abbey I stayed in was kind enough to arrange an interview with a monk and many of them also facilitated interviews with lay staff at the breweries. Though the extent to which monks were part of the day-to-day operations varied from brewery to brewery, the Trappist ethos was a constant thread. I aim to build on my discussions with both the monks and the brewing staff that further illuminate the unique understandings of silence on offer from these communities. Moreover, these conversations also provided insight not just into the importance of silence, contemplation, and equilibrium for Trappist spirituality but also into the extent to which these themes came through in the processes of producing, marketing, and consuming the beers.

My initial question in these conversations was always based upon the very first paragraph of Benedict's Rule. I wanted to know exactly how contemporary Trappists understood "listening with your heart" and the

---

2. Bernard of Clairvaux, *Bernard of Clairvaux*, "Letter 19, To Suger, Abbot of S. Denis."

general place that contemplative silence had within their communities. This grew into asking about the place that silence had within the realm of the breweries they maintained.

I pick up here with my stay at Abdij Maria Toevlucht and an interview with the monk responsible not just for organizing my stay but running the brewery operations—Brother Christiaan. He kindly made himself available during a break in the liturgy of the hours on the second day of my stay. Brother Christiaan also helped lead Zen meditation every morning before Lauds (the first service of the day) which I share here as an example of the Trappists respecting many contemplative paths toward insight.

As with each of the brothers that follow, the first question was "What does Benedict mean when he says that we are to listen with our hearts and how does this work its way into how the monastery operates?" Brother Christiaan responded,

> To listen with your heart, what does it mean? The first thing I think that is needed is that you are silent. That you are silent, and quiet, and listen. In a way, to interpret the things that are happening in your life. What's the meaning of what is happening right now? Because listening with your heart is a little bit different because you have to reflect. The people you meet, the places you visit, they give you a certain feeling of "what does this mean to me?" For example, what does it mean to me when I visit a monastery? Do I feel a certain connection with what's happening? If I'm in Church, or when I'm talking to the monks? For me, this is kind of the description: Listen with your heart, it's not with your ears. It is living and trying to discern what direction does life move in.

This contemplative silence leading to discernment and action serves as the foundation for much of what happens within the walls of both the monastery and the brewery. Moreover, this type of listening is understood as a gift from the monks to the rest of the world. The interweaving of silence and interpretation with regards to the directions that our lives might move in becomes a remedy for the anxiety and chaos that so many of us feel in our current context.

This is more evident in a follow-up question asking what he wants his guests to walk away with after their stays. He shared that,

> When people have stayed here and then go home, I hope that they, like with your first question, can reflect on being silent and interpret what had happened here. When they leave, I hope they have

been challenged. I hope they have been quiet and then can go and give direction to their own life. Whatever direction that may be.

Rather than serve as an outlet for overbearing evangelization, the abbeys are places of solace. Carving one's own path of human flourishing is far more important to the Trappists than any sort of doctrinal or dogmatic acceptance of preset values. In this sense, listening is tied to welcoming and hosting is tied to creating space rather than oversight.

The guesthouse master from another abbey, Koningshoeven, clarified this when asked the same questions regarding silence. Here I think he was far more hopeful about people's ability to be present than I am. Brother Jakobus pinpointed that,

> Normally, you're only listening to what another person says, and you look at the way they behave, you have a first impression of someone. But you "hear" visually and also by ear. So, listening with your heart, that means you try to meet the person you're talking with in terms of what that person means in the eyes of God. So, for God, every human being is His child, is worthwhile. According to the Roman Catholic Church it's also very important that every human being is worthy to be a person and to be seen and that can only be done with the heart.

Lest we forget that contemplation and action are intrinsically linked for the Trappist Order, Brother Jakobus continued with the practical application of such a conclusion. It is clear, listening with your heart is neither inactive nor to be confused with merely an auditory process.

> Because whenever you see someone on the streets a [housing insecure individual] for example, your first impression with your eyes is "oh, I'm going to walk on the other side of the road." Or this person might be smelly when you are in the supermarket. You listen with your nose, with your eyes, with your ears, yeah? And listening with your heart means that you see that person on the street, he might be of course in a certain state, but moving towards him instead of past him means that you recognize him as a human being. Not looking to the other side of the street, or to the ground, or somewhere else, that would be very good for people who are deep in their own troubles. You might be a drunk person or a smelly person or someone who's whatever, but you must see him as a human being.

In this way, listening with the ear of your heart is a combination of self-reflection, discernment, communal outreach, relationship building, and the elevation of human persons.

The Cistercian pursual of silence and the cultivation of this type of listening to grow along the path of spirituality isn't a secret kept from the rest of the world. It is something that must be sought by all if we are to truly love ourselves and others. The loudness of the world around us can lead us to forget what is truly important, to focus on the wrong things.

Brother Benedikt from Westmalle captured both the importance of listening and its difficulty even for those who have come to the monasteries to pursue it. His response to my initial question was telling,

> Yeah, it's very difficult to explain that. It has something to do with that you have to listen with your heart which is also with listening with your feelings, which are intuition. But it's difficult to explain, it is also something that is more difficult given our time because people are visiting only briefly, everything is going very, very quick and then it's difficult to hear things that are of a deeper level.

Of course, such struggles are partially the result of short-term stays versus the lifelong commitment to the Trappist life undertaken by the monks, but there is also a sense that our natural inclinations are impeded by the noisiness of society. Benedikt continued,

> But we remark that it's very difficult for most people because when they are coming here, the first thing that they feel is the murmurs of their inner-life. And then it is very difficult to visit in silence, in yourself, in the depth of yourself. It's a big problem. There's a lot of people that are coming here and then the first moment that you are here it is clear it is not for silence. Or is it to "receive" the silence? Or a lot of people also immediately demand, or directly ask, for a code for their phones. A WiFi code. There are also a lot of people that say, yeah we will not use that [their phone] during our journey here, and then after just a few hours they are coming here to ask for it. But it is an art to live in silence.

The dichotomy here is stark. The expectation that you can just upload contemplation, receive silence, or check a box for spiritual growth during your retreat is directly contrasted by brother Benedikt's portrayal of the monastic life as an artform. The beauty here is that it is not a question of possibility but a question of will. One of the most stunning things to come from the silence of these retreats at the abbeys is just how naturally such growth comes if given the chance. Moreover, there is no pressure from the monks themselves to pursue such growth.

Brother Xavier from Orval echoed as much in his response to my initial question. A completely open hospitality is what is on offer from the Trappists, one without judgement or pretense. He shared,

> Listening with your heart, is a precursor for Lectio Divina which we hope that everyone participates in while being here, but we do not have any expectation about what a guest will take away from their stay with us. It is about respecting the individual's conscience. We do hope that they realize the synergy between silence and the surroundings and ecology here but that is all.

The function of the cloister as a separation between the ways of the world and as bastion of living otherwise comes to the fore here and reflects not only the disparate nature of the two in terms of theory but the experiences of a guest master that sees this play out in practice. All of this is to say that the process of listening with the ear of one's heart is a question of commitment, intentionality, rhythmic praxis, and finding beauty in the mundane. Again, there is no pressure, but the beauty of the longstanding monastic tradition is there for all to partake in should they want.

In a sense, this is also a process which parallels what is going on in the brewhouses of these communities as well (I promised there would be beer!). The industrial whirring, clanging, banging, and whooshing that it takes to even produce the Trappist liquid in our glasses certainly does not seem like it would have anything to do with contemplation or silence. And yet, each of the breweries understands the intimate relationship between monastic values and the products that are made by them or receive their stamp of approval.

In 1997, the Belgian Trappist breweries, coupled with Koningshoeven in Holland and Mariawald in Germany, created the International Trappist Association (ITA) as a way of ensuring that products sold under the name "Trappist" were indeed associated with the Cistercian Order of the Strict Observance. This came in the wake of imitators of both the beers and cheeses attempting to profit from fake associations with abbeys, a trend that Westmalle Marketing Director Manu Pauwels says led many of the Trappist abbeys to momentarily pull out of both the US market and other continental European markets until clarity could be established. This clarity came when the ITA decided to create an authentication label for every "Authentic Trappist Product" (ATP).[3]

Three distinct criteria are mandated for being granted such a label, and the monks I spoke with also described the unofficial criteria of the Cistercian ethos being present in the production and distribution of the products. First, any product seeking the label must be made on or near the abbey's grounds. Second, supervision over the production of goods receiving this label must be in the hands of Trappists (male monks or female nuns). While this does not mean that a monk or nun must be involved in every step of the production process (though some are), they do have in-depth knowledge of the goings on in the breweries, cheese shops, bakeries, etc. and direct control over them. Lastly, the sale of Trappist products is not to be for profit. Any capital generated from things bearing the ATP label is meant for the sustainability of the abbeys themselves, solidarity and fiscal support for other Trappist communities, and for charitable donations to causes close to the hearts of each individual Trappist community.

This standard is utilized not just for the beers with which I am concerned but also for cheeses, bread, coffee, chocolate, liqueur, or any goods associated with these abbeys. The discernment process for creating both the ATP label and the ITA generally revolved around protecting not just authenticity, but quality, intention, and the proliferation of the values exhibited by the Trappists themselves. It is no surprise that I can trace the ways silence and contemplation shine through in these beers.

Readers should also know the importance of delineating categories when discussing these beers. The common usage of "Trappist beer" when talking about beers that are made by or under the supervision of these monks can be a bit confusing in that it seems to imply a distinct style. This simply isn't the case. Trappist is a designation, not a style. We cannot think of these beers as unified in a way that IPAs, lagers, saisons, or stouts are. Each brewery produces unique beers that fall under individual style categories (they may at times overlap) but there is no such thing as a Trappist style. I stress this here because careful attention to vocabulary creates a space for silence and contemplation to work themselves out in the discernment process of the breweries and brands associated with these Trappist communities.

For example, one of the most common methods of making beer shared across the abbeys is founded upon the notion that time, silence, and yeast

3. International Trappist Association, "About."

are foundational to the product itself. Though the beers all use ale yeasts (strains that ferment quickly), all the beers made at Trappist breweries are given much longer to more fully mature including some making their way to lagering tanks before being dosed with a second helping of yeast in the bottles for more development.

Such a lengthy production process is not conducive to most breweries. In the States, there is a predominant ethos that argues that time is indeed money. The storage space taken up by these Trappist methods along with the extended time to get to market is not at all in line with the culture of cranking out as many beers as fast as possible. The monks understand that you cannot rush yeast, it does what it wants at its pace. It is a living breathing aspect of the beer and needs to be given the time and space to ensure it is reaching its full potential. There is a rhythm to its cycle, much like there is a rhythm to the monastic life. The monks offer respect and space to the tiny cells that move the wort[4] along in its process of becoming beer.

Here I am struck by something that Brother Christiaan from Zundert shared in our interview with regards to the place of silence and contemplation in the brewing process. He put it brilliantly,

> The most important thing for Trappist beers, and for our beer of course is not to bow to commercial pressure. The beer is given time. In a way you could say the quietness of the monastic life is given to the beer. At least we try. Because, yes, we need money to live, to keep the buildings here in a good state, of course we do need it. But in a way, we try not to bow to those commercial pressures.

Their brewmaster and brewing consultant Constant Keinemans chimed in to echo this sentiment as well,

> Quality is the most important thing in our brewery, in most breweries. When the distributor comes and says, "we need the beer now because we've sold out." Normally you can stack out your fermentation, you can do it in seven or eight days. Some people might say, ten days. No, for us it is always fourteen days. Then it's ready. Fourteen days.

It is not about acquiescing to the ways of the world, rather it is a dedication to the contemplative life outlined by those cherished guiding texts. Both Constant and Brother Christiaan remarked on how they hoped that this

---

4. Wort is the liquid extracted from boiling grains which provides the base sugars for fermentation by the yeast.

type of mentality could seep into other facets of the brewing industry via their example—to stop and think about best practices and quality outside of just production and profit models.

They also shared that Zundert envisions their beers as sparking contemplation once they have been opened as well. Not just on the complexity of flavors on offer in their products, but also in the sense of motivating thought, curiosity, and conversation. When I was shown to my guestroom at Zundert, I was reminded of this by the guest master when given my allotted bottles for the evening, my bottle opener, my Bible, and shown where I have access to a desk and reading light. It also moves far beyond individual thought, highlighted by Brother Josef from Westvleteren pointing out that the common room that houses the beer fridge for guests at that abbey is also a reading room and set up for conversation but was to be used only after the completion of that day's liturgy. These beers and the praxis of reflection are not separated.

Brother Benedikt from Westmalle echoed similar sentiments in our time together as he focused both on the need for extra time spent in tanks and the monastic life to be reflected in the Extra, Dubbel, and Tripel on offer from the brewery.

> Yes, we are using lagering tanks. We think that time adds a lot of quality, our central aim with these beers. It's very natural for us to want to do as best as possible. It's about your faith but also the faith you are given because other people rely on you and rely on what you do being the best possible. This contemplative faith is certainly reflected in the products.

This was not just a gimmick either. Marketing Director Manu gave me unfettered access to the brewery that had me giddy as he poured me samples of Westmalle Dubbel from various stages in the lagering process. Though the room itself was impressive, housing more than two dozen cylindrical tanks, the diversity in flavor profile was immense and accentuated just what their famous house yeast could do when given the time and space it requires.

The aromatics of plum, fig, caramel, spices, banana, melon, and bursts of tropical notes highlighted both the uniqueness and complexity of the beer, which Manu assured me would not be nearly as prominent if rushed. The silence-fostered care was evident in each glass we sampled, and I was convinced that as much as each monk attempted to reinforce the separation between the breweries and the monasteries, this beer would not be here without the process of capturing Benedict's precepts in each bottle, at least not in any form that I would want to drink.

Indeed, the association of Trappist beverages with silence and contemplation is a far more unifying factor than the notion of style. The intentionality of pairing Trappist beer with these themes is clear and perhaps worthy of one more anecdote—La Trappe's motto "proef de stilte" or "taste the silence." For thoughts on how the monks at Koenigshoeven interact with the La Trappe brand, I return to Brother Jakobus and the end of our discussion on silence. I asked him how the brothers that don't work in the brewery understand this intersection. His answer highlighted the integral nature that monastic life plays in what consumers taste at the end of the process:

> We know our beers. We also know the mindset, the motto, "taste the silence" "proef de stilte." Silence is inside the monastery. It's not over there on the terrace or in the restaurant. There, there's no silence. It can be very crowded like two weeks ago when we did the Trappist Market. It was full of people. So, what we try to produce with the beer are the values of the monastic life so they can have a little taste of that, quite literally.

It was powerful to hear that an entire way of life is meant to be tasted in a sip of beer. Not every person enjoying beer on the terrace thinks in this way, much less people thousands of miles away, but the sentiment is worth sharing here as the opportunity of contemplation is certainly there for anyone who listens. Incredible beers that are value driven in this way are truly refreshing.

Chapter 3

Abdij van Onze Lieve Vrouw van het Heilig Hart van Westmalle

LOCATED TWENTY-FIVE KILOMETERS NORTHEAST of Antwerp, the town of Malle lies in the beautiful rolling meadows and farmlands of Flanders. The municipality also houses Westmalle Abbey, one of the most important Trappist communities with regards to the topic at hand—beer. As will be the case for each of the abbeys covered below, I introduce the history of this community before diving into the beers they produce; the ethos they incorporate into their brewing, marketing, and communal engagement; and the stories I have garnered from the monks themselves about these divine liquids.

I begin with Westmalle not because it is my favorite (it's impossible to make such a designation), or because I visited it first (that was Zundert!), or because it is the oldest of these communities (it isn't), or for any reason in particular outside of perhaps its continued influence on the ITA with regards to assisting the other breweries bearing that label. I must start somewhere. So, Westmalle's exciting, busy, and at times frightening story serves as the launch point.

Historical Overview

It began with a man on the run. Augustin de Lestrange, responsible for the instruction of novices (the stage of monastic life before one officially takes vows) at La Trappe Abbey in France was forced to flee the country in 1791.

The Constituent Assembly responsible for passing laws in the wake of the French Revolution had become increasingly hostile to anything religiously oriented—it abolished church property, confiscating it for the state, and auctioned it off to the highest secular bidders; outlawed religious orders generally and the taking of sacred vows specifically; exiled over 30,000 priests under threat of death; and ultimately replaced any form of organized religion with a Deist state cult. The reality for those that resisted the state was much more visceral, as people who refused to renounce their vows and didn't flee faced the guillotine.

Landing at La Val-Sainte monastery in Switzerland, de Lestrange was able to continue his vocational calling and increasingly became responsible for finding landing spots for fleeing monastic communities. Though the Swiss themselves capped the number of refugees accepted, de Lestrange was able to look to other countries as well. He sent one such group to North America.

En route, the group had to pass through Flanders and was invited by the Bishop of Antwerp—Cornelius Franciscus de Nelis—to stay within his Bishopric. This was not merely to show them hospitality on their journey. Bishop Cornelius wanted de Lestrange to allow the group permanent residence as he looked to bolster the monastic presence in the region. To sweeten the proposition, the Bishop offered the Trappists a piece of property to call their own. While the initial excursion continued as planned, de Lestrange left a handful of monks behind to form a separate community in Malle, and on June 6, 1794, the priory of Westmalle was founded. The implications of housing a Trappist community are the same, but a priory is a smaller community with less status.

The land that Bishop Cornelius secured for the monks had already been named by its former owners as *Nooit Rust* (never rest) because of the toil and harsh conditions associated with farming in the region. This was perfect for a monastic order dedicated to both labor and prayer but would also come to symbolize the constant upheavals that the community would face in its early days. The refuge that the Trappists sought from the ongoing political and religious struggle was not to be. Already by July the monks had to abandon the newly founded priory as the French Revolutionary Army crossed into their region of the Netherlands (Belgium did not exist as an independent nation yet). They briefly settled in Westphalia near Munster and by October of 1795 they had built their own community in Darfeld, always keeping an ear out for news about Westmalle.

By 1801, the edicts governing French territory had loosened somewhat as Napoleon was busy with various iterations of the Napoleonic Wars and had seen the legalization of Catholicism as a way of pacifying the masses that still had traditional affiliations with their faith. Specifically, Napoleon passed a concordat that allowed for the return of the religion into his empire as long as the government had control over electing bishops and the Catholic Church vowed not to pursue regaining any property that had been confiscated during the Reign of Terror. The monks felt the time was right to return to *Nooit Rust* as the property had been in the hands of faithful lay persons and they were ready to continue their original work in Westmalle. A dozen monks were sent back to the priory where they lived, worked, and expanded for nearly a decade under the tutelage of local bankers and merchants eager to return Flanders to its status as a Catholic stronghold.

However, the twists and turns of the monks' story were not over as they had misjudged the supposedly favorable conditions under Napoleon's Concordat. Pope Pius VII—himself a Benedictine monk—clashed with Napoleon over jurisdiction of the newly allowed return of religion. Napoleon's secular vision of religion did not have room for Papal oversight and looked down on Catholic institutional strongholds of any kind. This need for control became especially true of the Cistercians and their ties to the land on which they worked. Things came to a head in 1811 when Napoleon issued a decree officially tightening the government's grip on religion in the region which included closing all monasteries. As if to add insult to injury, the initiative also saw the conversion of parts of Westmalle into military barracks.

The close ties to the local community kept the priory alive in spirit as the technical owner of the property, Baron Peter Joseph de Caters, successfully objected to its confiscation under Napoleon's edict. One monk and two lay assistants remained behind in hiding under the Baron's care. Luckily for the brothers, a coalition of opposition forces recaptured Paris and ended the Napoleonic era shortly after their exile. In 1814, the Treaty of Fontainebleau not only brought peace and stability back to the region, but by August the monks had fully returned to the Westmalle priory *en force* with a community of over thirty persons.

The monks now found themselves under the political jurisdiction of the United Kingdom of the Netherlands headed by King Willem I. Tensions were not as bad as under the Napoleonic period, but Willem's favoritism of the Protestant faith and the enforcing of Dutch as an official language caused tensions among the Belgian territories in his Kingdom. Moreover, the 1814 Charter of Religious Freedom; a lengthy period under French secularist rule; and growing post-Enlightenment rejections of Church interference in the economic realm meant that the monastic orders could rely less and less on outside financial support.

These factors meant that in addition to supporting themselves, the monks at Westmalle needed to receive a declaration of "contribution to civil life" from Willem's government in order to remain open legally and provide for their community. Their working of the land as well as the founding of a medical clinic and trade school fulfilled these requirements, ingraining the priory further into the hearts and lives of the locals.

Belgian nationalist fervor simmering under the surface of the region's populace at the time would add another twist in the journey of the Westmalle community. Several social, political, and economic/industrial factors led to Belgium declaring independence on October 4 of 1830 and successfully rebelling against the Dutch forces stationed in Brussels. Belgium became a constitutional monarchy that elected King Leopold I to power and finally, for the longest period in its fledging history, the priory at Westmalle would see a period of stability.

Under a decree from Pope Gregory XVI, Westmalle was elevated to the status of abbey and recognized as a Belgian Trappist congregation. As the current prior, Dom Martinus was elevated to the status of the community's first abbot, and Westmalle took its next steps as a monastic center in Flanders as he also became Vicar General. April 22 of 1836 marked the first official day of the new designations.

Dom Martinus began building a brewery for the monk's own self-sustenance as Order observances entitled monks to a glass of beer with their meals. Brother Bonaventura Hermans and brother Alberic Kemps were put in charge of running the brewery and tasked with creating a recipe that utilized local grain. On December 10, 1836, the brothers at Westmalle collectively tried the first fruits of their brewing endeavor. Between *sekst* and *noon* prayers, with their *middagmaal* (lunch), they tasted the first official beer to come out of the brewhouse.[1] Though the brew was much different than any of the three offerings that leave the cellar house today and was not initially sold to the public, that winter afternoon would forever change the trajectory of the abbey.

---

1. Westmalle Abbey, "Our History."

Originally dark, sweet, low in alcohol, and avoiding bitterness, the beer served the monks well for decades solely as accompaniment for meals. However, as the region became more populated, local demand for beer grew. With the brewhouse capacity notably beyond what the monks could reasonably consume, abbey records show that around 1856 Westmalle began unofficially selling small quantities of beer to visitors. This included a stronger version of the original dark brew while the monks had shifted to a lighter "white beer" for in-house consumption. In 1861, the enterprise became official. Tax stamps and excise records show that Westmalle was allowed to sell commercial quantities from the gates of the abbey and eager pilgrims flocked to the grounds to taste what was already becoming known as a quality product.

Though the abbey continued to be sustained primarily by raising dairy cattle and farming the land, selling beer became an addition to the community's finances. The funds raised through beer sales allowed for a brewhouse expansion in 1861 and a second in 1897; while in 1899, the Church and cloister were completely renovated and partially rebuilt. The beer also began being bottled during this period to ease the way in which distribution at the gates might happen (pitcher service or wooden barrels were the only methods available prior to this). As he was describing Westmalle's history to me, Brother Benedikt also made sure to note that this growth was, as always, focused on hospitality as well.

> It is also so that a lot of things had changed since the 19th century. For instance, they could live a life with simple things, with just a farm. And as things changed, at the beginning of the 20th century, the needs of the community changed. At a certain moment they decided to brew more than they needed as a source of income because there were a lot of people coming [to the monastery] for help.

By the early twentieth century, the direction of travel for the brewery was only going one way. Between the industrialization of farming and dairy industries minimizing the market impact that Westmalle could have, the freedom that beer afforded the monks with regards to the labor-time commitment, and the penchant for brewing that was evident amongst the brothers, the potential for self-sustainability via brewing was clear.

However, the *Nooit Rust* moniker reared its ugly head again with the outbreak of World War I, which put a momentary dent into proceedings at Westmalle. The Germans invaded Belgium in August of 1914 and held onto the territory until the signing of the armistice and the re-establishment of Belgian independence. This meant that the monks, once again, had to seek refuge elsewhere as the world's tendencies interrupted their contemplative life. Though a few of the brothers stayed behind during the conflict, the rest found a temporary home.

With the Netherlands staying neutral during the war, the Trappist communities there could offer safety and security for the duration of the conflict. The same could not be said for the abbey structures at Westmalle as significant damage to both the cloister and the brewhouse occurred as a result of the war. The main church tower was destroyed by the Belgian army upon retreat from Malle in order to avoid offering the Germans an observation post, and the Germans themselves looted the copper kettles from the brewhouse for the war effort. Both sides utilized the abbey as barracks and a logistics center at various times in the conflict over Antwerp.

Upon returning in 1918, the brothers had quite a bit of work to do to restore operations. By 1921, they had not only rebuilt the brewery, but abbey records show that they had obtained licensure to sell beer beyond the gates of the monastery. Utilizing beer sellers, they began to distribute throughout Belgium and wider markets got their first taste of Westmalle. With the new brewhouse and expanded operations, the beer itself changed slightly during this period. There were two distinct styles being brewed— one for consumption by the monks and one for sale to visitors and beyond.

The former, Extra-Gersten, was a variation on the lighter "white beer" that had been brewed since 1856. Literally "spare-barley," the now blond ale came in at roughly 3.5 percent alcohol by volume (ABV) and was perfect for the monk's meal-time beverage. The latter was initially a version of the original dark sweet beer created by Brother Hermans but eventually shifted in profile. By 1926, the beer was marketed as the Westmalle Dubbel Bruin, a significant modification of that first offering. This stronger version literally doubled the malt profile and hop ratios while also adding candi sugar to lighten the body and crispen the mouth-feel of the beer. In doing so, the brothers created what would be a more appealing beverage to the drinking sensibilities of the wider Belgian beer-consuming populace. This beer has never been significantly altered and remains the recipe for the current Dubbel.

The early 1930s then saw yet more additions to the operations at Westmalle as the brewhouse expanded again to feature a full brewing hall with bottling and cellaring/fermentation rooms. Abbot Edmond Ooms coined the moniker "Trappisten Bier" to describe what the abbey was producing for commercial sale as business boomed in the expanded market. In order to celebrate the opening of the new facilities, a new beer was planned, tested, and finally released in 1934.

Branded as a "Superbier," this golden liquid tripled the initial recipe of the in-house monk's beer and would change the beer world more than any of the Trappists could have imagined. That original release was a far cry from what would eventually be a final recipe codified by Brother Thomas Sas as the Westmalle Tripel in the 1950s, but its general contours of being a pale, strong, aromatic ale, and having a distinctly dry finish were present from its earliest tasting notes.

There is some controversy over whether Westmalle's Tripel was truly the first ever of its style, as Hendrick Verlinden (a notable food-chemist) not only consulted for the brothers at Westmalle and the regionally famous Slaghmuylder Brewery but was the brewmaster at Drie Linden brewery. There he brewed a beer known as Witkap-Pater around 1931/1932, which was eerily similar to the early versions of what would become the Westmalle Tripel. The chicken or the egg conversation continues to this day.

The beer name itself, "white-hooded father/monk," was a nod to the robes of the Trappists, and Verlinden had spent quite a bit of time at the abbey advising during the building of the new facilities. This work included dialing in their new equipment as well as an extensive crash course on yeast-cultivation techniques, but I was told that this exchange was a two-way street with the monks sharing some of their long-successful approaches as well. Either way, the Westmalle Tripel would become an industry standard over the next few decades and continues not only to be synonymous with the style but is *the* gold standard (literally and figuratively) when it comes to style guidelines.

The modern version of the Tripel that is available was tweaked slightly, enlarging both the hop profile and the hop amount, by brother Sas in 1956. This will likely never be altered as the monks are ever slower to change in the wake of stability, and current head of brewing Lieven Van Hofstraeten told me there is no need to mess with perfection (Jan Adriaensens, his longtime predecessor, was continually on record saying similar things).

WWII was not as damaging to the monastery as the first iteration, and the monks were largely left alone. The 1950s and 1960s in Belgium were not as turbulent as other European nations impacted by the post-war era, and the cold war tumult was also not felt as heavily by the nation. This period saw stability and growth on the production side as well with several major brewery additions taking place in this period—most notably, the addition of an on-site water plant at the abbey in 1968 for use in all facets of the community but especially in the brewery (this was additionally augmented in 2011 to expand sustainability initiatives). The devastating aspects of the *Nooit Rust* theme I have been following have seemingly taken a break.

Contemporary Facets of the Community and the Brewery

The time I spent at Westmalle flew by in a flash, but the care and attention I received as I laid out my purpose with regards to the brewing aspect of my project were just as thorough and accommodating as the retreat aspects of my stay. Both brother Benedikt and director Manu ensured that I would leave with everything that I needed to paint as clear a picture as possible of their brewing operations, but also the relationship between the abbey and the brewery. In what follows, I hope to share what the beer nerds reading this have likely been waiting for, a thorough discussion of the beers that leave the gates of the brewery.

First, it must be highlighted that while all three requirements of the Trappist designation continue to be met by Westmalle (quick quiz, what were those again?), the day-to-day operations of the brewery are largely in the hands of lay workers. Though the brewing capacity is capped at 120k hectoliters per year—the capacity of the brewhouse is 135k to offer some wiggle room if need be—this is still far beyond what the monks could ever imagine handling on their own. There are currently fifty-two lay persons employed by Westmalle on the brewing side, including Manu and Lieven who were both quick to remind me that the monks have the final say on everything from ingredient selection to label design and marketing. This is ensured by Westmalle's advisory board, which is comprised of two monks and four lay persons, meticulously aligning with the standards set by the Cistercian ethos.

Brother Benedikt proudly described how many companies have maybe one meeting a quarter while Westmalle's meets a minimum of twelve times a year. The two monks on the board reflect the consensus decisions made by the community as a whole. This is similarly mirrored on the farming and dairy production side, which have three lay workers running operations. This oversight ensures that the meticulous standards of the Trappists are present within the products used to sustain the abbey but also allows the brothers to navigate the changing contours of their community.

While the precedence of prayer is clear in Benedict's Rule, there is also the stark reality that the ways in which monastic life has shifted directly impacts how the monks engage with the labor aspects of their vocation. Brother Benedikt shares that,

> There are seventeen monks living here in Westmalle, the youngest one is forty, and this is not a bad thing because the vocation isn't for, or living in a community, isn't meant for very young people. It's better to have, you need some, life experience. You need to have reflected on life before you decide to enter. We have older brothers from around Europe. Belgium, Holland, France, and Germany. But we are also living in a time where people are not really connected with religious life, which is different to several decades ago where religion was part of everyday life. There are not many moments of contact with religion these days. In this way, it's normal that less people are attracted to religious life because they don't know it. The religious aspect has disappeared from public society.

The monks not only supplement their labor force with lay workers but have developed an outward-facing hospitality that is ministerial in nature. The people employed at Westmalle do not just have increased contact with religion in an overt sense, but they also see the stark contrast between the ways of the world and the Cistercian ethos. For example, the brewery operations at Westmalle are conducted Monday through Friday and operation hours vary with the time of year to allow employees a functional family life with regards to things like the school calendar, holidays, and vacation times.

As the pinnacle example of this dedication to their lay workers, when I was touring the facility with Manu, I was shocked to see the sheer size of their bottling line. Given what I knew about their yearly output, there was simply no way that they needed something this big. This type of machinery would be better fit for a Stella or MillerCoors facility, and yet, here it was. When I shared my observation, Manu simply chuckled and said, "you are correct, we don't *need* this big of a bottling line."

Westmalle had invested several hundred thousand Euros above and beyond a line that would offer peak efficiency for their facility simply because it allowed them to keep the family-oriented structure of their schedule intact. It was more important for the monks to see their employees continue to thrive than it was to allow capital gains to dictate operating procedures. "This machinery is only expensive if you look at it from one perspective," said Manu. As an added caveat, the facility also installed soundproof paneling to absorb the noise associated with high-capacity machinery so as not to disturb the surrounding area—both human neighbors and the wider eco-sphere as well.

This communal aspect is instantly discernable in any part of the facility. To be frank, I have not really seen such a jovial working climate anywhere in my experience of the industry. Smiling forklift drivers, joking in the halls, an impressive employee lounge, lay workers stopping to greet a strange American wandering around the facilities, etc. (this is all the more impressive given the general sensibilities of the Dutch and the Flemish). This is not to say that there is a lack of seriousness around the place; the well-oiled nature of the facility is also impressive.

They may not be monks, but the lay workers at Westmalle seem to emit the values of St. Benedict's Rule in their own vocation. Hanging beside the employee entrance of the facility is a reminder that this approach applies to all who work at Westmalle. A simple plaque dedicated to the facility renovation of 2001 is adorned with Psalm 90—"Let the favor of the Lord our God be upon us and establish for us the work of our hands. O establish the work of our hands!" What is interesting is that the implication of "establish" here, *kownah* in the original Hebrew, implies that the fruits of this labor be both long-lasting and beneficial to others. Again, dividends for shareholders are the furthest thing from the mind here.

Such an approach is completely different from what commercial brewers are used to—here I am referring to more than just an implied influence of monasticism and spirituality on the brewery. I have friends that work at macro-facilities in the US that are run around the clock seven days a week and employee well-being is only to a level of minimum industry (or, more frankly, legal) standards. When production, consumption, and profit are the only modes of gauging success, three rotating shifts a day, long hours, and seclusion are the norm. The way in which St. Benedict centered labor around human development, communal growth, and tapping into our innate nature of creativity might serve as a better model than that of the soul draining market-driven aspects of corporate capitalism and the flashy pursuit of trends within the beer industry.

That is not to say that such an approach is easy or that starting a brewery with such lofty goals is even possible in certain contexts. The reality is that what the Trappist communities have built over the last two centuries is unique and potentially not applicable to the wider spheres of the industry.

There is truly a unique confluence of identity, approach, and particular moments of history that make the beer in your glass possible. Brother Benedikt commented on this as well when I asked him about not just the wider contours of the beer industry in Belgium/what he knew of it abroad ("How can one brewery produce so many beers? Do they not want to perfect one first?"), but also on the unfortunate shift in Trappist brewery numbers shifting rather than increasing.

Brother Benedikt lamented the loss of Achel's ITA designation—the last two monks from Sint Benedictus Abdij retired to the community at Westmalle in 2021, leaving no one to oversee the production of beer at Achelse Kluis. Achel was originally a daughter house of Westmalle (founded in 1846) and began brewing beer as a way of supporting itself in 1998. After accepting the retiring monks with open arms, Westmalle attempted to oversee the production at Achel remotely but ultimately discerned that this was not in line with the hands-on ethos that the ITA required, nor was it a genuine way of pursuing the in-community labor requirements of the Rule.

Even if the monks had been replaced, there is no guarantee of success with the Trappist ethos. Brother Benedikt continued by reflecting that,

> It's no longer the obvious choice to choose brewing in modern times as a community for self-sustainability. But those were very different times when the tradition started. And sometimes they also start in the wrong way because they think, well, if you start brewing, it generates a lot of money.

Here he was commenting on the other unfortunate side of the current Trappist brewing landscape, attempting to compete in markets that are not ready or not adaptable for such an ethos. The niche that the Trappist communities have carved in the Belgian and Dutch beer markets is unique and a specifically tailored number of exports also keeps a certain market mystique alive beyond their borders, but Brother Benedikt is correct in emphasizing the difficulty of breaking through.

For example, Spencer, the former brewery attached to St. Joseph's Abbey in Spencer, Massachusetts, about an hour West of Boston, accentuates this warning. The community took a crack at being the first US Trappist brewery (and the first outside of Europe) when it opened its doors in 2014 after years of conversation, learning, and planning with help from the ITA-certified breweries on the other side of the Atlantic. An incredible pater style beer branded as a "Trappist Ale" was the initial offering, which was followed up with an equally sumptuous "Monks' Reserve Ale"—a Belgian quadruple. When these beers hit the Chicago market, I was not only delighted but impressed.

The excitement was short-lived, as within a few years Spencer was churning out IPAs, imperial stouts, fruited Saisons, and even a pumpkin beer in its attempts to stay relevant within a growing craft-centered American context. Compromises on the Trappist approach were clearly being made while the barrel production was almost half of the initial ten-thousand-barrel target. By early 2022, Spencer announced that it was ceasing brewing operations and the primary labor choice for sustainability shifted back to fruit preserves and vestment production.[2]

Though I am sure that the brothers were happy to see some return on their initial investment, in an ironic gut punch, Trillium Brewing—arguably the most famous purveyors of the New England Hazy IPA—purchased the brewhouse equipment from the abbey. It is exactly this type of scenario that Brother Benedikt and the board of directors at Westmalle are all too cognizant and wary of.

Manu was clear on multiple occasions that overstretching themselves in terms of production and attempted market share is not just a quality-oriented concern, but a survival-oriented one as well. Brother Benedikt on the other hand adds a bit of nuance to the fact that there is balance to be found because of monastic vocational concerns as well. Over and over, at each of the abbeys, I am reminded that Trappist communities are monasteries that happen to have breweries attached to them rather than breweries that happen to be run by monks. More explicitly,

> We have only, and this depends on each monastery, 120,000 hectoliters per year and no more. It's not our purpose to augment that but to find the right balance between brewing and the monastic life. Of course, at that amount it is always a factory in truth, but that's what creates a permanent difficulty [finding this balance]. Yes, we would like to do without so much beer production but the reason we keep up with it is that we have to help not only ourselves but the other Trappist communities.

Thus, there is a balance between quality, commercial prowess, and the application of monastic ideals that must be struck at each of the breweries discussed here and was evident explicitly in my experience at Westmalle. The monks realize that brewing is not their true purpose, and yet it paves

2. Miller, "Only Trappist Brewery in the US is Closing."

the way for so much of the good that they are able to do. The push and pull of hospitality and service as outlined in the Rule is constantly at the forefront of how the brothers operate.

This includes taking responsibility for those communities that do not have the same production capacity as Westmalle does. Brother Benedikt shares that, "Zundert is [producing] only a tenth of what we do, Westvleteren also. But there is a demand, an expectation, to take responsibility for these other communities. Also, for this reason, the production at Chimay is yet more than we have here." He is referring to the fact that within the ITA there is a sense of cooperation rather than competition as the larger operations offer things like lab services, raw materials, equipment assistance, advice, etc. to the smaller ones. This type of comradery exists among the smaller craft producers in the US as well (I can't count how many times equipment, hops, malt, or even a bottling line had been exchanged among Chicago's craft producers), but for a large-scale producer to offer such services without charge is unique indeed.

Such solidarity just adds to the Westmalle brewing ethos that I hope has become evident here. Without such approaches their beers would be markedly different, or quite frankly, not exist at all. Though it is not necessarily a conscious application of monastic ideals that lead to a thriving brewhouse, Benedikt and other monks throughout my journey were quick to point out that a separation is intentional, when one conforms one's life to the Rule it certainly bubbles over infectiously into everything one touches.

Perhaps this is the beauty of St. Benedict's work in designing the guidebook to begin with. The spiritual growth and honing of virtues outlined therein are not meant to be a checklist. Instead, the intention is a wholistic shaping of the person over time, which can been noticed throughout everything that they do. However, if a visitor wanted, they could certainly find most of the chapter headings present in essence within the beer facility as well as the abbey. This synergy is most importantly present in the beers themselves.

> *Extra:* Described as a golden-blond, this is a 4.8 percent ABV light and refreshing beer. Manu made clear that the recipe is similar to the 1836 refectory beer, but its current form was perfected and has been unchanged since the 1950s. It continues to be used for its original intent, as a meal pairing. Thirst quenching, crisp, dry, slightly bitter, and with fruity aromas from the signature Westmalle yeast, Benedikt describes it as almost a Belgian-style pilsner—a description that I think works

exceptionally well. Light but sustained carbonation allows the white pepper, pear, banana, citrus, and ripe red apple esters of the Extra to flourish. Though originally available only for the monks and visitors of the guesthouse, it hit shelves in all Westmalle's markets to share a bit of the abbey with the world in the wake of the COVID pandemic.

Dubbel: Known locally simply as The Trappist, this a classic example of a Belgian style Dubbel. Though confusing, this is due to Westmalle coining the term when they released the beer for wide distribution in 1926. All subsequent attempts at mimicking the style came with the same name. At 7 percent ABV and with a reddish-brown hue, the dominant flavors of this beer are caramel, raisin, date, dark cherry, sweet toffee, and dark cocoa. Hop aromatics of pineapple, peach skin, and earth-spice couple well with yeast esters of black pepper, banana, and citrus. Due to a heavier body, the yeast also creates an initial pillowy creamy mouthfeel before the crisp dry finish characteristic of Westmalle beers. I would allow this beer to breathe as it continues to develop with each sip.

Tripel: The gold, or rather golden, standard. Sitting at 9.5 percent ABV, this is arguably the most recognizable Westmalle product and one of the most recognizable of all the Trappist-made beers. Clear and golden in color, the body of the beer is thin at first glance from the addition of additional fermentables via sugar. This is slightly misleading as there is still a full-bodied mouthfeel to the Tripel and a hearty, sweet booziness in the finish that leaves you comfortably warm. It holds up a creamy head and distinct lacing throughout consumption. A fine balance between spicy and fruity esters is discernable in the nose with a distinctly floral character present from aromatic hop varietals. Citrus peel, chamomile, underripe banana, and green apple skin are also present in the beer. Most discernable is a lingering bitterness that is shockingly pleasant and approachable—this is not only unique to the Westmalle Tripel, but also a hallmark that is rarely achieved elsewhere. If you could capture decadence in a bottle, this would be it.

Duo: Despite the weariness to over-tinker with a sure thing at Westmalle, brewers will be brewers and are constantly on the lookout for creative outlets. Duo became the first modern release at Westmalle. Just 5,000 barrels were produced in March of 2025 which were meant to be restricted to Belgium and the Netherlands and packaged in draft format only. When I heard that one keg of it was being tapped at Hopleaf (nothing nefarious occurred, Westmalle sent a thank you for their long-term partnership), I found myself in the car before I had even finished reading the social media post. In typical Westmalle fashion, the beer was exquisite. Coming in at 7.2 percent ABV, Duo is a blend of the Tripel and the Extra which highlights the best of both worlds. Crisp, refreshing, and lighter in body but full flavored with a lingering thirst-quenching bitterness. Six hop varietals are added for fruity and grassy aromatics. A kiss of light bready sweetness rounds out the beer. I sincerely hope that Duo joins the permanent portfolio.

Trip-Trap: Wait, another beer? Not exactly. This is a draft Dubbel topped off with some bottled Tripel made famous by locals and eventually a menu staple at Westmalle's Café Trappisten where it appears as "half and half." I ordered one of these during a break between prayers on my last day at Westmalle. A chuckle from brother Benedikt accompanied Manu's strong recommendation to try it, but I too now pass on the sentiment.

Ultimately, the beer making process is quite simple and requires the coupling of at least four general ingredient categories: water, a fermentable sugar source (usually a malted grain, and as we will see shortly perhaps an addition of candi sugar), a bittering and preservation agent (hops), and yeast. I am going to assume that those interested in reading this book have a general knowledge of how we get from these raw materials to the final product, but I list them here because Westmalle prides itself on the premium quality of each base ingredient in each of its three beers.

Beginning with water, the aforementioned purification system taps into underground streams within the Flemish subsoil layer—roughly 60 meters below the surface—to bring water up to the brewery, café, and abbey. This hard water (high minerality concentration) undergoes minimal treatment before use in the brewing process—Manu indicates that there is an iron removal procedure to avoid metallic flavors in the products and to minimize the impact iron deposits may have on the water system itself. While typically not understood in this way, I think the local water sets the tone for the overall dry and crisp flavor of the Westmalle beers that are accentuated by the other ingredients yet to come. This lack of extensive water manipulation again reiterates the Cistercian emphasis on stability with regards to the importance of a distinct sense of geographic home and loyalty to place.

With regards to the fermentable sugars present in the Westmalle portfolio, each of the three offerings relies on French grown barley which is then expertly malted by three maltsters that the brothers have been working with for decades. These partnerships provide Westmalle a level of oversight that ensures each delivery is tailored to their specifications for both quality and consistency. Though Benedikt and Manu stopped short of revealing all of the beers' secrets, Pilsner malts make up the Extra and the Tripel, The Dubbel relies on the addition of dark candi sugar for color while the Tripel sees sugar additions elevate the ABV and body consistency as well. The extra is brewed without additional sugar.

As for hops, perhaps one of my favorite questions, as someone who spent most of their time in the industry working for breweries that do not produce IPAs, was always "Do you have anything hoppy?" I would explain that all beer does indeed contain hops but they function differently in different styles—what they were really asking is if I had anything similar to whatever IPA was leading check-ins on Untappd. Manu and Brother Benedikt were amused by my experience and commiserated with the sentiment as Westmalle beers, and Belgian beers generally, are not typically categorized as "hoppy" despite the presence of multiple varietals and large additions throughout the brewing process.

There is a base bittering hop and five aromatic hops that make up three additions throughout the boil. Though the actual varietals and amounts are a closely kept secret, Manu does tell me that the hops "come from very traditional hop producing countries like Germany or Slovakia, Czechia, for example" and that the exact hop profile might fluctuate slightly to get the desired feel based on what is available. Despite Flanders being a hop-producing region since the thirteenth century, not using local hops seems to go against the trend with the remaining ingredients but the spicy and herbal varietals favored by Westmalle have been perfected elsewhere. When we tour the cellar in which the hop bags are stored, I am asked to turn my camera off and although I can see each of the varietals clearly labeled, the secrets of my generous hosts are safe with me.

There is one other surprise in the cellar as I am shown around, each of the massive shipping bags contains whole cone hops rather than pellets. Seen as requiring less storage space, easier to use, involving less guesswork, being cost efficient, and overall, less of a hassle, pellets and extracts are the industry norm now. Manu tells me that "The hops are freeze dried but fresh. It's not overly aged hops we are using" and when he sees my surprise at the presence of actual hops, adds, "Yes, they're real hop cones, we don't work with pellets. It's rare but we stick to it." For Brother Benedikt, there is also a sense of quality control present in whole cones given that you know exactly what you are getting and how you might make minor adjustments for consistency in the profile, while pellets come to you in their final form. The monks are slow to adopt change with regards to some aspects of the process, and with the quality of their beer, I don't blame them.

This leaves us with the final component—the yeast. The majority of the flavor profile as well as the aromatics of these beers come from these tiny single-celled organisms, making them invaluable and instantly recognizable. The essence of the spicey and fruity notes in particular would not be the same without the house-propagated yeast, and thus the character of Westmalle's products is foundationally related to these little guys. Functionally, yeast is responsible for the creation of alcohol via its feasting on the sugars provided by the wort but there are also byproducts of this process that influence the beer far more than by providing its inebriating qualities. From a gastronomic perspective, part of the process involves an enzyme present in the yeast (and unique to each various strain) called acetate transferase which causes esterification—responsible for those flavors and aromas we all love.

Manu outlined a bit of the process with regards to propagation of the yeast as we chatted. "We cultivate our own yeast. It's lab cultivated, but it's very well monitored. So, we use it and re-use it." Well monitored is an understatement. I have seen quite a few in-house set ups and toured labs cultivating yeast for a wide array of brewing operations, but the Westmalle lab was a thing of beauty.

Lieven Van Hofstraeten, the head of brewing operations at Westmalle, took a moment out of his day to introduce himself and give a brief layout of the lab. Interestingly, Westvleteren had just dropped off a case of bottles for analysis and a few lab workers were busy pulling samples. After a brief chat about my admiration for their beers, Lieven was off to one of the countless meetings an industrial-sized brewery demands—but not before telling me that if I have any follow-up questions to not hesitate to reach out. In an extension of the hospitality on the other side of the brewery wall, I do not think he was just being polite.

Each of the three beers made by Westmalle utilizes the same yeast strain. Though contemporary yeast labs might be able to tell the particular lineage of any given yeast strain, the lab is far more concerned with keeping their proprietary yeast happy, healthy, and thriving. Close examination allows for proper attenuation levels as well as knowing how many generations a particular batch might go through before needing replacement. This helps account for the durability of the Westmalle yeast, which is typically pitched at higher temperatures than most ale yeasts would be comfortable in and then raised even higher throughout the fermentation process. Hard work in strenuous conditions leads directly to the production of those sought after esters that have become synonymous with these beers—perhaps St. Benedict's insistence on labor for spiritual formation goes beyond humans...

The yeast is so important, in fact, that Westmalle's products undergo a refermentation in the bottle that is the product of introducing fresh yeast during packaging. This bottle conditioning ensures not only an accentuation of the flavor profiles of the beer but also ensures the longevity of the products. This is true with regard to the kegging of the Dubbel at the facility, where the introduction of yeast allows for further development and consistency of taste even when served on draft.

Westmalle Tripel is not served on draft. The primary reason is that it would compromise the beer's celebrated complexity—a trade-off they will not make. Additionally, natural yeast can make the beer appear hazy. With the darker Dubbel this is less visible; with the golden Tripel it is.

The first three of these ingredients come together in the brewhouse, which itself is a stark reminder of Westmalle's history. The shiny stainless-steel kettles and the fully automated brew system that was part of the most recent expansion are set up next to the old copper brewhouse and manual brewing faucets from years past. They were left there intentionally, not as a matter of aesthetics but as a proud nod to legacy, says Manu. Looking back on this with some time to reflect, this setup is a perfect encapsulation of the Trappist ethos. Unafraid of innovation in search of quality, consistency, and efficiency, but always with an eye on the past and the foundations it set. The brewhouse control panel also faces the abbey itself, aligning almost perfectly with the church's bell tower, another opportunity for the lay workers to remember the ultimate purpose of Westmalle. The wort then flows from the brewhouse to the fermentation tanks located on a lower level.

Once the yeast is pitched, the fermentation process takes roughly a week for its primary stage. The beer is then moved into conical lagering tanks so that the beer can further mature, and the yeasts/proteins fall out of suspension, clarifying the product. The Tripel spends up to three weeks in these tanks while the Dubbel and Extra are moved onto the next stage after two weeks. Lagering is not necessary for ale production, but it allows for the accentuation of flavor, body, aromatics, and other characteristics. As I walked among over a dozen of these tanks, Manu asked if I would like to try some Dubbel straight from the tank to see how the maturation process is going.

He goes off to find a taster glass while I attempt to hide my giddiness and then fills it. Though far from the taste and carbonation level that will eventually be present, I can see the direction the yeast is taking. Manu explains that this particular tank is about halfway through the lagering cycle. The candi-sugared sweetness, date, raisin, and dark cherry notes are overwhelming but will become rounded over time and I am nonetheless ecstatic about the hospitality shown to me in this moment.

From these tanks, the beer is filtered via centrifuge, reprimed with a sugar source, doused with yeast again, and pumped into the bottling facility where the aforementioned bottling line does its quick and beyond efficient work. The Dubbel and the Tripel are formatted in 330-ml, 750-ml, and, for special occasions, 3-L magnums, while the Extra is only available in the 330-ml format. A small adjacent kegging line is also available for the limited draft supply of the Dubbel. Once packaged, the beers continue the maturation process in a massive cellaring hall kept at room temperature. Well over 100,000 cases are kept here at any given time before heading out for distribution. Three weeks of warm-room conditioning here gives each of the three offerings the final characteristics they will acquire within the walls of Westmalle—this includes both carbonation levels and alcohol content alongside the flavor profile.

Once the beer leaves the facility, the monks still exude control over their product with regards to its presence in the market. Brother Benedikt shares that "every community has its own philosophy about how the product should be marketed and it's represented in the product. It's true that generally, it's all Trappist, it's all the same but there are little differences among the brands and that reflects how each community looks at commerce." For Westmalle this means several things, especially on the side of label design and aesthetic.

A prior career as an architect has given Benedikt an eye for detail that helps not just with the day-to-day operations of the brewery, but also with the simple, clean, and instantly recognizable packaging of each of the three products, the glassware on offer from the brewery, the coasters and beer tacker tins that mark the only promotional materials on offer at pubs, or approval of the limited merchandise made available by Westmalle.

Care for others takes precedence in promotion of the beer as well with both Manu and brother Benedikt highlighting that Westmalle does not utilize commercials or other traditional advertising methods in order to mitigate the fact that, let's be honest here, alcohol calls for responsible use; we therefore communicate soberly and emphasise responsible enjoyment. They want to express the need for responsible consumption and therefore they, and the other ITA-certified breweries, minimize the commercial aspects typically associated with other breweries. Contemplation, not partying, is the preferred backdrop for these beers and so, free promos, giveaways, discounted products, and open bar tab events are not in the Westmalle's marketing wheelhouse. In this way, they not only allow the beer and its lineage to speak for themselves, but they avoid unnecessary potential for harm. This is extended to the sphere of sustainability as well.

Long before Pope Francis issued *Laudatio Si*, the brothers at Westmalle were treating our earth with respect and under the assumption that it is a shared home that requires stewardship, not destruction. Brother Benedikt capture this sentiment perfectly,

> Well, we do an effort of course [for sustainability], like you said. The water treatment is always something that got a lot of attention even before it was regulated by the government. We have solar panels, to generate as much energy as we can. There are some intelligence systems to absorb the heat that is produced during the brewing process, and we can utilize warm water for the next batch so we hardly lose any energy during the production process. We are not capturing CO_2 but that's the next project for us.

There are no tax break incentives, no marketing gimmicks for "eco-friendly" beer, just a genuine concern for creation. The sustainability and stability of their home is of vital importance.

Ultimately, the guiding hand of the Trappist ethos is present in every aspect of the labor processes in the brewery and beyond. In my experience, Westmalle's monastic heritage, their hospitality, patience, focus, listening, and eagerness to constantly and consistently improve are as much ingredients as are water, hops, barley, and yeast. Some Trappists would urge caution when making such a connection as it is certainly not intentional (their true vocation lies in the cloister as we've seen) but the thought is infectious when spending time in community with the brothers at Heilig Hart. Brother Benedikt leaves me with one more gem when discussing what Westmalle's approach brings to the world around it.

> It would be a very useful way of life for young people to experience all of this, to share, to work together, to live in community, to respect people, that would be very, very enriching. We should be taking care of each other. Yeah, it's not about collecting and gathering as much as possible. It would be very therapeutic.

Quite frankly, it is also a thought I cannot shake every time I sit down with any Westmalle offering. Yes, I am reminded of Manu's brilliant tour of the facilities and of brother Benedikt's generous time in conversation, but I am also transported back to the giant elms that line the path to the abbey; to the meals shared in the guest house where I was welcomed with open arms; to the time spent in prayer during the liturgy of the hours; to moments of contemplation in my room; to rough notes of this manuscript made in the garden; and to the fact that my walk to the bus after my stay was full of wonder, awe, and a distinct emptiness that I was leaving a place where, even if ever so briefly, I belonged.

Chapter 4

Abbaye Notre-Dame de Scourmont

I NOW RETURN TO the very first line of this book and the beer that truly got me hooked. Located in the Hainaut region of Belgium, just a few kilometers from the French border, is Abbaye Notre Dame de Scourmont which oversees the production of Chimay beer. While it is true that the nearby town of Chimay has been significantly shaped by both the abbey and the brewery bearing its same name, the rest of the world has been as well. There is no brand that is more synonymous with Trappist beer than Chimay and there are no Trappist products that reach as many hearts, minds, and mouths as those that are made within its walls.

It might seem strange, given what you have read so far, to associate monks with a global brand, but with Chimay that's what we have. Moreover, moving from Westmalle to Chimay offers a stark contrast in approach and influence as I try to portray the uniqueness of each community within the Trappist fold. Chimay is for the French-speaking Wallonian Trappist breweries what Westmalle is for the Flemish with regards to stewardship and resource sharing, but it differs significantly in the commercial aspects of their ethos and the sheer scope of their operations. In what follows, I will try to show the extent to which such a presence and approach shapes not just Scourmont abbey, but the ITA, and the Cistercian Order as a whole. But first, a bit of background on both the brewery and the abbey.

Historical Overview

Scourmont's initial founding as a monastic community was in 1850. As part of the mid-nineteenth century swing back towards recognized Catholicism in Belgium, a parish priest—Father Jean-Baptiste Jourdain—was looking to expand the spiritual and material support system on offer for the region's iron industry. The wider social ills associated with the industrial revolution (hard living, poor wages, atrocious workplace standards, inaccessibility to economic growth for laborers, etc.) were starting to take their toll. A landed member of the gentry named Jospeh de Riquet—with the ceremonial title of "Prince" bestowed upon him—was happy to donate a parcel of land for the priest's purposes.

Father Jourdain initially wrote to Abbot Martinus at Westmalle who turned down any notion of sending monks to start another community. If you remember, Westmalle had barely established themselves and could not spare any brothers for the endeavor. Jourdain then turned his hopes to Westvleteren which was overflowing with monks at the time. A group of brothers was eventually sent to oblige the request and founded an official daughter house with the Order's approval.

In the high heat of July, seventeen monks arrived in the marshy, hilly, and rocky land parcel—one that put the *labora* aspect of their vocation to the test. Attempting to farm in this part of Hainaut was brutal to say the least. The majority of their initial months were spent attempting to clear boulders from the donated land only to discover that the soil itself was far from ideal for planting crops. This delayed the start of construction of the priory until 1852, with completion not coming until 1864. On September 8, 1865 the church was reconsecrated and the priory was officially recognized by the Order. Scourmont would go on to be elevated to the status of abbey in September of 1871 with Father Hyacinthe Bouteca elected as its first abbot.

Under his guidance, dairy production started to supplement income and provide self-sufficiency for the community while they struggled with their farming endeavor. A gift of fifty Holsteins (the famous Dutch lineage stereotypically associated with dairy cows) would kickstart this side of Chimay's soon to be historic identity. Though the cheese produced by the monks at Scourmont is arguably just as famous as the beer, these early days of the dairy were focused on butter making—which was sold with the bread that Scourmont was producing in their bakery. Abbey records show that it was not until 1876 that the community sent a brother named Benoit to

France to learn the cheese-making trade. Upon return, he perfected the semi-soft varietal which has become synonymous with Chimay. The shift towards dairy production was far more lucrative and less labor intensive than working the land and would become a staple source of income that continues to this day.

It is also under Dom Hyacinthe Bouteca's tutelage that beer production for the community's own consumption started. An official license for selling beer at the abbey gates was issued by King Leopold in 1861, and thus Chimay officially counts its first beer release as having occurred in early 1862. Interestingly, this means that the brewhouse and fermentation rooms were completed and functioning before the rest of the priory. Abbot Bouteca was initially trained as an architect, and he personally oversaw the construction of the brewery while also investing in steam engines to power production for all of their commercial undertakings. He famously utilized dynamite to blow away access to underground cisterns, ensuring that all water utilized by the brewery came directly from a series of newly created wells. In much the same way that each Trappist brewery's unique water source shapes the taste of the beer, Chimay's central characteristics took the shape of this fresh well water. The region's soil is not high in minerality and thus Chimay has what is described as a soft water profile.

The initial beer was much different than anything that we would associate with Belgian Trappist produced beer today and is described in records as a German-influenced lager with the name *Bavaria*. Some sources describe this beer as having been a "double beer," which perhaps indicates that it was made in the style of a doppelbock. This initial brew likely came about because of the German workers installing the kettles, but the beer was only produced a few times before the recipe was abandoned in favor of a more authentically Belgian style—a decision that was both market and ingredient oriented. Bouteca would take the lead in designing the recipe for Chimay's first commercially available beer, this time with the aid of expertise garnered from the monks at Westvleteren.

This new beer was dubbed *Bière Forte Hygiénique* (healthy strong beer) and was the precursor of what today is known as *Chimay Première*. In 1875, a second beer was made available for commercial release. *Bière Goudronné* was the same dark strong ale, but the beer was aged in pitch-lined oak barrels for two years prior to being sold. Both iterations were made available in what excise documents show was a one-liter corked bottle sold not just at the abbey but delivered to establishments in Chimay and Forges.

Outside of the brewery's museum you can still find delivery carts dating back to this era, which carried both thirty-liter oak barrels as well as forty-bottle crates (if only such a package quantity still existed!). As with each abbey, a *pater*-style beer was made for the monks' own consumption and for retreat guests.

The success of Chimay was immediate with Bouteca regularly fielding complaints that production could not keep up in those early days. As the lore of the oak-barreled beer increased, it went through droughts of unavailability that were exacerbated by a unique use of the beer. Though I might argue that Chimay heals the soul, these early iterations of the beer took the health moniker more seriously and were even prescribed by doctors in the region for the general well-being of their patients! The myth behind the beer was growing as people throughout Belgium began thirsting after Chimay. It quickly became clear that the original brewhouse setup just wouldn't do.

In addition to expanding the on-site maltster, a mill room and a separate space for bottling were completed in 1910—solidifying the commitment to beer production on a commercial level. A more industrial-oriented dairy facility with sections for cheese, butter, and milk production, as well as an adjacent shop were also completed in this same year. Additionally, farming continued to be undertaken for at least the internal uses of the community; a woodworking shop with a regionally famous joinery operated on site as well; and the monks operated a printing press. In this sense, it seems that Chimay was diversifying its interests and income very early on. The community itself was expanding, and the abbey housed eighty monks at the turn of the century. Growth would falter with the advent of World War I.

During enforced conscription after Belgium's neutrality was violated by the German invasion, not even the monks at Scourmont were spared. Though some were recruited as medics or even chaplains, many of Scourmont's brothers were mobilized to combat units in the Yser region held by the remnants of the Belgian army or served in French units for those monks that hailed from there. Dom Le Bail, the abbot at the time of the war, was himself taken into an ambulance unit while he continued to oversee and minister to his fellow monks both near and far via correspondences and journal publications.

The most famous of these was the recurring *Le Moine Soldat* (a nod to the "monk soldier" ethos first instilled by Bernard of Clairvaux) which provided devotionals, spiritual advice, and Order updates throughout the conflict. Through this engagement, Le Bail would solidify his standing in the Order as he went on to become a pivotal Cistercian figure in the interwar period and beyond.[1]

A monk by the name of Brother Maxime Carlier was another notable member of the Scourmont community that is remembered in various archives. Carlier's extensive diaries written from combat zones, ones which focused on adapting spirituality and the contemplative life to the trenches, provide unique insight into a scenario few Trappists have ever found themselves in. So much so that he was famously catalogued in Thomas Merton's *The Waters of Siloe*. Merton appreciated their shared approach to recounting their spiritual journey in writing and felt that his staunch pacifism was challenged by a brother that saw military service as potentially an extension of his calling. I highly recommend both Carlier's collected letters and the Merton text. Though Carlier was killed in September of 1917 at the Third Battle of Flanders, his body was taken back to be buried at the abbey along with the medals he earned throughout the conflict.[2] His story was a vital reminder that contemplative life can be ripped apart at any moment, especially in the tumultuous period of the early twentieth century.

Those monks that returned to the abbey would struggle with readapting to life in the cloister (many could not bring themselves to return at all), while those elderly monks that were spared involvement in the conflict had spent years in seclusion and with their own versions of worry and doubt. Nearly four-hundred members of the Trappist Order died in service of the Allied Powers while hundreds of others took on care for the wounded and disenfranchised victims of the war in the years that followed. This proved to be a logistic and vocational stumbling block as navigating a new context became taxing for Chimay.

The interwar period saw Dom Le Bail take on added responsibility within the Order as he was tasked with a host of administrative tasks stretching from being a member of the architecture commission that oversaw any new Trappist projects to writing and editing *Collectanea*, a publication that catalogued the general history of the Order as well as provided reflections on Trappist contemplation.[3] In an era of spiritual uncertainty wrestling

---

1. Veilleux, "Great Monastic Formator."
2. Collins, "Michael Carlier."
3. Order of Cistercians of the Strict Observance, *Cistercian Order of the Strict Observance in the Twentieth Century*.

with the devastation of the war, such engagement was vital in fulfilling the emotional aspects of Cistercian hospitality. There was a boom in vocational calling during this time of wider uncertainty and Le Bail was more than happy to take in new novices finding their place within the world.

A rededication to intellectual pursuit was also undertaken in this period as Chimay's archives and library grew significantly under Le Bail's tutelage. Thomas Merton would later praise the abbot as creating a balance of sanity and clarity within his community while being a respected leader within the wider Order as well. As far as the beer was concerned, the interwar era was equally positive. A refurbished and revitalized brewhouse began churning out both iterations of the *Bière Forte* for commercial purposes as well as the house table beer for internal use. The packaged beer now contained the phrase "*Pères Trappistes*" on labels, predating the ITA's official designation by nearly half a century. Just as things were looking bright, this mini renaissance was cut short in 1939 with the advent of World War II.

The conflict was devastating for Chimay. Initially, as the Allies officially joined the war, Scourmont saw two dozen of its younger monks called up for duty. By the time the German army crossed the border into Belgium a year later, conscription was mandatory for everyone under thirty-five. Le Bail and those elderly monks that remained attempted to continue their sojourn at Scourmont, but the Nazi onslaught made this an impossibility.

An initial forced evacuation from late May to early July during the invasion of 1940 was then made permanent from April of 1942 until September of 1944 when the German army would pull out of Belgium. The exile not only saw the Nazis set up a radar station on the plateau occupied by the abbey, but they stripped the brewhouse, cheese factory, and cloister of any materials that could be repurposed for the war effort. Additionally, three thousand German troops turned Scourmont's property into barracks, a field hospital, and a command post, meaning that a rebuild was necessary after the war. Le Bail began publishing *Le Moine Soldat* again in exile and restarted his correspondence with those brothers serving. The devastation caused by the second conflict was drastic for both the abbey at Scourmont and for the collective soul of Europe. After the liberation of Hainaut by American forces and the final retreat of the German army on September 4, 1944, the abbot and his fellow brothers were free to begin picking up the pieces at Chimay.

The years immediately following the war would be the most formative period for Chimay as far as beer production is concerned. With the amount of rebuilding that needed to be done, in every sense of the word, Le Bail wanted to ensure that the commercial success of the brewery could provide adequate support to do so. Not only was Scourmont to be rebuilt, but he thought its surrounding region's revitalization was the monks' responsibility as well. The Cistercian dedication to home, stability, and hospitality was on full display. With his own responsibilities focused on so many projects across the realm of the post-war rebuild, Le Bail delegated the brewing enterprises to others, specifying that only an "exceptional" approach to beer and this new undertaking would do.

This is also where the paths of my two adopted Belgian homes—the Trappist abbeys and Katholieke Universiteit Leuven—intersected in a major way. Once the brewery was rebuilt, with considerable expansion upon the original facilities, the abbot instructed one of the brothers to attend brewing school at KU Leuven to pursue that new ideal. Brother Theodore packed his study supplies and made way for the famed brewing program. The school was producing some of the finest brewers not only in the country but throughout continental Europe and had been since its founding in 1887. More importantly for Chimay's story, it had a unique focus on multiple facets of the beer-making process overlooked elsewhere.

Specifically, their pursuit of yeast strain isolation was cutting edge at the time and caught Brother Theodore's eye in a trajectory-altering way. Under the tutelage of brewing professor Jean De Clerck, the Scourmont resident would learn not just the basics of quality-centered production but the ins and outs of industrial-sized brewing (Leuven's very own Stella Artois was well on its way to world-wide success at this point and has had continued association with the brewing school). The two also struck up a friendship and working collaborative relationship that would stretch decades and shape the beers coming out of the abbey.

De Clerck graduated from the brewing school at KU Leuven before taking the reins as the head of the school from 1947 until his death in 1978. The university still has an endowed chair position named after De Clerck, such was his influence on both the beer industry and the school. His accolades included the following: founding the European Brewery Convention, which was aimed at uniformity in industry quality standards; authoring a two-volume guidebook compiling his expertise—*A Textbook of Brewing*—which has influenced hundreds of macro and craft brewers since its first printing in 1948; providing professional consultation not just for Chimay but also secular breweries like Moortgat; coining the term "microbrewery" during an interview while on an industry tour in the US; and most relevant to my purposes here, influencing the development of Chimay's beers.

De Clerck's emphasis on the details of every part of the brewing process meant that among Brother Theodore's first tasks in elevating the quality of the beer coming out of the abbey was an expansion and modernization of the brewery. This included the addition of an advanced chemistry lab aimed at finding a yeast strain that would provide the type of flavor profile he had in mind. Chimay's records indicate that although Brother Theodore was responsible for overseeing the lab, the abbey makes it a point to say that Theodore and De Clerck isolated the new yeast strain together. The mentor-mentee relationship continued until De Clerck's death and a specially allowed burial of his body on the abbey grounds. No matter where the praise for isolation goes, the initial work done on yeast development by the duo would forever shape the beer.

Later in Theodore's life, he reiterated the importance of yeast to flavor expression while also beautifully capturing the Trappist ethos by making clear that we cannot say Chimay's yeast was created in the lab, but rather that it was found/isolated. In this sense, its uniqueness and purpose reflect several painstaking years of trial and error. By 1948, the yeast profile was dialed in and its qualities included high temperature tolerance for fermentation, a medium flocculation level, and an instantly recognizable ester profile that is simultaneously fruity and spicy. The star of the show was ready for its debut.

Brother Theodore officially released *Chimay Première* on Easter weekend of 1948. The symbolism of resurrection and new life was not lost on anyone as the stubby 330-ml bottles (courtesy of a brand-new bottling line) flew off shelves across Belgium. Popularly dubbed *Chimay Rouge* because of the red labels and bottle caps, this new smaller format became the favored size among consumers. Interestingly, the development in capped versus corked bottles is noticeable (a product of oxidation potential) and so a preference for one over the other is not necessarily unwarranted.

The novelty of that year for Chimay would also include a Christmas release that was brewed by Father Theodore as well. *Spécial Noël* utilized the same yeast strain as *Rouge* but at over 9 percent ABV it warmed both body and soul for consumers that winter. The malt bill accentuated dark fruit, chocolate, and caramel flavors, while the yeast added spicy notes of coriander and clove—it was Christmas in a glass. It returned seasonally for a few years but as the demand grew, the definition of "seasonal" expanded to months before Christmas and after (seasonal creep is nothing new apparently!) and by 1954, it appeared as *Chimay Grande Réserve* and was available year-round. In the same way that *Rouge* became a moniker for the *Première*, this bolder beer became *Bleue* colloquially because of its cap and label.

Both beers derived their fermentable sugars from six-row barley grown in France and Belgium, which was then malted locally. With a transition to larger brewing operations, the community no longer attempted to malt on-site but did (and continues to) run a mill room at the facility that pulverizes the malt into a particularly fine consistency. According to museum notes, both "light and dark" malts are used in their core beers, but this might be a poor translation on my part of what is meant to be both "pilsner and caramel" malts.

Though Chimay currently utilizes wheat starch and candi sugar to some degree as additional fermentables (per the labels), the original recipes were entirely malt based. A switch in label indicators in 1997 reinforces this. Though there is some debate as to whether the continuity of Chimay's original lineup over the years can be considered uniform, I think slight alterations to original recipes for consistency and efficiency are a natural process when dealing with breweries of this size. I appreciate that the addition of wheat partially accounts for the fuller body of Chimay's products and the creamier head whose retention is typically higher than its other Trappist cousins.

The next major historical development with regards to the brewery would come with the 1966 release of *Chimay Blanche*, a Tripel that catered to the palates of the Belgian populace that had grown accustomed to the style initially made famous by Westmalle. There is no indication that there was any exchange between Brother Theodore and the monks at Westmalle and the character of the water and yeast at Chimay make the two beers quite different despite sharing the same style designation. To make *Blanche* and the other offerings more readily available without further disturbing the monastic life of Scourmont, 1970 saw the refurbishing and grand opening of the *Auberge de Poteaupré*, a restaurant, inn, and store under the control of the abbey. Visitors can enjoy beer, cheese, and world-class Belgian fare here, but I highly recommend traversing the grounds and museum—opened in 2012 under the name l'Espace Chimay.

With growing output at the brewery, 1978 saw the decision to expand enterprises beyond the abbey walls. Construction on a business administration center and bottling plant began in the nearby town of Baileux. Though the production of the beer itself remained on site at the abbey, this move would ensure that the monks would be able to continue their focus on contemplative life and silence while economically reinvigorating the region. Tankers now bring beer to the industrial sized bottling plant where they are filled quicker (55,000 units per hour after the latest update in 2019) and without disrupting the quiet of the abbey.[4] The administrative offices also provided job growth while alleviating many of the day-to-day commitments required of the brothers. Here again I heard the phrase "we are monks with a brewery, not a brewery with monks" several times when describing the need for such developments.

In the early 1980s another renovation shaped beer production at Chimay as open fermentation tanks were replaced by closed conical fermenters. With regards to the beer itself, this shift did several things. First, it cut down the fermentation time by several days—moving the window to under a week for full ferment; second, the switch allowed for the elimination of any contamination potential during this crucial stage of the brewing process; and finally, it likely altered the ester profile slightly given that it was working quicker and in an environment more conducive to happy yeast cells. Innovation and tradition make up delicate dance partners and Chimay is not afraid to be on the cutting edge of the former as a switch in fermentation alluded to.

The 1980s were also formative for Chimay's cheese production. A concerted effort to provide opportunities for regional economic growth saw a series of partnerships with local dairy farmers and producers for knowledge exchange established by the Scourmont monks. This included an expansion of the dairy facilities in 1982, which worked in the form of a cooperative bringing in milk from throughout the Hainaut region for production at the abbey. Since then, annual output has remained consistently around the 900-ton mark while paving a path for over 200 farmers to participate in the collective.[5]

---

4. For more on the bottling plant and cellaring operations see Wallace et al., *Trappist Beer Travels*, 97–99.

5. Wallace et al., *Trappist Beer Travels*, 103. Extensive descriptions of the cheeses and their production process are provided by Wallace, Wood, and Deahl.

Returning to beer, in 1983 Chimay began exporting products to the US and their core range was made available for eager American connoisseurs. This move would massively alter Chimay's approach to how they marketed their products, as success in the US opened new horizons for further export around the globe. The sky became the limit. Roughly half of Chimay's production would be marked for export from this point forward and at current count, over seventy countries serve as destinations for Chimay beers. Thus, the global brand identity unique to this Trappist producer was set in motion, and representation of the Cistercian ethos was made available to millions of people.

A busy period followed as 1986 saw the celebration of the 500th anniversary of Chimay (the principality). The occasion saw a rebranding of *Blanche* as *Cent Cinquante* in 750-ml bottles, a designation that remains to this day. While this name and label change may seem like a simple thing, I want to emphasize just how much it reflects the way in which Chimay is ingrained in its local context. The global availability of their beer did not change the sense of responsibility that the brothers had for their local community.

The virtues of stability and firm roots are reflected in Brother Theodore's insistence on *Cinq Cent* keeping its name beyond a momentary historical celebration. It was an acknowledgment that without the town and its people, there would be no brewery either. A gift of an older copper brewing kettle surrounded by a flower garden was another such sign of appreciation from the monks. Placed across from the "*Bienvenue á Chimay*" sign at the town limits, the display is perhaps the most iconic town entrance I have seen and speaks to the intertwined nature of the two entities. The decade was further demarcated by the installation of a new brewhouse in 1988, this time with an eye on massively increasing capacity (175,000 hectoliters was the average hit by the early 2000s and 200,000 hectoliters is not out of the realm of reality).

The 1990s proved to be another important decade for the abbey, especially with regards to the commercial enterprises of Chimay. In 1996, the *Fondation Chimay-Wartoise* was founded to manage all Chimay's assets. As the monastic community itself shrank, the business aspects of Chimay boomed exponentially, a clearer delineation between the pursuit of monastic life within the cloister and the continual generation of income needed to be made. *Chimay-Wartoise* became the primary shareholder of all Chimay subsidiary companies—the brewery, dairy/cheese factory, marketing firm, distribution arm, the Inn/Museum, and its real estate holdings—as well as steward of its charitable initiatives and educational programs.

Because the monks still have oversight of the foundation but not day-to-day labor in the facility, the achievement of streamlining operations and providing job growth is coupled with an ever-present commitment to the Trappist ethos from a distance. It also ensures that all aspects of the ITA designation are still met while giving monks the space to focus on their spiritual vocations. Though Chimay turning over their operations to a foundation is not unique amongst the communities discussed here, at their size and output it is certainly understandable.

The switch in structure came with yet more innovation. In 2001, Chimay began worldwide draft distribution of its *Tripel* which was then followed by *Rouge* in 2010 and *Bleue* in 2015. As we've already seen with some of these styles, this form of packaging can be a nightmare to deal with but one that can come with a reward. As I sit and author these very lines, I am sipping on a draft pour of *Rouge* at the Map Room in Chicago where it has a semi-permanent tap handle. Outside of the occasional Westmalle Dubbel delivery, even in a beer town as big as Chicago, the Chimay core trio is typically the only Trappist draft around.

The 2010s were a pivotal period as far as the beer nerds reading this are concerned. As the craft beer scene grew on both sides of the Atlantic, Chimay would begin a series of portfolio additions that ensured they remained competitive among changing palates and beer interests. The classics remained staples in the portfolio, but 2012 saw the creation of *Cent Cinquante* to celebrate the community's 150th anniversary. Characterized as a hoppy strong blond, just 150,000 bottles were made for the special release, but demand soared way beyond that and *Cent Cinquante* is now in their year-round rotation. 2013 continued trends of breaking through barriers as Chimay released their *pater bier* to the public. Previously reserved for the monastic community and guesthouse visitors, the table beer was branded as *Dorée* (Gold) and joined the permanent portfolio.

2015 would then take a turn that few would ever imagine a Cistercian community could, as Chimay announced the launch of a barrel program. Now, barrel-fermented or aged beer is certainly nothing new, especially in Belgium. Oak-fermented lambics, tar-pitched oak-aged pilsners, casked English milds, and even the original Chimay brews have storied traditions and places in the Belgian market. However, the trend of fermenting and/or aging beer on second-use spirit barrels was something developed on the

American craft beer scene in the 1990s. Greg Hall of Goose Island first put an imperial stout into used Jim Beam barrels in 1992, calling it Bourbon County Brand Stout, and turned it into a yearly release that has reached hysteria levels of epic proportions since. The technique quickly grew beyond Goose Island's walls to the point that today you would be hard-pressed to find any craft producer not dabbling in barrel-aging to some extent.

Nonetheless, a classic brand such as Chimay sourcing individual lots of used spirit barrels caused heads to turn. The base beer entering the barrels for secondary fermentation (before a third fermentation in the corked and caged bottles) is always Chimay *Grande Réserve*, but the finishing cask differs on a yearly basis. Branded as "*Grande Réserve* Barrel Fermented," it is an eagerly anticipated release that entices droves to make the trek to the Inn or to hassle their local beer buyer about obtaining some of the numbered and limited bottles. The original 2015 release was an ode to the classic oak-aged beers of Chimay's past and saw both French Oak and American Oak barrels used before back blending into a uniform batch. Since then, they have released a cognac edition (2016), rum edition (2017), whisky edition (2018), a second oak blend (2019), Armagnac edition (2020), rum edition (2021), whisky edition (2022), calvados edition (2023), and a brandy edition (2024).

The pivotal period of the early 2000s took place under the tutelage of Abbot Dom Armand Veilleux who served in this position from 1999 until his retirement in 2017. He remains an active member of the community and a beacon for the growth of Cistercian values as he focuses on lay Cistercian ministries. He perfectly encapsulates the balance of multifaceted vocation as his collection of homilies and spiritual commentaries is as impressive as the guiding measures he put in place for the brewery. Collections of those writings are available on the abbey's website should readers like to pair contemplation with their exquisite beer.

In portraying Scourmont's ebbs and flows over its rich history, I hope to have shown that it holds a unique place in the Cistercian beer-making community. Its sheer size and constant eye on growth and development are not only impressive from an industrial production and brand recognition perspective. What I do not want to be lost is just how much this approach allows for the foundational aspects of the monastic vocation to thrive. The charitable outreach and founding of daughter houses are done on such a massive scale that all other communities discussed here pale in comparison (not that it is a competition). Moreover, the extent to which Chimay is ingrained in the social fabric of the region—spiritual, economic, and otherwise—encapsulates exactly what St. Benedict outlined as community rootedness in the Rule.

Contemporary Facets of the Community and the Brewery

My trip to Chimay was certainly not as arduous as the one that the seventeen original monks underwent, nor did I have to employ the use of dynamite, but it was the longest and most difficult of my escapades from Leuven. Two trains and a bus got me to the town center while a second bus dropped me off at the *Auberge de Poteaupré*, a short walk from the abbey itself. The impact of the abbey and the brewery on the town are instantly noticeable. Outside of the copper brew kettle greeting visitors, it is hard to walk a full block in the town without seeing Chimay branding. It took me no time at all to find both Chimay beer and cheese as I waited on that final bus and took in the sights of the town.

The walk up to the grounds was secluded and gorgeous. Two huge pillars and a crucifix assured me that I was in the right place as I made the trek up the road towards the cloister and the church. A fork in the road instantly reminds visitors of the scale that Chimay has in terms of output as the brewing facility itself is entirely separate from the cloister and signs direct those on official beer business to continue down the road—this is in addition to the entirely separate bottling plant and offices in Baileux. My initial foray took me to the cloister in time to catch Compline on my first night. Abbot Dom Damien Debaisieux and the remaining thirteen monks, along with what appeared to be two novices, finished the evening with a rendition of *Avant la fin de la Lumiere* as the sun set through the sanctuary's windows. A peaceful end to a long day of travel.

An exploration of Espace Chimay the next day provided me with an incredible wealth of knowledge on the current brewing practices and operations. Unlike Westmalle, the disconnect between visiting Scourmont Abbey and having extensive access to the brewing operations at Chimay was cavernous. This was evident with the advent of Chimay Wartoise overseeing enterprises across Chimay's business portfolio, the operation is truly massive.

As the abbot shares at Espace Chimay, "since 1996 the foundation has had a clear objective. Concretely, its philanthropic objective is one of development of the whole region."[6] Nowhere is this more evident than in the production of the beer itself and the process's firm rootedness in the commercial thriving of the region. Though alluded to above, the extent to which the Cistercian values of locality and stability are present at Chimay is impressive. Between the brewery, the dairy, distribution roles, and the administrative offices, Chimay employs over 250 full-time workers with countless more involved in the supplying of raw materials used by the abbey's enterprises. This makes the abbey the largest employer in the region and a vital economic catalyst that prevents the all too familiar financial struggles of rural living.

This locally oriented approach is present from the very beginning of the brewing process where the regional barley used for mash bill begins its journey in February every year. Hainaut farmers sow the seeds of the six-row barley that will serve as the fermentation source in the final month of winter before tilling and organically weeding the crop in April. Harvest happens in August, it is lightly germinated/sprouted before drying, and then the grain is malted to Chimay's specifications before entering the mill room at the brewery. Additional fermentables are present via both candi sugar (though this occurs in a ratio of less than 5 percent of the overall base) as well as wheat grist.

That finely ground malt—a technique that Chimay argues allows for greater starch distribution during the mash—then enters the mash tun where it meets water from the still functioning wells which have been expressly protected by conservation mechanisms to ensure their continued purity. Chimay employs a quality control expert that also has a focus on environment management to avoid soil contamination of any kind. The laboratory set up on site at Chimay is more impressive than in any other production facility I visited, and extensive labs are run at every stage of the beer making process, including checks on the raw materials themselves. This focus on water purity and conservation is extended to farmers in the region as well. The soft water remains untouched by the hands of time/environmental degradation and is just as recognizable as the rest of the base ingredients.

The water and fermentables are brought together via step mashing. Before being transferred to the industrial kettles from the latest brewery expansion, Chimay utilizes an impressive filtration unit to separate the

---

6. L'Espace Chimay, "Museum Tour."

spent grain from the wort. In the boil, Chimay's proprietary hop blend takes center stage.

Unlike other Trappist producers, Chimay makes it a point to use hop extract rather than a majority addition of whole cone hops or pellets. Chimay has done so since the days of Brother Theodore. He favored the level of control on offer with extracts as he kept an eye on consistency, fearing that whole cone hops are too unpredictable. Ultimately, the form of hop utilized comes down to personal preference and quality can come from either method as exhibited by the range of Trappist beers.

Though the exact blends are not known and likely vary occasionally, Chimay's beers feature some hops grown in the Pacific Northwest's Yakima Valley. For the aromatics, Chimay draws on the Hallertau Mittelfrüh varietal which, despite its German origins, is grown locally as well with an eye on revitalizing the local agricultural economy. The perfect blend of citrus, fresh flowers, and an earthy spicy tone comes together in this particular hop and pairs nicely with the profile created by Chimay's yeast.

Though I covered Chimay's distinct yeast strain in my overview of De Clerck and Brother Theodore, it bears mentioning again. The qualitative oversight done by Sandrine Selves—who has been at Chimay for over twenty years—and her microbiology team continues the rich heritage of focus instilled by that original Chimay yeast duo. They have collections of lab sheets dating back decades and directly to the original isolation of Chimay's strain to ensure quality and consistency.

There are also several labs, including the one at the brewing school in Leuven, where yeast is archived just in case. At three to five days for primary fermentation time, Chimay's yeast is also the quickest acting of the Trappist products discussed here—though secondary fermentation does continue in the bottle after a second dousing of yeast. During the centrifuging and clarification process, Chimay pulls residue and compresses it into multivitamin tablets, which are available in the shop—those nineteenth-century doctors may indeed have been onto something!

After that initial primary fermentation, the beer is transferred into clarifying tanks so that any remaining sediment/suspended protein can drop out. Though held at low temperature for a few days, this process is not fully considered lagering but is vital for stabilization of the beer and reaching a visual consistency that Chimay is happy with. Once this occurs, the beer is pumped into tanker trucks that make the five-kilometer trip to the packaging facility where the liquid is doused with another portion of yeast for secondary fermentation. After it finds its way to its final glassy home, each of the Chimay products is stored at cellar temperature for twenty-one days before heading to distribution.

The keg line at the production facility is also a busy place as Chimay's draft offerings far outnumber its other Trappist cousins—a conscious decision to make shipping more economical and less environmentally detrimental when beers make their way to places less keen on recycling and renewing resources. Excluding the barrel aged offerings, all Chimay beers are available in 330-ml, 750-ml, and draft format.

Though the labor of beer making is complete at this point, Chimay's employees are not quite finished yet. The global presence and brand power of the beer did not come to fruition miraculously and the marketing team picks up where the brewers and packaging technicians leave off to ensure such prowess continues. Unlike other Trappist breweries, Chimay sees promotion, marketing, and branding as an extension of the Cistercian values and an elevation of the gifts of the people involved in these processes. The social nature of theological anthropology comes to the fore here as other communities favor conservative approaches to these aspects of production.

A dedicated YouTube channel featuring videos for each of its offerings;[7] a plethora of tackers, coasters, keychains, giftsets, neon signs, glassware variations, mail-in certificates, posters, and other promotional materials; sponsorships of events from the Brussels Film Festival to the Giro d'Italia cycling race; and an active social media presence are just an introduction to the labor put into these beers once they leave the production line. A multi-member stateside team with several reps in the Midwest has been beyond helpful with follow-up information for this book.

It is no surprise that Trappist beer and Chimay have virtually become synonymous among connoisseurs throughout the World. The latest tagline, "Tasty. Meaningful. Authentic." carries weight that other marketing teams can only dream of. Production, distribution, and promotion all work in tandem to get the beers in the hands of consumers while sustaining both the abbey and its various charitable projects through its distinct portfolio of offerings.

> *Première*: This Dubbel pours a gorgeous ruby red in the light but has tones of copper brown or perhaps hazelnut as well. Given refermentation, the beer should also appear slightly cloudy at first pour. Incredible

---

7. Chimay Beer, "@1862 Chimay YouTube Channel."

head retention lasts throughout consumption and leaves creamy lacing behind in its wake. Initial aromas of peach, apricot, honeysuckle, and overripe berry from the yeast profile meet the spicy tones of the Hallertau hops and the caramel, fig, and subtle banana from the malt profile. Biscuit, clove, and lightly perceptible cacao notes come through on the body, while a kiss of molasses sweetness lingers in the aftertaste. At 7percent ABV, the *Rouge* is extremely quaffable, and the slightly elevated alcohol content is not noticeable on the palate. The soft water adds to this inherent drinkability.

Grande Réserve: Though not officially categorized as such, the heaviest hitter in the portfolio can be helpfully described as quadruple adjacent. Technically a Belgian dark strong, the Bleue has some of the same base flavors as the *Rouge* but ups their intensity—especially with the dark chocolate and dried fruit elements. Pouring a very dark brown, the creamy head associated with Chimay's beers is still present, albeit beige in this instance. The aromatic profile created by the hops, yeast, and malt bill is also reminiscent of the *Rouge* but clove, Christmas spice bread, and a hint of booziness round out its profile—the 9 percent ABV is noticeable. Still easily potable for those so inclined, but the *Bleue* is a bit more of a mouthful than any of the other Chimay offerings. It is no surprise that it was quickly moved from the seasonal to the year-round category. I highly recommend picking up a few bottles of a singular vintage and opening them at differing intervals over the years. The *Grande Réserve* lives up to its name and ages beautifully, developing flavor characteristics in the peppery, chocolatey, and bright candied fruit categories with time.

Grande Réserve Barrel Fermented: As described above, the barrel program at Chimay has really boomed since its founding in 2015. It takes a bit of searching to find these Stateside, but doing so is well worth it. These give any other barrel aged "whales" a run for their money. The beer coming out of spirit barrels is only as good as the beer that goes in so the success of this project should be a surprise to no one. Contrary to popular barrel aged beer opinion, I would drink these as soon as you get them so that the barrel characteristics do not fall off over time.

Cinq Cents: Pouring bright gold in color, the creamy head is a bit thinner than the *Rouge* or the *Bleue* but present. Aromatics of freshly cut grass, newly dried flowers, and spices show the utility and range of the yeast, while the hops and malt provide a backdrop of muscat, green raisin, and bright red apple to round out the nose. A body with a hint of vanilla leads into a crisp sharp boozy finish of clove. At 8 percent ABV, it is once again a dangerous reminder that strength and heaviness are not synonymous.

Dorée: This 4.8 percent *pater* beer still packs a flavorful punch. Pouring lighter gold than the *Cinq Cents* and with a bit more yeast retention, its refreshing nature is present at first sight. The gorgeous lacing associated with quality is still present but dissipates quicker than its more robust siblings. Aromatics of orange peel, lemon zest, coriander, bright green apple, and a hint of cinnamon are produced by the yeast and meet the earth tones and spicy character of the hops. Banana bread, carrot cake, and brown sugar come through in the body. Thirst quenching but with a crisp lingering bitterness, *Dorée* calls consumers back again and again. I am glad we no longer live in a time where this beer was reserved for monks.

Cent Cinquante: The last and newest of Chimay's offerings, this hoppy strong blonde is fitting for its purpose of celebrating Scourmont's 150th anniversary as it is pure joy in a glass. This beer is hoppier, brighter, more floral, and overall, louder than Brother Theodore's original Tripel. It is a confluence of the uniqueness, quality, and character present at Chimay. Gold in color with minimal sediment, the crispness of *Cent Cinquante* instantly catches the eye. A bouquet of floral notes reminds enjoyers of the hop prominence here while the yeast comes through as mint, bergamot, lime, and dried stone fruit. The body is incredibly well rounded and a bit lighter than what one might expect. Spiciness and citrus intensity are the lingering tasting notes, etched in memory long after drinking. At 10 percent ABV, it is the booziest of Chimay's offerings, a feature present throughout the drinking experience. Whether checking off a momentous milestone or simply making it to the end of the workday, *Cent Cinquante* fulfills its original celebratory purpose well.

In these offerings, the essence of Scourmont is perfectly captured. Classic and innovative; technically excellent and yet easily approachable; distinctly rooted in their surroundings but available around the globe; exquisite but humble; and beckoning invitation with every pour. As I catch an early bus out of Chimay, the first leg of what will ultimately be a journey back to the States, a local café proprietor is preparing his outdoor seating for the day. He unfurls Chimay-branded patio umbrellas just as I take my seat and the driver starts off. A fitting end to a wonderful stay at the place largely responsible for my journey.

Chapter 5

Abdij Maria Toevlucht

I NOW TAKE A quick jump across the border to Holland and the most novel of the Trappist abbeys that support themselves via brewing discussed here—brewing its first commercial batch in 2013—Zundert. About fifteen kilometers from Breda in the Netherlands, Zundert is most famous for being the childhood home of Vincent Van Gogh, which one may visit in its contemporary museum form—along with a gallery and countless monuments around town.[1] My purpose in making the trek was much different as Abdij Maria Toevlucht was the first stop of my Trappist adventure but passing by the gorgeous window displays of the museum en route to the main country road was a pleasant addition.

    I had my college-aged brother in tow on his own summer excursion. Having taken art history more recently than I have, he was able to fill in our five-kilometer walk with all sorts of facts about post-Impressionism while I gave a rough sketch of both monastic life and the Trappist propensity for brewing. This would turn out to be a perfect start to my stay at Zundert with their emphasis on stimulating contemplation and conversation with their beer. Moreover, I would come to learn that both the abbey and the brewery take the importance of the *terroir* to a level beyond the other Trappist communities. Taking in the surroundings via my walk would thus prove to be vital in understanding their approach and the intrinsic influence of the land on Zundert's beer. A light drizzle accompanied us, kicking our olfactory systems into gear as we passed by agricultural fields and cow grazing pastures before turning down a wooded path to the abbey grounds where

---

1. Vincent van Gogh Huis, "History and Building."

snails made their way along the wet pavement to greet us. A very modern gift shop and office space was the first building we encountered as we began our stay, giddy that this project was tangibly underway.

Historical Overview

Not only is Zundert the youngest of the Trappist brewing enterprises, but the community itself is also the youngest covered here. Founded in 1900 as a daughter house of Abdij Onze Lieve Vrouw van Koningshoeven (which houses the La Trappe brewery), Zundert lives up to its name as *Abdij Maria Toevlucht* literally means abbey of Mary our Refuge. The community was founded with a distinct purpose in mind as the anticlerical context of the eighteenth-century post-revolutionary period and Napoleon's own aversion to non-state religion continued to impact Cistercian communities in the region, particularly with secularization laws at the turn of the twentieth century.

1879 saw the removal of clerics from positions on state funded hospital boards and non-profit organizations; the passing of the Jules Ferry Laws in the early 1880s removed Catholic control over education and severely limited its place in secular classrooms; the Goblet Law of 1886 removed priests, monks, and nuns from teaching posts entirely; 1901's Law of Association placed all Catholic education under the direct control of the State; all of which culminated in the 1905 Law of Separation of Church and State which among other things abolished the Ministry of Religion, banned religious symbols and phrases on public buildings, and confiscated all Church property as national property that was then "generously" loaned back to the church for use.[2]

The Monts-des-Cats abbey and its abbot Dominique Lacaes saw the writing on the wall amidst this return to secularism and attempted to find land elsewhere that could provide a safe haven for them and other French monastics should things escalate. Koningshoeven, a town outside of Tilburg, proved to be just such a place and in 1881 a community was founded there as the first of many sites of refuge for French Cistercians in Holland. Dutch Catholics took it upon themselves to counteract what they saw as unfair treatment of religious orders and the landed gentry especially sought to offer land grants to those fleeing secularization. Zundert itself became the site of one of these donations as Lady Anna Catharina van Dongen

2. Bruun, *Cambridge Companion to the Cistercian Order*.

gifted a parcel of her holdings to Koningshoeven's abbot, Dom Willibrord Verbruggen in 1897.

In the Fall of 1899, the abbot sent brothers Nivardus Muis and Dorotheus De Vries to ascertain the viability of the land and begin planning the buildout of a priory. They were hosted by a local farmer as they surveyed the future home of the community on his property which was nicknamed "De Kievit," or Lapwing, a local bird particularly attracted to the intersection of wetlands and open farmlands—a creature that became a constant feature of Zundert's story.

Ten more monks from Koningshoeven joined the original two and a monastery was constructed alongside a modest chapel. The Church was officially consecrated by Dom Verbruggen on May 24, 1900. The priory was placed in the hands of Father Muis as superior, and the brothers began the arduous task of making the thirty-seven acres of land arable. This was no easy feat given the marshy nature of the property and the less-than-ideal soil (this seems to be a recurring theme with regards to the type of land donated to Cistercians). The addition of dairy cattle and other livestock via donations from the local congregation helped to supplement the meager agricultural returns and would point to the potential for the later reconfiguring of the community's business practices as primarily cattle based. Unfortunately, struggling with the landscape was not the only problem that the abbey at Zundert would face early in its existence.

In the summer of 1909, financial constraints beyond the control of the abbey at Zundert came to the fore. Dom Willibrord in Koningshoeven had stretched his community's finances thin and defaulted on a mortgage. The only feasible way to remedy the situation, according to the abbot, was to sell off Zundert's property and material possessions. In this period of uncertainty, the brothers at Zundert went from refuge providers to refuge seekers. For six months from June to November they moved in with the monks at Westmalle while the Cistercian Order stepped in to try to find an amicable solution. Ultimately, Dom Willibrord was removed as the abbot at Koningshoeven while the Order helped refinance.

In the wake of this, the brothers of Maria Toevlucht left Westmalle and returned to the abbey at Zundert. The community became more independent financially through some generous land, resource, and monetary donations from local landowners including sizeable pledges from the De Schooten family which were demarcated for the building of a more impressive church on the grounds.

The period of WWI did not impact Zundert in the same way as it did other Trappist communities given Holland's neutral status during the conflict, but it was both stressful and formative. If you'll recall, Maria Toevlucht continued to live up to its namesake as it served as a refuge from the monks temporarily seeking shelter away from Westmalle, but even before this, hundreds of civilian lay refugees fleeing the German army crossed the Belgian border to seek shelter at the abbey. Some stayed just a day or two before moving on, while others spent the entirety of the war there. Sustenance was provided by the farm itself, and though extreme rationing was the norm as the brothers adapted to their newly expanded scope of hospitality, the abbey served as a beacon of hope in this time.

The addition of the brothers from Westmalle for the duration of the conflict was said to have revitalized the spiritual vigor of the Maria Toevlucht community and they were also able to pitch in with regards to finishing various construction projects around the priory. This included the completion of the sanctuary in 1915 and the addition of smaller chapels around the cloister as well. In the wake of the conflict Zundert actively sought to help other abbeys that needed rebuilding via both material and financial means, continuing its growth in prestige and the attraction of new members. This helped facilitate its official movement from a priory to an abbey in September of 1938 with Dom Muis remaining in charge of the brothers under the title of abbot which he held until his passing in 1942.

Though Holland was occupied during the second world war, Zundert itself was minimally impacted by the Nazi regime and navigating this conflict was again much different than what other Cistercians underwent. Abbey historian Godfried Bomans notes that not only did the community experience joy and tranquility from its newly elevated status, but that it recorded a record harvest on the farm, hit a new high of sixty-five members, and proudly avoided deviating from the performance of its daily liturgy even during the initial invasion.[3] The remainder of the war saw little alteration to this calm outside of a few instances of German soldiers seeking shelter to treat their wounds or to check that the monastery was not housing collaborators.

The community surpassed seventy-five members by the end of the war, a testament to its creation of a sense of normalcy amidst chaos. The only casualty of the war, if he can be called that, was Dom Muis whose quickly declining health was triggered by stress. The community elected

---

3. Bomans, *Trappistenleven*.

Brother Alphonsus van Kalken to replace him and when liberation came in 1944 and then the abbey helped pick up the pieces of many Cistercian monasteries impacted around Europe. For example, Oelenberg Abbey in Alsace was rebuilt and revitalized after suffering near catastrophic damage during the war through financial support and the relocation of several Toevlucht monks.

In the post-war period, Maria Toevlucht would reach its peak size in 1950—numbering eighty. The main source of income for the abbey was still the raising of dairy cattle and agricultural production, tasks made easier by the number of brothers participating in the monastic vocation. This would set the tone financially for a period of renovation and modernization in the 1960s. Led by newly elected Dom Schuurmans, this reinvigoration was both liturgical and structural as the Church, the grounds, and the cloister received upgrades, while the decision was made to switch from Latin to Dutch for religious services. Following Schuurmaans, Dom Hieronymus Witkam led the community for over three decades (1967–2001) in a similar fashion, undertaking a full rebuilding of the cloister to allow private quarters for each brother. This was also partially facilitated by a shrinking community.

Contemporary Facets of the Community and Brewery

Unlike the other communities above, I have covered Zundert's history and have not yet discussed beer. This is because the brothers at Maria Toevlucht adequately supported themselves via their agricultural and cattle endeavors until the early 2000s when several factors led to a shift. First, an ecological survey made clear to the community that although the viability of the land was just fine at that moment, long-term degradation meant that productivity would increasingly decline over the coming decades. With the changing economic landscape piling pressure on smaller producers, alternatives were necessary. Second, with a shrinking and aging community, the physical strain and time consumption necessitated by raising cattle and farming the land was an added factor for consideration.

Or, as Brother Christiaan put it, "having a cattle farm, or whatever kind of farm, takes seven days a week. In fact, it's twenty-four hours a day because yes you have to be milking but they also give birth, get sick, etc. It really takes up seven days a week to work on a farm. And then the number of monks decreased and this happened more and more while adding stress on the brothers." The longevity of the community and the monks' religious focus were on the line, so Zundert began to consider a route familiar to many regional Trappists—brewing beer.

By 2007, Dom Daniel Hombergen had been elected abbot and made the decision to close the cattle farm amidst this changing reality. The abbey's land was still in its possession, but eventually its stewardship would be entrusted to a conservation organization focused on maintaining natural habitats in Holland. Simultaneously, Dom Hombergen set up a research group among the monks to map out the economic viability of sustaining Maria Toevlucht via brewing, including the feasibility of transforming its current facilities into a brewery.

Consultation with other Trappist breweries certainly played a role but Brother Christiaan was adamant that the numbers as well as the transition in labor needed to make sense for the Zundert community itself. After extensive dialogue. Brother Christiaan shared, "we had to have another source of income. We started thinking, and in the end, by a vote, we decided to have a small brewery. Not a big brewery attached to a small abbey but an abbey with a brewery of appropriate measure." The decision to shift to brewing was made official in 2008, but the hard work was just beginning.

The brothers needed to ensure that the Trappist ethos guided the transition both in terms of building out the brewery as well as crafting the beer profile itself. Brother Christiaan sought outside consultation in addition to communal discernment. "We went on thinking and thinking and then we met Constant Keinemans, our lay brew master, and went about the process of developing and designing the brewery." The decision was made to repurpose the former cattle stables as a brewhouse—a nod to the past with an eye on the future. The guiding principles of stability, locality, and a conscious focus on ensuring that the contemplative life of the monks was protected were essential in the process. Brother Christiaan went so far as to say they would not jeopardize or compromise the essential parts of their vocation.

Constant chimed in and reiterated this importance,

> We began engineering the brewery and decided upon how we wanted to solve [local issues] and to build the brewhouse in a way that can help the community. Not in the sense of building a large brewery that a lot of people need to staff, but how can we build the brewery in a way that can help the monastery to survive and to stay? Because yes, we had to build the brewery, but the monks are not coming into the abbey to become brewmasters. They come into the monastery to give themselves to God.

As he said this, it dawned on me that this was the only community I would visit that gave me direct access to the people responsible for the founding of the brewery. The insight on offer was truly unique and meant that I was cataloguing what many still consider the initial growth stage of Zundert. I was literally getting to pick the brains of the people there for the conception and execution of the beer I had the evening before!

Returning to Constant's insight, the focus on keeping the brewery small is reflected in the operational size and the conscious staffing of Zundert. It is by far the smallest capacity brewhouse of the Trappist producers—40 hectoliters per batch on a gorgeous fully automated Joh Albrecht built system. This means they cap production at an average of 3,000 hectoliters annually, though their output could be closer to 5,000 hectoliters should they choose to expand. Fermentation takes place in just six cylindrical lagering tanks placed vertically in the production facility. Bottling has been done off site since they began their operations (at La Trappe's brewing facility).

The nature preserve designation installed in 2011 along with the agricultural lifestyle of their neighbors also necessitated care in approach with regards to the size of operations. Brother Christiaan jokes, "You've seen the environment we live in! So, it was quite a process to get permission to build a brewery because when we said to people in the neighborhood that we wanted to build a brewery they said, 'Oh no, not a brewery!' because they were very imaginative about what it was we were going to do." They had to ensure that the scale was adequately conveyed to their neighbors, that this wasn't going to be anywhere near like what Zundert's mother house had going on. "The first thing we did was to inform the neighborhood what plans we had developed and it was a whole procedure to go through with the governing township. During this, we had time to think in detail about the development and design of the brewery."

The approval process was completed and by October of 2012 construction was ready to begin, though again, this would not be as vast an undertaking as at other facilities and the brewery was ready for its first commercial sized test batch in October of 2013 and the plaque designating the opening of the brewery was affixed on December 6. Officially, Zundert's brewery was dubbed "Trappisten Brouwerij De Kievit," a nod to the original plot of land to which the monks arrived and the local bird which would eventually feature on the beer labels.

These conscious touches of identity are found throughout the facility itself which includes extensive glass paneling on the walls, ceiling, and entrances to the brewery (a decision as theological as it was aesthetic); a statue of St. Arnold, the patron saint of brewers, overlooking the kettles; and vaulted wooden beams eerily reflecting those of the sanctuary. Brother Christian recalls the importance of partnering with a build team that understood the project's ins and outs. "We found a guy to build the brewery with an eye for detail in the last few things, like conserving water, concentrated brewing, a steam generator where all of the heat is coming back into the water, re-feeding the water supply for the steam generator. The tanks are bigger so that we can have two batches fermenting in one tank. We only brew one beer so having bigger tanks saves energy for cleaning, it saves time, and it's good for developing the unique taste."

It is important to reiterate intentionality here in size and design. Brother Christiaan reminds me that contemplation, liturgy, and other religious vocational aspects come before any labor aimed at sustaining the community. For this reason, only two brothers participate in the brewing process at Zundert. Initially the brewing related tasks fell in the purview of brother Christiaan and brother Guido, but since the election of the latter as abbot in 2017, brother Christiaan began training another monk to step in. It is not that Zundert is not welcoming and open to the surrounding lay community, but they want to ensure that their true monastic calling is at the forefront of everything they do. "Outside of Constant, the bottling advisor, a commercial manager, and the accountant we have no other lay workers. So, every month we have a meeting to discuss brewing questions and items." The community is still in charge of all matters related to production.

Which brings us to the beer itself and one of the most unique approaches to recipe design in the Trappist community and beyond. At Zundert, I was not only given an inside look at the community and brewery but was guided through the creation of their product from the very first stages of its inception. Brother Christiaan and Constant were overly generous, and I am happy to share the story of how Zundert's beer moved from an idea wheel, focus groups, and sensory panels to the glass in front of consumers. It all began with a conscious focus on uniqueness and distinct identity. Or, as Constant put it, "when we started thinking about a recipe, we immediately said we don't want a copy of another Trappist Abbey, we want our own recipe."

Of course, brand identity is important for any brewery but when you have the proven track records of places like Westmalle, La Trappe, Chimay, etc. as both examples and readily available resources within the ITA family, it may seem strange to pursue this line of thought. Consumer palates and wallets are already geared in a certain way and Trappist-made products are no exception. I was intrigued to say the least, and brother Christiaan made it abundantly clear that this was not just about branding, marketing, or consumer trends. The ethos of Maria Toevlucht needed to be found in everything that they do, liturgy, beer, or otherwise and the Cistercian focus on stability and locality became a linchpin for moving forward. Brother Christiaan echoed as much when tracing the beginnings of the beer,

> As you already know, monks that follow the Rule of St. Benedict start at a certain abbey and then they stay at that abbey. This is the vow of stability. So, we have our roots in a specific environment and a specific place. So, we wanted to develop a beer recipe with connections to our surroundings, to the place in which we live. Again, we didn't want a copy and so we started thinking about the beer with Constant and a beer sommelier and we had nine brothers participate in the process. They [Constant and the sommelier] organized a taste party for us, but no Trappist made beer, just all other kinds of beers.

Though the monks naturally looked forward to the opportunity for bonding over beer there was work to be done. The focus group of nine brothers selected for this process was a way of ensuring that the decision on what type of beer would be made at Zundert was not only reflective of the *terroir* but would be reflective of the community itself. Their like, their dislikes, the varying tastes brought together under the singular roof of the cloister, and ultimately, this communal input would ensure that the beer was a representation of the abbey in all of its facets. Brother Christiaan says,

> Before we started tasting, we had a sort of conversation or a brainstorm session. We noted and named all of the aspects we found important in our monastic life. Because monastic life has a certain aspect of endurance, of being stable, but also an aspect of caring for the environment. You could call it a mind map I suppose. There were several key words that we collected, and they were grouped in themes. Then we started tasting.

The fact that the beer started out in this way was a microcosm of the product to come. Tastes, esters, malt profiles, hops, all of the things I have been describing in the descriptions of the other Trappist breweries were of secondary importance to the fact that this was to be a Trappist beer in the spiritual sense, reflective of Maria Toevlucht itself.

When finished, the mind map was organized into larger themes and sprinkled outwardly from there to lesser associations. Zundert as a monastery, the contemplative life, seclusion, hospitality, nature, and the property of De Kievit were among the bigger reflective points that would need to make their way into the beer. The brothers wanted to make sure that they had a complex theoretical launching pad for the product they would be making and the time to discern its ins and outs properly. Patience, attentiveness, and purpose are monastic virtues of course!

Constant was able to highlight the necessity of such an approach perfectly,

> "It was important for us to start with that. We easily can make a recipe but to make something special we have to see what's new in the Trappist world versus what is conferred to them. But for us, it was important that it's a beer of this Abbey. The monks need to be proud of their beer so it's important to take them along in the process. Where are we going? What do you want to do? What do you want to produce? The look and the feel of the monastery, for the Abbey it's really important. And also for the monks, from the beginning they were going to brew only by themselves."

The monks were then ready to see if they could find parallels to the outline they had created for the beer. Constant illuminated that the beers on offer in the blind tasting that followed came from as wide a spectrum as possible.

The tasting itself was exceptionally analytic in nature with a full range of questions being asked of the brothers as they worked through the beers in a diagnostic fashion. "We didn't ask them simply did you like this beer or did you like that beer? But we asked them, here's a sour, what do you think about it? What do you like about it? What don't you like about it? We noticed certain things and analyzed them." Grasping the nuances of such an array of styles is no easy task but Brother Christiaan was adamant that Zundert did not want to be limited by the accepted norms of what Trappist beer "is." Because Trappist is a product designation and not a particular style, this approach allowed for the creation of a beautifully novel beer.

With focus on a singular beer rather than a larger portfolio, they had to get this process spot on. "The color was different, the alcohol was different, everything was different about each beer [tried]. And so, we tasted and tasted. One of the first things that we decided upon was the color. First, we made the decision that we only want to start at one beer. That's now called the 8. Back then it was called just Zundert. Not multiple beers, just one. Now, the color that's not very difficult for a brewmaster, neither is the alcohol percentage. But the taste profile is more difficult. We tasted all of those beers and in the end we mixed them together [to create a profile]." This was not as much an arbitrary undertaking of mixology as it was a careful description of what stuck out about each beer.

The translation of the concepts from the brainstorming session into the tangible aspects found in the beers was also an important part of this task. The monks thought they had created enough of a vision map to move forward to the stage of test batches, but Constant and the industry expert needed the brothers to be sure. Brother Christiaan smiled as he recalled, "They said, 'no, the beer has to be appreciated both in summer and in winter. Because in summer your perception of the taste is different than in winter.' So, we had another round table tasting evening."

Constant, echoed his reasoning for the secondary tasting. "Yeah, we did it twice. Once in spring and once in Autumn. We had our fingers crossed because we had to do it with entirely different beers. So, when you try a sour, you can take a gose from Bohm, or you can take another version. We tasted a different small beer, we mixed up the order and lineup placement. We removed the labels from the bottles so that we could really understand what they want." Such sensory depth, consistency in vision, and attention to detail more often than not would produce differing results. The outcome was not what I would have expected in such a secondary tasting as Constant remembered just how far the thorough attentiveness and refined tastes of the brothers got them. "So, for us, it was again, fingers crossed, did we come out with the same results after half a year? So, they don't have in their mind, 'okay, this I like, this I liked yesterday, and this I'll like tomorrow. I know what I like.' But we came to the same results, it was very nice!"

So, what exactly was it that they had brainstormed in a now double-blind experiment? The basic characteristics were as follows: the amber color and roughly 8 percent ABV were coupled with a mix of earthy spice tones and sweeter caramel notes, herbs were a must for the nose, added complexity after some aeration was preferred, it was to have an exceptionally dry finish while still retaining a creamy head throughout, and most importantly, a sense of subtle peated smokiness was to be found in the beer. With this in mind, Constant was able to start brewing pilot batches as a distinct recipe was dialed in. Amidst this process, in addition to his expert guidance in learning the ins and outs of their new brewing system, Brother Christiaan and Brother Guido also underwent further training and collaborative information exchanges with other ITA members to perfect their new craft. All of these moving parts came together and leading into Christmas of 2013, the first commercial batch of beer was ready to hit the market.

Now labeled as Zundert 8 Tripel Trappist, it reached each of the envisioned notes and flew off the shelves from the very first distribution run. With no intended malice, I would say anyone opening a bottle should be weary of any style associations they may have with Tripels. The uniqueness planned from those initial viability discussions is the predominant conceptual characteristic that comes through in this beer. One would not think of a cloudy amber color nor a bouquet of herbs, spices, smokiness, and peat. Yet those are ever present in this beer while the aromatic hoppiness of a traditional Tripel is replaced with hints of caramel and clove. The perceived booziness certainly isn't as high as the label suggests, at least initially. It tends to increase and linger as the beer warms, an indulgence that we must allow for ourselves, shares Brother Christiaan—its complexity is to serve as a backdrop for contemplation and conversation. In more ways than one, the entire experience is more akin to sitting with a scotch than with a beer. Especially the peat, I simply cannot get that out of my head.

Constant asks me during our interview what I thought of the beers that were brought to my guest room the evening before, and I am quick to mention I have never had anything like the 8. I asked my hosts whether they were using peated bog myrtle in the beer and they both looked shocked while congratulating me on my discerning palate. Brother Christiaan noted not only that it was a staple ingredient but asserted why. "Yes, it's one of the herbs we use. In Latin it is called *myrica gala*, but I think the English is gale. It's an herb that grows here in the habitat nearby. Before, long ago, there was a lot of peated turf and when the peat was gone and plowed for wheat fields there was still some remaining gale. It took nearly two centuries to remove the peat and change the landscape." Ironically, it was one of the facets of the landscape that made it so difficult to farm initially but the locality and stability aspects outlined in the brainstorming session ensured that it would make its way into the beer.

Constant moved beyond a philosophical approach and added,

> It's also important that when you add something you are aiming for the right balance for people's tastes. It's not that when you add, for example, strawberries that you automatically say "Oh, I taste strawberries!" No, let them go through the subtle process of

tasting and smelling and ask, "Oh, what's that?" So, for the gale, we use very little so that it's not overwhelming. A long time before the usage of hops, it was used by brewers. They used several herbs together and gale was one of the most important for brewing. So, it adds bitterness but is also important for the shelf life of our beer. It's also very good for taste.

I have tried to focus on the importance of locally sourced ingredients throughout my presentation of these beers, but Zundert takes this facet to a new level. Well water from the abbey grounds, regionally produced malts and hops, and specifically cultivated yeast have been the norm throughout my Trappist beer excursus, but to go outside of the traditional ingredient profile to literally incorporate the abbey's land is truly beautiful. Moreover, its functional purpose in the beer both for taste and the sparking of palate contemplation makes this beer a perfect reflection of the Trappist ethos. It is also stunning to be able to see the translation of an idea map into the liquid found in my glass so flawlessly. I only wish that other brewers approached their products with such intentionality.

This sparked a conversation about production and marketing approaches as both brother Christiaan and Constant had a lot to say about the beer industry's obsession with ever expanding portfolios. Adjusting his glasses with an air of disappointment, brother Christiaan says, "I don't know about the United States but in Holland there has been the development of a large amount of small breweries and they are each producing a dozen beers with different tastes. That's not the way we want to work." Oversaturation in terms of the number of breweries and the products they put have certainly been factors in the craft bubble bursting over the last several years. Longevity and stability are not at the forefront of most breweries' minds and the immediacy of trends reigns supreme.

Constant chimes in by adding, "Yeah, they need to renew all the time. Every month they come out with a new beer. We see it with some of the small craft rooms in the Netherlands, if they don't come up with a new beer every month then they will lose their place in the market." This deviates into a conversation about the inability for this type of approach to provide stable employment, consistency in product quality, longevity of brands, and an overall inability to build unique brewery identity. It is evident how much thought, passion, and care the pair put into their craft, their community, and the beer that leaves their doors.

The remaining ingredients outside of the focal point of gale reflect this approach as well. With regards to developing a yeast strain, Zundert had access to a whole catalogue of strains from the ITA but chose the route of developing their own locally influenced yeast. Constant described the initial process of development by sharing that "we don't use a stock Trappist yeast. It's also a central part of our process because 60 percent of your taste comes from it. So, we did a lot of tests with different kinds of yeast, and we found the perfect one." They needed a yeast that could create both the 8 percent ABV of the beer while also not producing esters that would overpower the other aspects of the beer.

Similarly, because of the smaller sized capacity, they concentrate brewing batches and ferment two turns in a singular fermentation. Though this naturally increases the pitch rate, the work-horse aspect of Zundert's particular yeast also alleviates some of the strain here. Constant proudly mentions that they get six generations out of each propagation without impacting outcome. The brewers also employ a technique called "drauflassen" which allows the yeast to begin fermentation in a half-filled fermenter that is then topped off at the height of yeast productivity—the microscopic critters are just as happy as the cattle grazing in the surrounding fields. The yeast typically takes three to four days for initial fermentation, but it does spend an additional four weeks in the lagering tanks for maturation and clarification. A secondary dose of yeast is added before bottling at La Trappe's facility for refermentation in 330-ml bottles (a small percentage of the beer produced is also kegged for draft availability).

Zundert specifically chose characteristics in its house yeast that avoid development with age. If you will recall, Chimay prided itself on the ability of its beers—especially the *Grande Réserve*—to change, grow, and mature over time. Its ten-year shelf-life touted on the label is reflective of this. Oxidation, flavor drop off, hop bitterness degradation, etc. are all real factors that are present when dealing with beer and change is ultimately unavoidable, but Christiaan was adamant that they wanted to get as close to stasis as possible. "When we produce a beer with a certain taste, we want to have that taste for three years, for five years. But, your beer, there is yeast in it, there is always something going on in the bottle. It's not a balanced beer if it's always changing. So, it's also a process to get consistency." They want to know that the beer their customer buys tastes as close to the form it left the brewery in. No guessing games, no frills about vintage fluctuation. Just consistently beautiful beer.

With regards to the water used for brewing, they do not have the same direct draw well systems as some of the other Trappist breweries but the municipal water being used still carries unique regional characteristics and is ready to go without many alterations. Constant tells me that "we are really happy in the Netherlands, we can drink our water, our tap water. The quality here for our water is unbelievably good. So, we don't need to do anything with water outside of running it through the steam generator and adding a bit of softener because you don't want calcium or some other harsh things in it. But for the rest, we don't need to treat it."

As for the malts, the specific ratios weren't shared with me, but the utilization of five different types of malt including two-row pale malt, caramel malt, and a bit of chocolate malt make up the malt bill. This helps to explain some of the complexity of the beer as well as its color. A portion of the malt is also peated, adding to the flavor profile provided by the gale. It is subtle so whatever the ratio, it's just a small portion. A small grain silo and mill room are housed within the brewery itself, and the malt is brought to the brew deck via chain driven pipes.

The hop addition comes in two phases, the first for bitterness and the second for aromatics. However, the locally picked gale—an amount overseen by the conservation society put in charge of the land—also enters during the first addition. The powerful bittering and flavor presence of the gale, along with the need for its subtlety in the taste profile, means that each brewing turn utilizes just a few grams of it. Neither the bittering nor aroma hop varietals were shared with me—although my hosts paused slightly before confirming it was a secret. Given the importance of locality, I would venture a guess at the Brabant region's proclivity for Saaz, Hallertau, and Cascade, but don't take that as canon.

The majority of these ingredients go into making Zundert 8, but the brewery also produces two other beers. After five years of steady production, a second beer was added to the commercially available portfolio; while in typical Trappist fashion, a *pater* beer for the internal use at monastery for both monks and guests has been brewed alongside the 8 since 2023 as well. I'll briefly introduce these other two offerings.

Zundert 4 Refterbier: A passion project of Abbot Guido's, this beer fulfilled his wish of being able to offer a beer for visitors while also continuing the tradition of Cistercians adopting the local beverage within the cloister. It follows the same process outlined above but the recipe is vastly different from the 8. Though some two-row malt enters into the frame, the 4 also includes wheat malt and rye malt. The presence of the gale is still noticeable but not as much as in the 8. Constant highlights that they would not back away from the tradition of incorporating part of the De Kievit landscape, but it needed to be tailored to the style. It is available in the guesthouse for contemplative consumption and 330-ml bottles are made available in the gift shop as well. Similar floral notes accompany the 4, while it is lighter in alcohol (4 percent ABV), body, and taste. The rye and wheat dominate the flavor profile but come together in a way that is both surprisingly refreshing and rather complex for this style.

Zundert 10 Quadrupel Trappist: Coming in at 10 percent ABV, everything about this beer is bigger and bolder than the 8 while retaining contours that are uniquely Zundert. Heavy on dark malt and chocolate malt, a warm sweetness resonates throughout with cocoa, licorice, dark fruit, and a hint of dried apricot lingering long after first taste. As this beer aerates and warms to room temperature, its nuances grow, including a bit of a coffee element accompanied by a resounding date character. Its beautiful creamy head keeps its shape to the very last sip, though it is closer to beige than the white of the 8 or 4. The spicy character and gale presence are elevated, while a healthier dose of bittering hops also makes its way into the brew. Though available on draft in town as well as in the typical 330-ml format, the gift shop also has a small amount of 750-ml bottles that you can purchase in a gift set.

Each of the three beers are labeled and marketed in a way that reflects the attention to detail paid to recipe building. The 8 and the 10 have purple-colored labels mirroring the color of gale blossoms, heather flowers, and hibiscus growing in the region, while the 4 dons a yellowish green that perfectly encapsulates the hues of the moss and marshes of the region. The lapwing (kievet) which adorns each Zundert product pokes ever so gently out of a patch of grass eerily reminiscent of the outline of the sanctuary and is positioned on the background of a keystone found on many of the abbey's buildings. This keystone shape is cleverly incorporated into the coasters made available for bars carrying their product, one of the only promotional materials in use. The "d" in Zundert is set apart from the rest of the font on the bottle and is a nod to the calligraphy used in copying scripture throughout Cistercian history. The bottles are as aesthetically complex as the beer inside.

During my stay at the abbey, I did many of the cliché things one might when arriving in Holland. I borrowed a bike from the brothers to traverse local paths between prayer services, I ordered Pannenkoeken at the restaurant a few kilometers away from the abbey, and I tried the few phrases and prayers I had learned in Dutch only to realize I was completely butchering the vowel sounds. But I quickly realized that nothing was as I had expected. Novelty, uniqueness, and a one-of-a-kind cultural identity met me in the cloister and in my glass. As I took in my last moments at the guesthouse, I was able to enjoy one more beer with grazing cows in the background. Likely descendants of those that had sustained this community before they transitioned to brewing. I couldn't help but smile. Despite being the new kids on the brewing block, Zundert is fundamentally rooted in tradition and upon first sip instantly becomes a classic.

As an addendum to the original text of this chapter, as this manuscript was submitted for review the abbot of Maria Toevlucht submitted a request to the General Chapter of the Trappist Order for dissolution of the abbey. The passing and retirement of a number of the monks at Zundert throughout 2024 necessitated a rethinking of the community. As Dom Guido Van Belle said in a press release on the topic, the remaining monks "are still vital and can make an active contribution to the community life of another monastery. It is a very painful but also unavoidable decision. We became monks to live a life of prayer, not to manage buildings. By choosing dissolution, we can close everything out in our own way and close the door behind us with our heads held high." The final decision will fall to the Superiors of the Order when the General Chapter next meets in September of 2025. By the time you are reading this, there might be one less Trappist brewery in the world. I have left this chapter in print purposely as a reminder of the quality, beauty, and vibrance that was lost and as a prayer for the renewal of monastic vocations.

Chapter 6

Abbaye Notre-Dame de Saint Rémy

"*Bienvenue a Rochefort!*" declares the Smurf as I exit the bus that had stopped on a roundabout in the center of the quaint Belgian town. A mural of the smiling cartoon creature greets visitors to Rochefort from the wall of a residential building. The gem of the Namur province and a stone's throw from the famously scenic Ardennes, Rochefort sits atop a plateau of luscious rolling meadows, hilly limestone deposits, and an entire network of caves formed by the Lesse River. Visually, it was the most stunning of the landscapes I encountered on this trip—almost mythical in its beauty, and thus a fitting backdrop for the Smurf looking down on me. Though not many know that the world-famous blue mischief makers hail from the region (conceptually), I was brought there in search of a completely different creature: the iconic and style-defining yeasts of the Rochefort beers brewed by monks at Abbaye Notre-Dame de Saint Remy.

Before I delve into both the history and the current contours of the brewery, I must include a brief note for this abbey. Due to an ongoing construction project at the time of my sojourn in Belgium, the guest house was not open for me to stay in. This meant that I visited the Saint Rémy community daily while staying in the town of Rochefort rather than living as a guest of the abbey. Similarly, the brewhouse was off limits to me at this abbey, and therefore my first-hand accounts and the use of interview material are limited in a way that they were not elsewhere. I hope to paint as clear a picture of the monks at Saint Rémy and the beers of Rochefort as I can with these limitations. With that being said, my stay in Rochefort was still formative and the abbey's influence on the region was just as apparent as the influence of the other Trappist communities on theirs.

Historical Overview

The history of the Saint Rémy abbey could fill an entire book on its own. Its beginnings predate the existence of the Trappist reforms by several centuries and the community's roots reach almost back to Bernard of Clairvaux himself. Founded in 1230 under the name *Succursus Dominae Nostrae*, the original monastery was not inhabited by monks but by Cistercian nuns that had acquired the land. Poor soil, a harsh climate, and lime deposits throughout the property made agriculture difficult—the abbey's name translated to "The Help of Our Lady," perhaps more a plea than an assertion. Additional land donations from the local nobility, including holdings in the town of Rochefort itself, aided the sustainability of the community and the nuns scraped by for two centuries.

The early fifteenth century was a fraught time for Catholic vigor in Western Europe and took its toll on monastic vocations. As the community shrank in numbers, its ability to generate enough income to ensure survival did as well. 1464 saw the General Chapter send observers to take stock of the community's viability. Abbots from nearby Jardinet and Moulins took on the task and wrote up a full report ascertaining that the nuns could not continue at the abbey and that they should be replaced by monks which might be better suited to exploit the property's rich marble quarries. Abbess Marguerite Spangneau and her nuns moved to Abbaye Félipré in France, with Abbot Arnould de Maisonneuve and his monks moving the other way. The switch benefited all involved.

Prosperity was short-lived for the community as a series of religious wars ravaged the region in the wake of the Protestant reformation. First, the Eighty Year's War (1568–1648) saw the Dutch rebel against Spanish rule. With Dutch Calvinism on the rise as a unifying force in the region, attacks on Catholic Churches, iconography, and relics became commonplace. The monks' fears were realized at the outbreak of the war as Calvinist soldiers occupied, plundered, and ultimately, destroyed large parts of the abbey. To add insult to injury, the Spanish Catholic governor of the Netherlands, Don Juan of Austria, occupied and caused further destruction to the abbey in 1577. Don Juan's successor, Alexander Farnese oversaw a period of peace in the region as he favored diplomacy to battle, and the monks were able to return to a bit of normalcy despite a need to rebuild.

Importantly, this period also saw the first officially catalogued brewing take place at the abbey. Though it is possible that the monks had been doing so since their arrival in 1414, abbey tax records show that in 1595 beer production was in full swing.[1] The beer was made from barley and hops grown on the abbey grounds and was only for community use. Though its profile has virtually no resemblance to the beers made by Rochefort today, this technically makes it the oldest Trappist made beer discussed here and allows the monks at Saint Rémy to claim a centuries-long brewing heritage.

Shifting allegiances and a potential power vacuum meant that the Eighty Year's War was drawn into a wider conflict embattling the whole of Europe known as the Thirty Years War (1618–1648). Though its impacts were broad, the major importance of this period on the monastic community at Rochefort was that France took Spain's place as the superpower of the region and despite its Catholic faith, aligned politically with the Protestant forces. This war itself was a devastating conflict that caused depopulation, economic turmoil, a series of plagues and famines along with political uncertainty which manifested itself in the further destruction of Saint Rémy when the French armies took over.

Just after the conflict, these same soldiers abused their newly found power to pillage the abbey, oust the monks, and repurpose the property as a military encampment, purposely desecrating the altar to add insult to injury. The brothers fled to nearby Marche where they stayed until 1654. Upon their return to Rochefort, they found their home utterly destroyed with significant damage to both the cloister and the church. The sanctuary would not be reconsecrated until 1671, though Dom Phillipe Fabry would defiantly adopt a new motto of resiliency for his community and the newly opened church: *Curvata Resurgo*—"bent over, I stand up straight again." And stand up they would. Construction on the property did not stop with the sanctuary. Some of the buildings from this period survive to this day amongst a hodgepodge of styles, architectural approaches, and color schemes that point to the long but tumultuous history of Saint Rémy.[2]

The community at Rochefort was also impacted by secularization in the wake of the French Revolution. Without rehashing history extensively,

---

1. Trappistes Rochefort, "Brewery."

2. For more on the layout of the abbey grounds and discussion of the architecture see Wallace et al., *Trappist Beer Travels*, 73–74.

the nationalization of church property announced in November of 1789 was enforced by the French occupying forces after taking control of the region in 1794, though some monks themselves were influenced by the Revolution and requested Pope Pius VI to secularize their holdings in 1792 meaning that the abbey was not much of a religious community by the time of the troops' arrival. What the invaders did not plunder was left to be picked off by locals (some of whom held onto religious objects, artwork, and vessels that would eventually be returned once the abbey was reestablished). The monks that were still practicing were dispersed to various communities outside of French reach, Saint Rémy was confiscated and sold by the occupying government in 1805 to a local that reconverted his new holdings into a farm. Nearly one hundred years would pass before Rochefort's monastic and beer tradition would restart as the property passed from secular owner to secular owner.

That cycle ended in 1887 when the property was sold to the abbey at Achel by Victor Seny, a retired chaplain that wanted to pursue the monastic vocation in his later years. Anselme Judong was named superior of the revived Cistercian priory and in addition to rebuilding the cloister, the church, and the farm, at Christmas of 1888 he told the monks under his tutelage they would be building a brewery as well. Construction was not completed until 1899 and initially the brewery's output was of meager size, questionable quality, and not used to support the community via sales. Instead, Judong wanted to make sure that the brothers were reflecting the Rule's allowances for partaking in the local beverage of the people. As a lack of agricultural viability in a competitive industrial farming age became more and more apparent, the idea of commercial production was brought to the fore to supplement income.

Under the guidance of superior Henri Kuypers, elected to succeed Judong in October of 1909, the transition to commercial production began in earnest. Kuypers also saw the elevation of Saint Rémy to the designation of "abbey" in 1912 serving as its first official abbot. It was a busy but exciting time for the community on both the religious and brewing fronts. Monks were sent to the famed brewing school at Leuven as well as gaining insight and inspiration from both Achel and Chimay to facilitate growth in production and quality. Though a refectory beer continued to be brewed for internal use, Chimay's *Bière Forte* and Achel's *Patersvaatje* served as models for a strong beer. Production was stable but the majority of the abbey's income was derived from the farm, the quarry, and cattle raising.

This would be changed by the devastation of World War I and the shifting landscape in its wake.

The Siege of Namur broke out in late August of 1914 after which the German forces overwhelmed and occupied the Belgian province for the duration of the war. Though liberated by the British in November of 1918, the conflict's devastation on the region (primarily from heavy shelling during the siege and looting of materials for munitions manufacturing) meant that the monks at Rochefort had to rebuild the brewery when they returned. This was done with the aid of the community at Scourmont whose expertise and commercial acumen was growing, leading to post-war brewing at Rochefort resembling that of Chimay while the decision to market widely and make the beer available far beyond the abbey walls was mirrored as well—success that was sadly halted by World War II.

Initially captured by Germany after the Battle of Ardennes in May of 1940 and King Leopold's capitulation, Rochefort the town suffered initial damage while the abbey did not. In fact, the monks at Saint Rémy continued to brew throughout the occupation as the Germans allowed the community to function practically as normal. In this sense, they were luckier than some of the other Trappist communities discussed here—a trend that would continue during the Battle of the Bulge in 1944 which saw the liberation of the Namur region.

The town itself was not destroyed like others in the Battle of the Bulge but casualties were severe, and dozens of buildings were leveled. The monks of Saint Rémy offered spiritual and financial support in the rebuilding of the town, though they themselves would hit a few bumps in the road during the 1950s with regards to sustainability and the future of the brewery. Ironically, the monks from Scourmont that had been so influential on the Rochefort brewery would be the source of a major headache in this period.

If you'll recall Chimay's story above, this period was one of success for their brewery, success that directly impacted Rochefort. Less than ninety kilometers apart, the commercial expansion spearheaded by Chimay's renewed vigor and increased quality meant that bottles of *Chimay Première* showed up in Rochefort's "distribution territory." Though not the equivalent of a cease-and-desist letter, the monks at Rochefort asked Chimay to limit how far east they sent their beer. Chimay refused to alter their model but in a move that makes no sense to those with free market inclinations, they also offered to help put Rochefort on a quality and distribution level that could rival theirs.[3]

Cistercian solidarity took center stage as Chimay brought brother Morsomme for training at their facilities while De Clerck took on a consulting role at Rochefort for several months. There was quite a bit of work to do if Rochefort's beer was to compete with the prestige of their western neighbors. First, De Clerck could not believe that the monks were still using a brew system that had been cobbled together in the late nineteenth-century when the decision was made to start beer production. By 1952 this had been remedied with the construction of a modern facility, one which would serve as a standard among Trappist breweries until it was replaced in 2020, though portions of it remain as an ode to Rochefort's past. Aptly described as the "cathedral of beer," the copper brewhouse was surrounded by floor to ceiling windows and stained glass, reminding the monks that they are to be a light to the world in all that they do.

Second, De Clerck needed to implement the type of lab rigor that had led him and brother Theodore to isolate and then maintain Chimay's famed yeast. Though this leads some to speculate that Rochefort utilizes Chimay's yeast, the beers at Saint Rémy are made with their own proprietary strain. As a fascinating caveat, when discussing Rochefort's yeast with the lab technician at Omega Yeast in Chicago, he brought up that when they ran genetic diagnostics on Rochefort's yeast they came back with genealogical connections to British ale yeasts. Over beers with Yvan De Baets of Brasserie de la Senne (a famed Brussels based craft producer) it was further illuminated that the brewing school at Leuven had extensive contacts with British producers at around this time as they attempted to recover and reset after the war.

Third, the facility changes included a switch to a mechanized bottling line making its way to Rochefort in the mid-1950s. This meant an immediate increase in quality due to sanitation procedures. The facilities were now a force to be reckoned with, and Rochefort was ready to make its mark on the beer landscape as agricultural pursuits took a back seat in sustaining the community.

The period of the mid-1950s, in the wake of these improvements, was also one in which the recipes were retooled, and the commercial portfolio grew. The pinnacle of the hard work in shaping the brand came in the form of a Belgian dark strong ale released in 1952 and dubbed *Merveille*, partially

---

3. Van de Steen, *Belgian Trappist and Abbey Beers*.

in hopes that the beer would grow into its namesake (a wonder). The original refectory beer was not produced for consumption outside of the abbey and was abandoned in its original format entirely within a decade of this renewed commercialization. The other beer crafted in this renaissance at Rochefort was the *Spéciale*, or "special one," which originated as a Christmas release but was in permanent rotation by 1955.[4]

The recipes have only been slightly tweaked since this period and are now known as Rochefort 10, 6, and 8 respectively—or color-coded with a blue cap and label insignia, a red cap and label insignia, and a green cap and label insignia. The numbers are not correlative to the alcohol content or any sort of multiplication of ingredients but rather represent a holdover measurement system of the beers' specific gravities—Belgian degrees. This system was initially used as a way to collect the proper taxation amount on beer and differs from degrees plato in that it accounts for higher acidity levels in wort.

These changes not only allowed Rochefort to compete in the market but turned around their financial fortunes and to sustain themselves entirely by beer production. An annual output of 15,000 hectoliters meant that any agricultural or cattle subsistence was obsolete by the early 1980s. Though, like most of the other communities discussed here, the abbey at Saint Rémy gradually incorporated more and more lay workers into the mix while the monks took on administrative and decision-making roles in production—an especially prudent shift given the decline in vocations during the later decades of the twentieth century.

Contemporary Facets of the Community and Brewery

Each day, as I jogged from the town center in Rochefort to the abbey to participate in the Liturgy of the Hours, I traveled along the Lomme river. As I cut through cobbled hilly streets to get to my route, I passed countless adverts for the abbey's beer, morning deliveries of the plastic yellow cases emblazoned with "*Trappistes Rochefort*" made to stores, restaurants, and cheese shops alike, and on one occasion, an elderly gentleman with his morning paper, a cigarette, and a bottle of Rochefort 6. By now, readers should know the close connection that each of these monastic communities shares with the surrounding populace, but with Rochefort this aura seemed stronger, perhaps even defiant.

---

4. Hieronymus, *Brew Like a Monk*.

I would soon learn from the hosts at my bed and breakfast that the monks had been embattled in a lawsuit on behalf of not just the abbey but the town itself, defending a local water source—the Tridaine spring—from the Lhoist mining company. With Lhoist wanting to take advantage of the region's lime and chalk deposits, the monks were worried about the impacts on the spring which feeds not only the brewery and the abbey, but the town as well. Assurances from the mining company that they would help dig a supplementary underground cistern linking the spring to the abbey by an unpolluted route were rejected. A series of court cases were tried at multiple levels in the Belgian court system and the monks of Saint Rémy triumphed each time because of an 1833 land deed which stipulates that the property's water source cannot be altered in any fashion.[5]

Though numbering just a dozen monks—with a few novices there—such leadership and solidarity have continued to be exhibited by the brothers as they navigate their current context. Brewery revamping took place in 2002 and most recently in 2020 as well as Rochefort expanding production to over 75,000 hectoliters at current capacity. Though this means that the cathedral of beer set up only functions as a museum display, the increased production allows for upkeep of the abbey and the employment of over two dozen lay workers across the facility, administrative, and marketing teams. Rest assured, the monks still have control over every part of the process, including a weekly sensory panel that enforces quality control measures before any batch can officially leave the premises.

On the cloister side, a fire swept through the grounds in 2010, which took over seventy firefighters from multiple towns to put out and destroyed four of the abbey's buildings—the residual effects of which were still being addressed by the construction, impeding my stay. The quickness of response saved the sanctuary itself, the brewery, and Rochefort's archives, preventing any casualties among the monks as well. Perhaps a cosmic nod of thanks for saving the Tridaine spring, the production of beer and celebrating the liturgy continued unimpeded. Which leads me to the portfolio itself and the reason for the initial excitement of walking off of the bus.

To begin, the water that the monks worked so hard to protect plays a pivotal role in the construction of each beer. Unlike the soft water of the Chimay beers that influenced those initial brews in the 1950s, Rochefort's water plateau can be described as having "harder water," meaning the minerality is much higher than many of the Trappist brews discussed here

---

5. Verstl, "Trappist Monks Beat Quarry Owner in Water Battle."

Time, Silence, and Yeast

(including a high concentration of calcium). The lime and chalk deposits come through in the water quality and are largely unaltered in the brewing process, meaning that it lends itself to darker and fuller beers to begin with as it can handle a more intense profile.

The fermentable sugars come mostly from caramel-Munich and Pilsner malts sourced from a variety of European countries, but the higher gravity beers necessitate the addition of dark Belgian candi sugar as well. The base flavor profile of the 6, 8, and 10 are largely the same but increase in intensity alongside the ABV of each. Like many of their cousins, Rochefort beers utilize a step infusion mash to ensure the production of complex sugars as well as to optimize protein breakdown. Though the exact rest times and number of water additions are secret, the ability of the Rochefort products to have both a full mouthfeel and a crisp finish attests to the importance of continuing this technique.

With regards to the hop profile of the Rochefort beers, they are subdued compared to some of the spicy characteristics of other beers discussed here. There are just two hop additions during the boil, one for bittering and one for aroma, both utilizing two varietals in pellet form—Hallertau and Styrian Goldings. The low alpha acid level of both reiterates that they are there mostly to accentuate the spicy character of the yeast rather than elevating the perceived bitterness. Like Zundert, the boil at Rochefort also sees an addition of dried herbs in the form of coriander. A miniscule amount goes a long way and its subtlety has been finely tuned to balance the beer rather than overwhelm the palate.

The wort makes its way to primary cylindro-conical tanks for a week and then to lagering tanks for a three-day secondary fermentation, where it is time for that famous yeast to do its work. Technically a mixture of two strains, each batch of yeast works its way through the 6, the 8, and the 10 before being discarded.[6] Reusing yeast occurs at most Trappist breweries because it is economical, efficient for kickstarting fermentation, and arguably adds consistency throughout multiple batches, but Rochefort is unique in seeing its yeast batches through the entirety of their core portfolio.

Because of the completely unique strain profile, Rochefort's yeast produces a flurry of surprising yet welcome esters in its beers. Green apple, pear, fig, and plum dominate the flavor characteristics of the yeast, and a complete lack of phenolic undertones reiterates this standout among Belgian and Dutch Trappist breweries. Another dose of yeast along with a

---

6. Hieronymus, *Brew Like a Monk*.

small amount of sugar are added as the beer makes its way onto the bottling line for packaging. The 6, 8, and 10 are only available in 330-ml bottles and spend ten days in a cellar at room temperature before making their way out to the world.

Rochefort 6: The beer that launched the modern identity of Rochefort. It pours beautiful ruby-amber in color with a white head that is not as creamy or lacy as other beers described here. It has a slight cloudiness depending on how long it has been conditioning, and the spicy aromatics quickly dissipate into a well-rounded green apple fruitiness. Caramel, date, and coriander come through upon first sip and only grow in intensity as it warms and breathes. The malty sweetness is balanced nicely with the crisp finish produced by the yeast. It is incredibly quaffable for a 7.5 percent ABV beer and though resonating with some aspects of the quintessential Belgian Dubbel style, it is uniquely Rochefort.

Rochefort 8: Though mistakenly billed as a beefed-up version of the 6, the 8 is its own beer. Coming in at 9.2 percent ABV, the malt profile and fermentable sugars come through in strong notes of caramel and chocolate across each sip. Dark fruit like plum, dates, and cherry are also joined with a unique hint of a berry mélange (blackberry, blueberry, and raspberry). The coriander and hop spiciness are not as pronounced on the nose as the 6 but their presence does well to make this beer balanced. A deep brown hue and off-white foam are telling signs of the booziness and complexity to come, but you will find yourself returning again and again for another sip.

Rochefort 10: Pouring burnt-molasses in both color and thickness with a darker-beige head, the heaviest hitter in the lineup comes in at 11.3 percent ABV. The yeast and coriander addition come through with almost a cinnamon characteristic on the nose while hop bitterness is almost imperceptible. Dark fruits dominate the majority of the profile. Milk chocolate, caramel, and coffee come together in what can be described as a lingering latte taste. Unsurprisingly these flavors make the 10 the most sought-after product in their lineup. Refermentation keeps it refreshingly carbonated to the last sip, even if you take it slow.

Rochefort Triple Extra: First released in 2020 to mark the 100th anniversary of the post-WWI boom, it rounds out their portfolio nicely. Now permanent in their line-up, this is also the only one of Rochefort's beers to feature on draft—though it is also available in bottles. The addition of orange peel alongside coriander and hops adds to the range that this beer has. Golden in color and 8.1 percent ABV, this is anything but a classic Tripel as Rochefort's yeast makes for a unique take on the style. Elevated hop bitterness, citrusy brightness, and a lingering sweetness are present throughout the beer. Marketed as utilizing a purple label to represent friendship, I recommend splitting this with loved ones.

On my last evening before departing Rochefort, I sat at a café and had the entirety of their lineup—don't worry, it was served alongside ample portions of local cheese with each beer, and it took me several hours. As I took in the tasting notes presented above, a young woman's eighteenth birthday pub-crawl arrived. Their cans of Jupiler Pils had to be discarded before they could enter, a prerequisite to which they begrudgingly obliged. As they approached the bar to order a quick round before departing to the next stop, most of them ordered whatever was cheapest but the birthday celebrant was presented with a draft of the Rochefort Triple Extra by the barman. A classy celebratory nod that mirrored the importance of the occasion. It was quite beautiful really, a momentous occasion for her, the trip of a lifetime for me, and random locals just out on an average evening, all drinking the same beer. It was appropriate for each of us in its own way, ordinarily mundane and yet historic simultaneously. The monks a few kilometers away would certainly have appreciated the moment had they not been busy with evening prayers.

Chapter 7

Sint-Sixtusabdij Westvleteren

ANTICIPATION. A LENGTH OF cars around a kilometer long were parked alongside a country road in Westvleteren, West Flanders. The scene is like many I have witnessed in the past. Places like The Alchemist Brewery, Treehouse Brewing, Russian River during Pliny the Younger, or the queue to enter Three Floyd's Dark Lord Day beer festival come to mind. But to see this outside of a monastery in Belgium was not what one might expect. I certainly did not, even with forewarning of the famed brews produced by the monks of Sint-Sixtusabdij—commonly known simply as Westvleteren.

Many of those reading will likely wonder why I did not start with this community when profiling breweries, as "Westy" is by far the most closely associated with the Trappist brewing tradition despite being the second smallest producer. Moreover, they have no interest in growing beyond their current capacity and frequently and proudly proclaim their wishes to be left alone in the quiet and solace of monastic life—an attitude which only adds to their mystique. They scoff at the prestige that others crave, and they only begrudgingly acquiesce to the reality of their fame.

With regards to my own anticipation, nothing about my experience at this abbey or with these beers would be as expected. I left a changed person for reasons far beyond what I could have imagined, even with the allure surrounding this place in popular beer culture. I hope to capture the essence of Sint-Sixtus below, in all its unexpected, glorious humility.

My trip to Westvleteren started as it would continue, a true adventure. Taking the train from my apartment in Leuven to Poperinge was marked by uncharacteristic delays and missed connections. Upon arriving to Poperinge, the bus to Westvleteren was also not running on its normal schedule, the bike rental shop was closed for a short holiday, and rideshare simply does not exist in the area. I would most likely be late for my check-in at the guest house with Brother Jos. In a panic, I managed to find a taxi service on Google that was just a short walk from the station. I booked a ride on their online portal and swiftly walked towards what I assumed would be a dispatch garage. To my surprise, I found the correct address in a residential cul-de-sac.

Stood at the end of an empty driveway, I could not believe my continued luck. Bewildered Flemish children were playing soccer in their yard next door as their mother stared at a strange tourist completely out of place in her tiny town. A van with an elderly woman and what I assumed was her grandchild pulled up beside me just as I was set to turn around and give up. Equally as shocked as her neighbor, the woman exited the van and, in Flemish, asked me if I was lost. Bumbling my words, I showed her my phone with the taxi reservation pulled up as she let out an exasperated sigh. Through the broken English of her grandchild, it turned out that her son had started the taxi service a few years prior and had since abandoned it without taking the website down. She hurriedly shuffled the teenager inside, opened the passenger door and ushered me inside the van. "Christina," she said with an outstretched hand, "I will take you where you go."

There I was, driving the short ten-kilometer ride, with a woman I had never met, in hopes of making it to Sint-Sixtus before the monks closed the guesthouse gate and returned to their daily tasks between services. A rosary hung from her rearview mirror swinging back and forth as we drove in awkward silence. She broke it first. "You go for the beer?" I explained that her assumption was partially true and with the help of my translation app and my rudimentary Flemish, I outlined my book project for her. She was both bewildered and amused that someone my age and from another country would be so interested in the intersections of monastic spirituality, contemporary life, and beer. I scrolled through photos of the other abbeys I had visited, and she told me about going to mass at Sint-Sixtus since she was a little girl.

The importance of the abbey for both Westvleteren and Poperinge was articulated clearly by Christina despite the language barrier as she navigated back roads with ease, arriving at the gravel driveway of Sint-Sixtus with lightning speed. I told her that she would get a few lines in the book as I attempted to give her whatever cash I had for gas money. She smiled and said thank you for the former but refused the latter, telling me that this was to help my project and to make sure that people knew about the monks. I insisted and with her final retort she invoked the Rule of St. Benedict before getting in her van and rushing off.

I walked up the path, rang the bell to the gatehouse, and was greeted by a smiling brother Jos who couldn't be less bothered that I was late as he asked why my friend did not want to come in. I share this story not just to fulfill a promise, but to highlight the infectious hospitality of the region, something I am sure is not entirely separable from the presence of the Trappists in their midst.

Historical Overview

Brother Jos began showing me around the grounds as is customary on these visits. He shares that in an earlier career he was an emergency room nurse, and we bond over the fact that many of my introductory theology courses are specifically geared towards the nursing cohorts at my institution. As he shows me to my guestroom, we pass the Sint-Sixtus library and archives, full of not only important historical information on the abbey, but also contemporary magazines and newspapers. This balance between history and the present, seclusion and openness to the world is vital to understanding the community at Westvleteren.

Technically, Sint-Sixtus declares its founding as having taken place in 1831 under the oversight of prior Franciscus van Langendonck along with a few other monks that made their way to Westvleteren from the French Mont-des-Cats abbey. Unofficially, they were joining a hermitage where Jan-Baptist Victoor—a widowed Poperinge resident and hop trader—had been living on his own since 1814. The surrounding area was also home to a group of Bridgettine monks (an order that follows the Rule of Saint Augustine) between 1615 and 1784, as well as a convent in the thirteenth century.

The new community continued in the Trappist tradition and fell under the jurisdiction of Westmalle in 1836 as it grew in both size and construction. The sanctuary was consecrated in 1840, and the community had roughly thirty monks that subsisted off the land, produced cheese, had a carpentry workshop, a book bindery, and supplemented income by running a primary school. During the buildout of the monastery the monks at Sint-Sixtus also purchased a brewhouse. Initially, they produced a low ABV *paterbier* meant for the monks' own consumption as well as to supplement the daily wage of the laborers tasked with building out the monastery. In April of 1839 King Leopold granted a brewing license to Sint-Sixtus and with the expertise available from Westmalle, the first batch was soon ready to enjoy. By 1849, the community had outgrown its original confines and a newer cloister along with a revamped church were constructed.

The 1850s saw Sint-Sixtus serve as both a founding monastery for a new community and a much-needed lifeline to another failing community. In the former instance, Westvleteren sent monks to start the abbey at Scourmont at the request of Father Jean-Baptiste Jourdain. The latter saw the brothers respond to a call from Father Francis Xavier Kaiser at the Petite Clairvaux abbey in Nova Scotia, Canada. The community was initially founded by Vincent DePaul but had struggled to find success and relocated first to Rhode Island, and then to St. Joseph's Abbey in Massachusetts (briefly discussed in relation to Spencer brewing above).

In 1860, a land grant from a local patron expanded the size of the monastery grounds—mainly for agricultural production—with Prior Dositheus Kempeneers steering the community to a membership of over fifty monks. The property added a solo standing guest house, a number of barns and sheds, along with a revamped brewery over the next several years.

By 1871 the monastery was elevated to the rank of abbey, an honor that coincided with the first public sales of beer at the community gates in modest amounts. Benedictus Wuyts was the first abbot of Westvleteren and under his leadership brewing occurred infrequently and was not seen as a viable source of economic stability. Outside of personal consumption and occasional supplementary income, brewing was on the back burner. This would change in 1877 under Abbot Albericus Verhelle, who looked at the success of other Trappist breweries to fine-tune a recipe for a second, stronger beer.

The beer was made available at the *In de Vrede* tavern across from the abbey (a partnership which continues) and sales soared. So much so that in 1896 Sint-Sixtus began to expand its brewery again. Following this, Dom Bonaventura De Groote (elected in 1910) made the decision to sponsor a series of taverns in addition to *In de Vrede* to make Westvleteren offerings readily available out in the world.

Despite this growing success, the early twentieth century still saw dairy and agricultural production as the main means of fulfilling the *labora* and stability aspects of the community. However, the ordinariness of life would change with WWI. Unlike other Belgian Trappist monasteries, Sint-Sixtus never fell into the hands of the German army. For this reason, the monks at Westvleteren wrestled with what their vocation meant during such a disastrous time from the safety of their home. Outside of half a dozen monks called up to be medics or chaplains, the rest stayed at Sint-Sixtus.

The archival records of the abbey reference three diaries and an unofficial abbey history kept by monks during the conflict which map out their contributions to housing, feeding, and providing beer for French, English, and Belgian troops (in that order) throughout the entirety of the war. King George V himself paid a visit to the abbey as he inspected British troops stationed there in 1917, including his son Prince Edward, arguably the most famous guest of Westvleteren.[1]

Over the course of the war, they had 40,000 allied troops stationed on the abbey grounds. This is in addition to hundreds of refugees that sought shelter from the destruction caused by the Germans throughout Belgium. There were times of tension between soldiers and refugees, but the monks at Sint-Sixtus insisted they make accommodations for non-combatants. At times the brew kettles themselves were repurposed for the cooking of large quantities of soup, such was the need for aid.

Because these were not invading forces, the goods that the abbey produced had to be purchased by soldiers. Cheese, bread, fruit, firewood, electricity, and linens were important commodities but most abbey excise receipts from this period were for beer as sales of the strong ale quadrupled during the conflict. With such fervent customers, the monks could hardly complain when the grazing pastures were destroyed by soldiers playing football matches in their spare time (the diaries make note of this on several occasions). The Sint-Sixtus brews were so famous amongst officers and enlisted men alike that when the boiling apparatus broke due to overuse on one occasion, the Belgian army engineer corps rushed to fix it lest the supply be delayed. This is not to make light of the harsh realities surrounding WWI, but to show the potential for the abbey to offer solace in such moments.

The interwar years saw continued success for Sint-Sixtus and its brews. In March of 1922 the brewery expanded once again and in 1926 the monks dug a well on the abbey's property to draw from directly for the brewery. With this addition, a steam engine was installed to speed up the brewing process in 1927 which also allowed for increased sanitation. The

---

1. Sint-Sixtus Abdji, *Golden Book of Signatures of St Sixtus Abbey*.

1920s were such a successful decade that 1928 saw the beginning of an abbey renovation without the need to take on any outside financial help.

The brothers were so busy with the brewery that they employed a dozen or so lay workers to assist in multiple brews a week. Still utilizing wooden open fermentation tanks, the brewery produced four offerings for public sales at this time (*Dubbel*, *Spécial Extra*, and *Abt*) alongside the refectory beer (*Ordinaire*) made for internal consumption and visiting guests. Eventually, the names would be replaced simply with their degrees plato (2, 4, 6, 8, and 12) and continue to reflect this nomenclature today.[2] This period of plenty would be halted by WWII.

Like with WWI, the monks at Sint-Sixtus were not impacted in the same way as other Trappist communities during WWII. This is not to say that their experience was easy, but the Germans treated Flanders differently than other segments of their occupied territories. Without side-tracking into political history extensively, Flemish nationalism and collaboration with the Nazis was a predominant attitude in the region (though there was a strong anti-fascist resistance based in Antwerp—the White Brigade). The Vlaamsch Nationaal Verbond, commonly known as the Black Brigade, dominated the scene and their vision aligned with that of the occupiers. Sint-Sixtus itself did not share in this sentiment—it served as an underground resistance site that housed Jews escaping the reach of the Reich and a few of the monks sought refuge in other communities to avoid the evil air of collaboration.

The brewery was not dismantled for material and continued production, albeit in a limited capacity, and the abbey itself was not damaged. Wider distribution of the beer was no longer possible during the occupation and therefore the abbey reverted to selling only at the gate, a move that would become permanent after the war. Poperinge was liberated in September of 1944. Though rebuilding was not necessary after the war, once the community returned to a sense of normalcy there were some heavy decisions about the future of the abbey that needed to be made. Under the leadership of Dom Gerardus Deleye, elected in 1941, there was a turn toward spiritual renewal and a conscious choice to downsize the brewery's production which he felt had become a stumbling block to their true calling.

Distribution licenses were pulled, the brew schedule was downsized, the lay workers were given notice to find other jobs, all tavern partnerships were ended—with the exception of *In de Vrede*—and beer sales were

---

2. Hieronymus, *Brew Like a Monk*, 80.

limited to in-person pickups at the abbey while production was severely cut. A close friend of Deleye's, Evariste Deconinck, leased the business license from Sint-Sixtus and began brewing the beers commercially at his St. Bernardus brewery in nearby Watou. Deconinck's takeover was not his first venture into monastic products, having purchased a cheese factory from the monks of St. Bernardus in 1934.[3]

Initially contracted for thirty years, St. Bernardus utilized the Sint-Sixtus yeast, its recipes, its material supply chain, and even took in its former lay brewmaster Mathieu Szafranski (offering him a generous salary and a stake in the brewery). The lease itself was priced astronomically but also included the payment of annual royalties based on sales. It was a win-win for all involved. The deal was so lucrative that it led to Deconinck selling off the cheese side of his business in 1959 to expand the brewery, and a renewal of the partnership for another thirty years was agreed in 1962 (the deal was actually struck at the wedding of Deconinck's daughter, presided over by the abbot himself).

Sint-Sixtus underwent changes beyond the beer realm under Dom Deleye via an expansion and modernization of the guesthouse in 1964 and the building of a new sanctuary in 1968. His no-frills legacy was reflected in the simplicity of the church's construction and is my favorite of the Trappist sanctuaries I visited. Its central features are light colored brick, a high vaulted ceiling with plain wooden beams, and non-decorative windows letting in plentiful light for services. There is no marble or stonework altar, just a simple wooden one with a matching lectern. A plain cross and a stone baptismal font offer the only other material presence in the sanctuary. The ideal setting to spend time in silence or to observe the liturgy of the hours.

Following Dom Deleye, the election of Herman-Jozef Seynaeve as abbot saw a bit of a renewed focus on brewing. Though St. Bernardus continued to produce the commercially available licensed beers, the number of people seeking beer from the abbey directly was growing. The success of not just the lay produced beer but the growing recognition of quality associated with Trappist brews across Belgium meant that the beers at Sint-Sixtus regularly sold out. Under the guidance of Brother Thomas from Westmalle as a consultant, a few tweaks were made that ensured the revitalization of sales were met with an expansion in quality. He introduced Westmalle's yeast for fermentation (it has been utilized ever since), altered the recipes, and emphasized the importance of consistency.

3. Kearney, "Once a Trappist."

Structurally, the monks installed a mill room in the brewery along with an automated chain-pulled grain conveyor belt to bring malt to the brewhouse, purchased new industrial quality fermentation tanks, and built a lab in the brewery to meticulously test each part of the process. 1976 also saw them replace the long used coolship with a closed top wort chiller and six open top fermentation vessels as well as building out a beer pickup lane next to the abbey to better facilitate sales without disturbing the monastery. In 1979, under the direction of newly-elected Abbot Remi Heyse, the monks installed a high-capacity industrial bottling line. Production, quality, and demand remained steady throughout the 1980s before another monumental era in the 1990s.

An external firm was hired to streamline the brew processes and equipment at Sint-Sixtus in 1987 and by their recommendation construction on a fully automated, state of the art, stainless steel brewhouse began in 1989. Completed and ready to run in 1990, the fifth (and currently used) brewhouse in Westvleteren's history saw an almost immediate change in the region's beer landscape. The license for contract brewing held by St. Bernardus was up in 1992 and the monks did not renew the agreement, bringing all production bearing the Sint-Sixtus mark back under the control of the abbey.

There were many reasons for this move which included ongoing deliberations about what it meant to label something as Trappist. Though the ITA discussed in the introductory chapter was still a few years from forming, the notion that "Trappist" was a unique designation which included being made under the supervision of the monks and at an actual monastery was being established through various legal proceedings in both the beer and cheese worlds. Moreover, changes in structure and leadership at St. Bernardus and a shifting beer scene amidst the explosion of Belgian macroproducers reinforced that it was time to bring things in house.

The separation was amicable and the relationship, to the extent that it exists, is still friendly. The monks offer advice when they can and have allowed Bernardus to continue using the original recipes that they contract brewed. For its part, St. Bernardus does not use any Trappist nomenclature and has even removed the "monk" from their labels—the figure no longer wears Trappist cowl nor dons the white cap. The secular brewery has since been purchased by another entrepreneur (in 1998) and has far outgrown the capacity and market reach of Sint-Sixtus. Though the beers are completely different, many consumers still associate St. Bernardus with the

Westvleteren products they do not have readily available to them. While great representations of various Belgian styles, the St. Bernardus products do not fall into the scope of my exploration here.

The end of the twentieth century saw the solidification of the Westvleteren brewing portfolio into what it is today. The *In De Vrede* café requested that the monks brew a blonde beer to accommodate the cyclists that frequented the space and they obliged. In celebration of a remodel of the café in 1999, the Blond was launched, replacing the lower ABV Dubbel/4 while the 6 was deemed superfluous. The Westvleteren Blond, 8, and 12 thus became the core beers produced by Sint-Sixtus with no deviation since. Production was capped at 5,000 hectoliters annually and the abbey chugged along just fine, accommodating to-go sales and supplying *In de Vrede* at a steady but not overwhelming rate. There were no restrictions on how much beer could be purchased, nor did there need to be. Pickup times and release days were announced by a simple signboard at the end of the abbey's driveway. The beer occasionally sold out, but a quick call to the brewery could prevent customers from being disappointed as a recorded message informed which beers were in stock. A sense of mystique certainly surrounded the beer, but it was manageable. That changed in the early 2000s as the pandemonium that is associated today with Westvleteren first began.

Contemporary Facets of the Community and Brewery

When I first emailed Sint-Sixtus about this project, the response was swift and not what I had expected. Every other community up until this point of planning had been happy to accommodate my visit and organize tours and interviews but Westvleteren replied with what appeared to be a stock rejection email. I was informed that neither interviews with brother Jos on the brewery side nor tours of the facility were possible and I was provided with links to videos about the brewing facility and an interactive "tour" at *In de Vrede*. The message was clear, the monks are not interested in being a locale for beer tourism.

Though my stay was eventually facilitated after the monks researched some of my other theology publications, and I gained ample material via discussions with the monks and a look at the brewhouse, the initial weariness stood out. How could it be that the hospitality so enshrined in the Trappist tradition could have been stretched to a limit with regards to

Westvleteren? The answer lies in another Trappist value being undermined: silence.

The rise of social media in the early 2000s amidst the growing availability of the internet impacted the beer scene as much as it did any other community. The advent of RateBeer.com and BeerAdvocate specifically changed the trajectory of Westvleteren's beers. Precursors to Untappd, these platforms allowed users to share descriptive information, rate, and comment on the quality of any beer they came across. Though RateBeer.com ceased operations in early 2025, it spent over two decades as *the* platform for beer nerds. BeerAdvocate (now owned by the parent company of Untappd) continues to serve in such a capacity and is highly regarded as the gold standard both for crowdsourced beer ratings and beer tracking. When both platforms picked up on the quality, uniqueness, and beauty of Westvleteren's beers, Sint-Sixtus partially lost the quiet contemplative days they so desired.

First checked into BeerAdvocate in 2001, the Westvleteren 12 quickly rose up the ranks to number one in the quadruple category, and top ten in beers overall with an average score of 100/100. Though it has fallen to the forty-fourth best beer in the world today, the 100/100 rating remains. When RateBeer.com released their first ever list of Best Breweries in 2002, Westvleteren was ranked number one. This was followed up with Westvleteren 12 earning the "best beer in the world" tag in 2005 and remained there until Dark Lord overtook it in 2008. Then the 12 jockeyed for first with Pliny the Elder from 2009 on, alternating with the Russian River flagship beer until the site shut down. When both the Belgian and US based media got hold of the story that something special was brewing in West Flanders, the hype train could not be stopped.

Cars began to line the gravel roads leading to the abbey, cyclists and hikers brought camping tents in the lead up to release days, the local magistrates went from having nothing to do to serving as traffic wardens and crossing guards, helicopters flew overhead to document the growing insanity, and even the Minister-President of Flanders, Yves Leterme, endorsed the beer as being his go-to night cap. The situation was so untenable that in September of 2006 a pre-order system was introduced to try to ease pressure on the abbey. They did not increase capacity, keeping it around the 5,000 hectoliter mark, but they did want to ensure a sense of fairness to acquiring their beer. Calls would be placed to the brewery where the buyer's information was taken down and limits were put in place on the quantity of beer per customer—five total crates. The local phone system crashed in the opening minutes of the launch. Because of these realities, there is no need to speak about the marketing side of the Westvleteren operation as it is virtually non-existent.

Unfortunately, it was not just the beer that was sought after, but the profit it could generate on the secondary market. Amidst this early craze—and because Belgium does not have the three-tiered system of alcohol sales prominent in the US—once the beers left the drive-up at the abbey, the monks of Westvleteren had no control over where they went next. Fake information was used to create multiple accounts, mules and ghost buyers proliferated, Belgian and Dutch tavern owners made the drive to the abbey with dollar signs in their eyes, and there was even a famous case of Belgian grocery chain Jan Linders deviously acquiring hundreds of cases to sell at a premium (public comments made by the abbot quickly ensured that this last instance never occurred again).[4]

These practices persist to this day, and I saw Westvleteren beers for sale in Bruges, Antwerp, Amsterdam, and Brussels beer shops and bars for anywhere between €15.00–€35.00 a bottle (a far cry from the €2.50–€3.00 at the brewery or the €4.00–€6.00 at *In de Vrede*). It was also fascinating to see customers not blink twice at ordering Westvleteren at these establishments. At almost every place I saw it available, I also saw someone drinking one. The bar staff made sure to always open the bottle in front of the customer, a practice that one patron told me stems from the fact that greedy barkeepers would not only partake in these unsanctioned sales but also refill Westvleteren bottles with other Belgian offerings of similar style to dupe unsuspecting tourists.

Shockingly, these European markups were nowhere near as steep as the bottle of Blond I came across in Philadelphia for $50.00 or the bottle of 12 I was offered in Toronto for $85.00 since returning home. These types of black-market dealings completely undermine the Trappist approach to sustainability, affordability, and communal stability, ultimately skewing the anti-profit and pro-charitable work requirements of the ITA designation. I have made it a point to regularly call out stateside buyers that participate in such blemishing of Westvleteren's name and encourage others to do so as well. The mystique is not worth a bastardization of the beer's ethos.

While the hype is less than what was experienced in the early 2000s, it was still eye-opening for me. As I stretched before my morning run one

---

4. Knox, "Monks Who Make World's Best Beer Have a Message for USA."

day, surveying the scene of waiting cars, Brother Jos popped out from doing some gardening alongside the front of the abbey gates. He saw my bewilderment and said, "This is nothing like what it used to be, thank goodness." Though some of the decline in chaos is due to the craft beer bubble bursting in Europe as well as in the States, most of it is due to the adaptation and foresight of the monks.

Sales are now done via an online portal for both pickup and, if you live in Belgium, home delivery while also being monitored more strictly. Limits have been reduced to four total cases per customer with a limit of two cases of each beer style (in avoidance of persons overstocking on the 12). Sales are directly tied to user accounts which include both your driver's license and your car's license plate, and orders can only be placed once a month per customer.

Any irregularities in purchasing can result in the canceling of accounts and orders—an infrequent but necessary occurrence informs the monk working the pickup line. I snap a few photos as we chat, and the well-oiled machine works through arriving customers quickly. Individual bottles and six packs can still be purchased at *In De Vrede* for a slight markup and can also be ordered for on-site consumption with lunch. Outside of these avenues, Westvleteren products cannot be purchased in good conscience.

With regards to the brewery and its processes, Sint-Sixtus continues to operate in much the same way it has since the installation of the latest brewhouse in 1990. Though the brew system was fully automated then, the open top fermentation vats along with the lagering tanks have since been updated and automated as well. Additionally, 2014 saw the purchase of a new bottling line—a requisite given that the previous one was almost thirty-five years old. All of this has streamlined the process to require less labor from the monks.

In addition to Brother Joris being responsible for overseeing the quality control and logistics/planning of the brewing and sales, there are only two other monks involved in the brewery. One to help Joris on the brewing side, and one on the packaging side. All three brothers involved are paired with a lay compatriot in their respective duties. In this sense, the monks at Westvleteren have more hands-on involvement than any other Trappist brewery save Zundert. Thus, though less monks are required as modernization has occurred, they are still intimately involved in each part of the process.

The current 6,000-hectoliter capacity is brewed on forty-two official brew days each year. This is divided among singular turns for the Blond and Part-Gyle method brewing for the Westvleteren 8 and the Westvleteren 12—a process in which multiple runnings are taken from a singular mash at separate times and moved to separate kettles for individual boils. Thus, the higher gravity runnings are used for the 12 and the lower gravity runnings comprise the 8. This allows for not only efficiency in beers with similar profiles but is an astute use of ingredients. Whether step infusion mashing is utilized or not was not revealed to me. Similarly, the length of the boil is a secret but given the number of complex sugars and flavors present in the 12 I would assume it is a 120-minute boil while the 8 might be a 90-minute boil with the Blond in the 60–75 minute range.

The wort is brought into the open tanks for fermentation where fresh Westmalle yeast is added. The Blond takes four to five days for primary fermentation while the 8 and the 12 take around a week. The beers are then pumped to lagering tanks for secondary fermentation in a section of the brewery that was revamped in 2016. The length of their stay is determined by style and the time it takes for any remaining sediment to clarify (five to twelve weeks). There is no filtration, pasteurization, centrifuging, or addition of clarifying agents so the process of allowing these living beers to take their own time requires more patience than most.

The bottling line installed in 2014 re-douses 330-ml bottles with sugar and yeast before they are capped with green, blue, or yellow crowns (for the Blond, the 8, and the 12 respectively). Another recent development is the addition of labels matching the color of the crowns for each beer with a "best by" date, pouring instructions, and the ITA stamp. The bottles themselves have the words "Trappisten Bier" engraved on the neck. At least initially, every beer is also packaged into the now famous wooden crates embossed with "Trappist Westvleteren" on their side for cellaring. The warm room/bottle conditioning cellar houses the Blond for a week while the 8 and the 12 take roughly two weeks before they are ready to be picked up during the allotted times.

All of this brings me to the ingredients used at Sint-Sixtus and the profiles of the beers. Beginning with water, the region surrounding Poperinge has what can be described as extremely hard water. The brewing school archives at KU Leuven indicate that a survey taken in the early 2000s found 530 parts per million of bicarbonate in the water of the area (almost twice as high as the next highest region in Belgium). This means that unless the monks want astringent metallic tasting beer, they must treat the water by raising the pH level. They take this alteration of the water so seriously that they installed a state-of-the-art water treatment plant on the abbey grounds. With this in place, there is no fluctuation of water quality or properties and the neutral profile allows other aspects of the flavor profile to flourish.

The malts utilized in all three offerings are one varietal of pale malt and one variety of Pilsner malt, sourced from Mouterij Dingemans. Additional fermentables come in the form of a sugar addition during the boil. Beer writing legend Stan Hieronymus has speculated as to how the 8 and the 12 achieve their color given the lack of dark malts present in these recipes, a question which I also asked but did not have answered.[5] However, given the ability to alter their water down to practically the molecule, alkaline profiles allow for the caramelization of sugars which can impact color. Additionally, their relationship with the maltster might allow them custom kilning time for the malt which can generate darker color without the use of classically darker varietals. Lastly, if a decoction mashing technique is used by Westvleteren, this would also caramelize sugars resulting in darker hues.

While other Trappist producers have utilized hops from all over the world, including Chimay's focus on Yakima Valley produced varietals, Westvleteren purposely sticks close to home. Poperinge and the surrounding area are known as the hop capital of Belgium and many bike trails and hiking paths crisscross the hop fields surrounding the abbey. Large wooden poles stick out around the horizon, supporting wire trellises for the vines to grow on. Though they would not be ready for harvest for another few months after my stay, the aromatics were palpable on my morning runs. The exact mixture of hops is also a guarded secret, but the most common varietals grown in the region are Northern Brewer, Challenger, Cascade, several strains of Golding, and Hallertau. Whatever the potential combination, spicy, earthy, and grassy notes accompany these varietals, and high alpha acids make them perfect bittering hops. Despite the influence of Westmalle on Westvleteren elsewhere, extracts and pellets are favored over whole cone hops.

The yeast utilized at Westvleteren is the same Westmalle yeast introduced in the Westmalle brewery profile above. I will not re-describe it here, but it is important to note that although a large portion of the perceived flavor comes from these little critters, these two breweries produce

---

5. Hieronymus, *Brew Like a Monk*.

entirely different beers. Open fermentation adds to this diversity slightly as do different pitch rates and fermentation temperatures. There are still Westvleteren samples brought to Westmalle for extra analysis when needed and the yeast is picked up fresh on brew-days by the brewers at Sint-Sixtus rather than cultivated on site. Despite this, each of the three Westvleteren offerings is completely unique compared to Westmalle's.

Westvleteren Blond: Coming in at 5.8 percent ABV, it pours a beautiful golden blonde in color and is slightly cloudy due to active yeast and refermentation. A creamy white head persists throughout the entirety of the drinking experience with majestic lacing left on the glass in its wake. Aromatics of fresh cut grass, lime zest, and a bit of honeycomb sweetness from the yeast make up the nose. An exquisite balance between a light mouthfeel but a full body and medium carbonation makes for a unique drinking experience. The bitterness does not linger but dissipates into a dry finish, leaving you refreshed between sips. I find it an exceptional example of the style, even if it is unexpectedly hop forward. Candidly, I think the wrong Westvleteren offering caused all of that commotion in 2005.

Westvleteren 8: Pouring dark amber in color, I would categorize this as a Dubbel. Aromatics of banana bread, plum, caramelized pear, nuttiness, and a slight hop spice are immediately apparent. The off-white creamy head lingers and laces the glass throughout drinking. The carbonation level is a bit higher than expected but works well even at 8 percent ABV, allowing for a dry finish and well-rounded beer. Classic dark fruit, toffee, clove, and a bit of honeydew come through in the taste from the malt profile. The earthy hops are barely perceptible on the tongue and nowhere near as prominent as they are on the nose, but their presence certainly mitigates the overall sweetness of the beer. Warmth from the alcohol increases as the beer breathes but is not overwhelming. One can see why it is provided in the shared guesthouse lounge to stimulate conversation.

Westvleteren 12: There are similar characteristics as there are with the 8 but far more ramped up in this Quadrupel. Sitting at 10.2 percent ABV, the dark amber color is pronounced and viscous. The head is creamy beige and both the lacing, and the carbonation linger without dissipating. The booziness is certainly present on the nose but so are a whole host of other complex notes including chocolate, raisin, cigar leaf, caramel, roasted nuts, and characteristic yeasty esters. Fresh sticky dark fruit and molasses are not only perceptible in terms of flavor but describe the body and mouthfeel as well. This is a big bold beer that grows in intensity as it warms up but never lacks smoothness. From first sip to last, the 12 lives up to the hype—much to both the chagrin and joy of the monks at Sint-Sixtus.

It has been my tradition to open one of the offerings from each brewery as I finish these profiles. I had to bring back bottles of Westvleteren given I could not just go down to Beer Temple to pick one up (nor would I even if they managed to get it in). They patiently sat in my beer fridge developing away as I transcribed, researched, and wrote. Anticipation. As I poured the Blond into a Sint-Sixtus chalice, one of the only branded items made available by the brewery, I rotated it to allow the yeast to settle and chuckled as I read a slogan printed on the back. This is the only thing resembling marketing from Westvleteren that I have seen, and it says *Ut vivant me coquunt, non vivunt ut me coquunt* . . . They brew me to live, they do not live to brew me.

As good as each of the three offerings is, my stay at Westvleteren was not memorable for the beers alone. The sale of these beers, like for all the Trappist breweries, allows the brothers to shift their focus to contemplation, charitable endeavors, and hospitality. The nineteen monks living at Sint-Sixtus today are led by Abbot Manu Van Hecke and they fulfill their vocational calling with standards of excellence reminiscent of the beers produced at Westvleteren. Despite their seeming disconnect from society, heightened by the shirking of fame associated with their beer, the monks at this abbey care deeply about the world.

Between the liturgy of the hours, the brothers asked me questions in the garden about what it is that I do, about how things in America have become so polarized, and what it looks like to teach theology in our modern context. They were not sheltered from current events. In fact, they seemed to know more about the world they were sending their beer out to than most unconcerned citizens or the beer hunters lining their driveway. Their prayers for the spiritual healing of barriers to human hospitality were genuine, frequent, and palpable. The brothers were not of the world, but they were certainly for it.

After my initial interaction with brother Joris by email and the subsequent secretiveness about their ingredients, processes, etc., I was under no impression that extensive interviews about the beers would be wanted or approved and even getting the photos and information that I did should be considered a victory. As I was practicing *Lectio Divina* on the third morning of my stay, I heard a knock on my guest room door. Brother Jos was there to inform me that Dom Van Hecke did not want to be interviewed about the brewery and that Brother Joris had to alter an extensive tour of the brewery to circumvent an issue they were having with yeast. Despite my disappointment, I was not surprised by either. What I did not anticipate was that I would actually get the lengthiest and most intimate sit-down with monks of my entire trip. Before he turned to leave, Brother Joris nonchalantly said, "Father Abbot would like to invite you to give a lecture to the community in the cloister."

At first, I thought I had misheard him. He continued, "Perhaps you could present on your most recent book? I will pick you up after dinner and you will have until we dismiss for Completen." I'm not sure if I even answered before he said, "Good, I will see you then." I scrambled to my laptop to prepare some lecture notes on my recent monograph discussing contemporary political theology through the lens of Dorothy Day and the Catholic Worker movement. I put more work into that presentation than any conference paper or visiting lecture prior. I could not believe that I was being invited into the cloister, let alone being given a chance to teach the monks I had learned so much from.

The cloister itself is an architectural marvel as the monks commissioned renowned architect Bob van Reeth to design it. Belgium's first ever National Architect, Van Reeth has worked on everything from museums, municipal buildings, and hotels to the Ark Floating Theatre in Antwerp. Despite his fame, van Reeth is on record saying that the Sint-Sixtus commission is the most beautiful project he has ever been assigned.[6] Completed between 2008–2011, the cloister redesign was necessitated by foundational damage and sinking in the prior construction.

Famously funded by a special release of Westvleteren 12 shipped to the US (a one-time occurrence that made the regular pandemonium witnessed in West Flanders pale by comparison)[7], the simple, sleek, and square design is based around a courtyard at its center. Charcoal in color on the outside with plain white walls on the interior, it is unplaceable into a particular school of architecture, something that van Reeth prides himself on. Floor to ceiling windows line the hallways allowing for the central garden to be viewed as the

---

6. Van Reeth, "Bob Van Reeth about the Saint-Sixtus Abbey in Westvleteren."
7. Chappell, "From Belgium to Piggly Wiggly."

brothers walk to and from the sanctuary while outward facing windows are prevalent as well. Twenty-seven rooms line the second floor with a scriptorium, meeting hall, infirmary, kitchen/dining area among the spaces on the first floor. It seamlessly blends Sint-Sixtus's past with the modern sensibilities that brought me into the cloister to deliver a lecture.

The presentation of my book went well despite my nerves of being front and center in a room of Trappist monks devoting their lives to spiritual pursuits and communal living—themes present in my work on the Catholic Worker—but the response was shockingly beautiful. Genuine curiosity came to the fore about the life of Dorothy Day, her struggles, her exploits, etc., and the conversation grew organically into an assessment of our current world. There were a few cliché questions like "Is our cloister kitchen better than the McDonald's you eat?" or "Does everyone in America really have a gun?" but these grew into discussions on overconsumption, greed, violence, spiritual malaise, and the importance of my vocation. I shared my own involvement in mutual aid initiatives and the work that my wife does as a public-school teacher in a neighborhood abandoned by the system. Some of the brothers took notes, even though many had to do so through their fellow monks translating on the fly and at a whisper.

My allotted time quickly ran out as the bells rung for the next service—I inadvertently made all of us late for Compline—and the monks gave me a round of applause before we were dismissed. I promised to return later in the summer to drop off a copy of the book to add to their library—which I eventually did—and we made our way to the sanctuary. Father Abbot approached me and extended his hand, "Thank you, Professor. It is not often that we get to hear from theologians, especially from the States." I had traveled half-way around the world to experience this community, their hospitality, and their beer, yet I was the one receiving thanks.

The rest of my stay was spent in a continued state of normalcy as I returned to the schedule necessitated by the Rule, but lingering in the background was this extraordinary occurrence. A vivid lesson in both humility and compassion exhibited in the leadership of Dom van Hecke that will remain with me forever. As I packed my things and got ready to depart on my final morning, one of the monks—Brother Daniel—shuffled across the lawn in full habit at a speed I did not think was possible. "Professor, I wanted to catch you before you left. Please know that we will be thinking of you and praying for you as you continue your important work in Chicago. Your wife as well. Do not forget your time here." As if I ever could.

Chapter 8

Abbaye Notre-Dame d'Orval

"You're absolutely correct. Trappist beers are not a style. 'Trappist' is merely a designation. People that think otherwise have no idea what they are talking about." This blunt, perhaps even harsh, assessment was not what I was expecting to hear from a man clad in a Cistercian habit. Yet, Brother Xavier Frisque was very clear on this point in my interview with him at Abbaye Notre-Dame d'Orval and seemed to break character from the delightful exchange we had leading up to the question which elicited such a response. "Given that Trappist is not a style, what makes Orval unique among the Cistercian produced beers?" Brother Xavier has held multiple roles at Orval and in the Order—including sitting on the ITA board, overseeing the board of the company officially in possession of the Orval brewery, playing the organ at services, and just a few weeks after I left the guest house, becoming the Superior—he was the perfect person to capture the essence of Orval.

The necessity to differentiate themselves from the other Trappist produced beers and to clarify the importance of the Cistercian values undergirding the brewing endeavor was present not just in Brother Xavier's response, but throughout my experience at Orval. This was also true on the abbey side as well—a strict delineation between the beer and the Trappist community were emphasized in my interview. Everything from the size of the guesthouse (there were thirty-eight diners at lunch my first day) to the magnitude of the majestic and storied ruins on the grounds and the hundreds of people visiting them daily reiterated what was now a common theme, an oscillation between Trappist unity and the true uniqueness of each community.

Located between Villers-devant-Orval and the town of Florenville, the Orval abbey sits in Southern Belgium near the French border. Technically in the Gaume region, it neighbors the Ardennes and shares much of its beauty. Hills and rolling meadows break into a densely forested valley as you approach the abbey, making for a gorgeously picturesque backdrop and serving as one of the main reasons that the abbey grounds are such a big tourist attraction. Cyclists, hikers, bird watchers, history buffs, and beer hunters all flock together at *A l'Ange Gardien*, the café operated on the abbey ground, where they can stop for a meal, a beer, and rest in the shadow of the towering sanctuary behind them.

The parking spots lining the walkway up to the monastery are nearly full as I arrive early in the morning, so much so that a few cars sit idling with their flashers on as crates of Orval are loaded into trunks. I make a wrong turn on the grounds and end up at the brewery rather than the guesthouse and see fully electric semi-trucks being loaded up on a much larger scale than the tourists' trunks, but to equal excitement for their ultimate recipients, I'm sure. Steam billows from a building at the center of the brewery and the smell of the first brew of the day fills the air. The bells chime at the monastery, announcing the beginning of another service observing the liturgy of the hours. My sojourn at Orval abbey begins in a moment of perfect harmony.

Historical Overview

A brewery worker in coveralls taking a cigarette break kindly interrupts me as I take in that moment. *"Tu cherches quelque chose?"* I tell him that I am looking to check in at the guesthouse and he points me in the right direction. It is a bit too early for my room to be ready and the guest master—a lay worker from the local parish—kindly holds on to my bags and sends me to the giftshop/visitors center, also staffed by lay workers. Later, brother Xavier would tell me that, "As monks, with regards to hospitality, we no longer run the guest house. It is staffed by volunteers that see it as a spiritual vocation. Yes, guests may request to speak to monks, but the day-to-day operations of the guest house are a charitable ministry for the local parish." I procure my ticket for the museum, nature trails, and ancient ruins on the abbey grounds as I wait for the next liturgical service and my accommodations.

The wealth of information on offer with regards to the abbey's history is far beyond the possibility of encapsulating here and I recommend visitors do not forgo this aspect of Orval's hospitality.

Both the museum displays and the historical material made available by the Orval abbey website interestingly start their descriptions of the abbey's origins far earlier than any of the other monasteries. The first panel in the museum starts its presentation of the abbey 165 million years ago. Declaring that the North Sea covered the region before receding during the last ice age and leaving behind ochre stone which would eventually be used in the monastery's construction. Beyond historical facts, this solidifies the Trappist focus on stability and sense of place. Orval traces its literal foundations to the region, a reminder of just how much locale matters to those adhering to the Rule of St. Benedict.

The story picks up from there with the arrival of the first monks to the grounds in 1070, making Orval the oldest community discussed here. This date precedes the establishment of the Cistercian Order or the stricter observance undertaken by the Trappists. The original community migrated from Calabria in Italy, a stronghold region of the Benedictines, during a period of growth for the Order. Arnould de Chiny, a local lord, welcomed them with open arms amidst his many projects of support for religious communities. Several years after its foundation, the Benedictine monastery gained a second, more prestigious benefactor—Matilda of Canossa, Countess of Tuscany.

Matilda's own story is like something out of a Soprano's episode. After the assassination of her father, Boniface of Canossa, Matilda inherited the vast holdings and wealth of the House of Attoni. This position came with not just status but also danger as she was now thrust into the political milieu surrounding the Holy Roman Empire. A power struggle between the Emperor, the monarchs within the Empire, and the Papacy—often referred to as the Investiture Contest—saw Matilda fervently support the Papacy's right to oversee the appointment of bishops, abbots, monarchs, and even the emperor. She became a close friend and confidant of Pope Gregory VII (to the point that rumors circulated of a romantic relationship), and at odds with Emperor Henry IV. She financed the military operations of the Papacy against Henry IV's armies and, on occasion, even led troops into battle herself. So how does her story intersect with Orval?

In 1069, Matilda married the Duke of Lorraine, Godfrey IV (colloquially known as Godfrey the Hunchback for obvious reasons). The union was fraught from the off as it was meant to unify two powerful factions amidst the aforementioned controversy, but Matilda and Godfrey found themselves on opposite ends of the conflict. When their newly born daughter died in 1071, Matilda saw no reason to keep up appearances and lived apart from her husband, returning to Tuscany to oversee her own holdings. Godfrey's politically motivated assassination (stabbed to death on his toilet in Antwerp in 1076) necessitated her brief return to Lorraine, where she stopped at the fledgling Benedictine community and her narrative moved from history to legend.

Matilda is said to have stopped by a fountain at the edge of the spring that provided the Benedictines with water where she spent time in contemplative prayer. Thinking about her marriage, the direction of her life in the wake of the controversy, and what to do with her new holdings, she was playing with her wedding ring and accidentally dropped it into the spring. Contemplation turned to prayer as she fervently begged God and the Virgin Mary to return the memento of her marriage.

In response, a trout swam up graciously returning the ring with its mouth. A shocked and thankful Matilda exclaimed "*C'est vraiment une val d'or!*" (truly this is a valley of gold) from which the area and future monastic communities attained their name, Orval. The trout with the ring in its mouth adorns not only the Orval beer logo but are utilized in the community's crest as well. Matilda went about her hectic life but financially supported the monks and provided further land grants as well. She was eventually buried at St. Peter's among the Popes for her service to the Church and her role in the Papacy's eventual victory in the Investiture conflict.

Whether one believes that story or not, it has become not only part of Orval's lore but a distinct part of the beer's brand identity (the importance of its water, the story's prominence on the label, the ancient connections). You can visit the spring on the abbey grounds to this day and a mural of the legend adorns the wall behind it as visitors throw coins into the water hoping for their own good fortune.

Ultimately, her donations allowed the Benedictine monks to begin construction of a monastery and a sanctuary, neither of which were completed before the community sought refuge elsewhere after forty years of inhabiting the grounds. Whatever their motivation, the Benedictine community's absence was soon filled by a group of priests who were invited to continue the build out of the church by Arnould's son, Othon.

By 1124, the community had finished construction, and the sanctuary was consecrated by the Bishop of Verdun. A lack of economic stability due to the drying up of financial patronage led to affiliation with the Cistercian Order. Bernard of Clairvaux agreed and put Orval under the immediate care of Abbeye Trois-Fontaines, the Order's shining star. A group of seven monks arrived to oversee the transition of Orval to the Cistercian tradition in 1131. This likely included the first brewing of beer given Bernard's allowance and emphasis on purifying water via the traditional means of each monastery's region.

More importantly, the community would avoid financial frustration via this transition due to the Cistercian focus on autonomy and self-sustainability. Manual labor came in the form of farming on land donated beyond the monastery grounds, taking advantage of the resources offered by the surrounding forests, and the leasing of land for ironworking. A century of prosperity followed, including the refurbishing of the sanctuary and transitioning the common house to a full cloister. In 1252, the monastery grounds were devastated by a fire that required nearly a century to recover from. Having just poured so many finances into construction, the repairs left Orval crippled and at the brink of dissolution. Coming through this tribulation, largely due to the help of the wider Order, stability was the norm for centuries.

The monks navigated the ups and downs of the various religious wars covered elsewhere in my abbey profiles, and Orval was an outlier in a sense during this period. Unlike the Flemish and Dutch Trappist communities, Orval grew and reached a community of nearly fifty members by 1620. Orval adopted the reforms of de Rancé and the Trappist strict observance officially in 1674 under Charles de Bentzeradt for another boost (130 members by 1720). In the mid-1720s, Orval was impacted by the Jansenist controversy, and a number of monks left the monastery as apostates.

The tumult of the French Revolution saw the cloister destroyed and the monks ousted in 1793. As the property passed through the hands of multiple secular owners, the ruins stood charred, abandoned, and were frequently plundered for building materials. The story of Orval as a community was put on hold for over a century.

In 1887, the De Harrene family acquired the lands on which Orval's ruins sat. 1890 saw the parish of Villers-devant-Orval obtain government protection over the site as having ancient and religious importance. Sympathetic not just to the Catholic faith but to the Trappist Order itself, the

De Harrenes donated the land to the La Trappe abbey in France in 1926 in hopes of reviving a monastic community on the site. Charles De Harrene petitioned King Albert directly to help finance the revival and officially approve the donation. Dom Jean Marie Clerc of La Trappe had the perfect plan for reviving the once flourishing abbey while finding a home for monks escaping another wave of French anti-clerical legislation passed in the early twentieth century as well as those from a failed communal foundation in Brazil.

He sent a group of seven monks to Orval in March of 1927. They were joined by brother Albert Van der Cruyssen from La Trappe who became the first prior of the community as he put his secular construction skills to work. He had not only been a builder in Ghent but had also served as an engineer in the Belgian army during the first world war. A conversion after the conflict saw him leave behind a thriving construction business to pursue monastic life. When he left La Trappe to undertake Orval's reconstruction, it became instantly clear that the dilapidated ruins could not be repaired. Construction of an entirely new abbey was necessary.

Famed Belgian architect Henri Vaes, a friend of Van der Cruyssen's from his secular days, was brought on to help design the layout and buildings of Orval while also incorporating the ruins into the field of the abbey grounds. Those pre-historic beginnings mentioned by brother Xavier would come to the fore as Vaes was insistent on using stone from the area. He also attempted to find a unique balance between simplicity and grandeur, between modernity and the past, between facilitating contemplation of God and reflecting the creative gifts that God bestows. In an interview with a Catholic Belgian publication, Vaes shared his approach to the gargantuan task before him and Van der Cruyssen,

> It was not only a question of rebuilding an old abbey, loaded with historical and religious memories, but also of recalling its remote origin, its eight centuries of sorrows and joys, and giving to its new features such an aspect that it would always be a living thing in time to come. A home of prayer of that kind must be immutable. The walls made of bare stone, the semi-circular arches, the ogive, symbol of prayer, all these are elements whose expression, at whatever epoch, will always be indisputable and understood by all. As early as the 12th century they were the soul of the Cistercian architecture, which was considered as monastic art in the highest sense of the word.[1]

1. Varneux, "Our Lady of Orval Abbey and Philately," 26.

The result was a mixture of the design features of the original abbey along with an art deco influence taken from Vaes's secular work (see for example his Palais de l'Agriculture). Construction began on August 18 of 1929 as Prince Leopold laid the cornerstone of the sanctuary, and the Bishop of Namur oversaw the groundbreaking ceremony. Work would not be officially completed until 1948, but the community was able to function normally throughout the process, even re-attaining its status of abbey in 1935 with Van der Cruyssen installed as abbot on February 29 of 1936.

The central feature of the abbey is the sanctuary's sixty-foot façade adorned by Mary holding a baby Jesus which guests can see far off in the distance. The duo overlooks a gorgeous set of gardens and a long pond that evokes both awe and contemplation. Ultimately, the balance that Vaes found was so appreciated by Dom Albert that he was also commissioned by the Order for the construction of the Clairefontaine and Sorée abbeys. When the sanctuary was officially consecrated in 1948, the church was raised to the rank of Basilica.

Though there was financial aid from other Trappist communities, support from Ghent's middle-class residents, and grants from the royal family, Orval still needed to find alternative means for economic stability. Initially, the *labora* of Orval was undertaken in the realm of farming, baking, and cheese making. Vaes designed the cheese factory and the bakery, providing consistency in style. However, given the grandeur of the construction project, they needed to supplement income, and the idea of a brewery came to the fore. By the time that the first stone of the abbey was laid, the choice to pursue brewing had been made and Vaes drew up architectural plans for a brewery while the monks made careful decisions on their logistical approach to beer making.

"From the very beginning, the brothers decided that they would not have a direct hand in producing the beer. They were occupied with agricultural work and monastic life," brother Xavier says matter-of-factly. "Secular employees were entrusted with the beer making to provide financially for the community and it has remained so." Brasserie d'Orval was formed in 1931 with ownership shares being sold to local benefactors that wanted to see the revival of the monastery (the De Harennes being among them).

The monks at Orval still had control over every aspect of production, direction, marketing, etc., but three secular men took the lead on building out the brewhouse, designing the Orval recipe, and dialing in test batches before Orval's first release to the public in 1932. German brewmaster

Martin Pappenheimer was joined by Honoré Van Zande as director of the brewery and John Van Huele as assistant brewer. Together, they enshrined a unique approach to production that would set Orval apart from its Trappist counterparts.

First, it was decided that Orval would only produce a singular beer rather than a portfolio of offerings. Thus, aligning with the influence of Pappenheimer's German roots and the lengthy periods that Van Huele spent working in England. These ties also explain a second unique factor, the rejection of step mashing or decoction in favor of a single infusion mash. Third, dry hopping the beer has been part of the process from day one, a technique that originated with British pale ales. This addition of hops during secondary fermentation provides aromatics more than adding any additional bitterness and why Orval is described as the "hoppiest" of Trappist offerings. Lastly, part of the fermentation process at Orval now involves the addition of Brettanomyces, a wild yeast strain that produces funky flavors described as barnyard, hay, and my favorite, horse blanket. Because Van Huele and Pappenheimer used a cool ship and open fermentation tanks, naturally occurring wild yeast (including Brettanomyces) joined the pitched yeast utilized in Orval and developed generational character due to purposely lax cleaning process. Pappenheimer, correctly, believed that the beer's original flavor profile was directly tied to the hardened yeast cake buildup in the tanks and therefore refused to scrub them.

The trio dialed in the recipe and hit the ground running. National distribution of Orval began with its initial release—making it the first Trappist beer available throughout all of Belgium—as the now world-famous bowling pin-esque bottles made their way into the hands of thirsty consumers. Vaes's architectural duties included designing the bottle, its distinct shape being a function of trying to keep yeast sediment from being poured into the Orval chalices (another Vaes creation) utilized by eager drinkers. The bottling itself took place at a secondary facility in Brussels due to the lack of an industrial sized bottling line at the abbey. Success was immediate and Orval became a household name prior to the outbreak of WWII.

Occupied by Nazi Germany for the duration of the war, Orval continued to produce its beer (at a limited capacity) and the monks were allowed to pursue the contemplative life under the regime. After the war ended, several major changes came to Orval with regards to the production of beer, including a "mistake" that nearly ended the beer as we know it. Changes in leadership at the brewery meant that the abbot sent monks to Chimay to train under brother Theodore and become more acquainted with the beer making process. Additionally, Jean De Clerck was brought in for outside consultation. A modernization of processes and equipment followed in 1950.

Moving away from cool ship production and implementing a rigorous sanitation regimen meant that Orval had scrubbed away the yeast cakes, and the naturally occurring Brettanomyces present in the original beer no longer featured. The unique funkiness of Orval was nowhere to be found and consumers complained. Under the guidance of De Clerck and the microbiological prowess of Theodore, the monks did not compromise on the new processes, but they did find the naturally occurring Brettanomyces still thriving in the wooden beams lining the rafters. They were able to isolate it and utilize it under controlled parameters.

Brother Xavier recounted just how important both the primary fermentation yeast (a more traditional Belgian Saccharomyces strain) and the blend of Brettanomyces strains are for Orval, "twice a year we return to KU Leuven to re-pitch batches of our house yeast culture. The yeast utilized in secondary fermentation is harvested here on site. Similar to the lambic styles made famous in Brussels, that yeast is cultivated naturally and spontaneously here. This makes Orval unique." There are two distinct strains of Brett noticeable in Orval today and the blend is added not just in secondary fermentation but utilized in bottle conditioning as well.

Contemporary Facets of the Community and Brewery

As I prepared to sit down for my interview with brother Xavier after the midday meal, I navigated past two dozen guests in the dining hall. Among them I was able to find guests of all ages, all backgrounds, and even several detectable languages beyond just the usual French and Flemish. In this sense, the hospitality aspect of Orval is truly remarkable. A community of just thirteen monks, with the help of local parishioners, impacts the lives of so many guests daily.

This is especially true, Brother Xavier tells me, in the late spring months as students prepare for exams. A program popular among Trappist communities, retreat rooms are offered free of charge to students during this time so that they may have the space to study, rest, and recharge. My own PhD advisor worked on his dissertation in such a way while studying at KU Leuven. Though my stay occurred too late to run into these students,

I could not help but think about the joys of such a program and reflect upon its need in my own home context.

As I weaved past guests returning their plates, a part of me wondered why so few attended the liturgical services each day. Of all these people, there were only three or four of us recognizable from mass. Brother Xavier later offers an important lesson; it is not up to the monks to dictate what type of retreat or hospitality each guest needs. Some stay for the gorgeous scenery, others want to experience the history of the site, some want to contemplate silently in their rooms, and others might attend each service. How they meet God, if at all, is up to them as the Rule argues that God is present even in the most mundane moments.

Although the monks are available for dialogue, there is no pressure to pursue such interactions. Or, as one guest at Orval said a bit more crassly, "they don't ram religion down your throat here, which is unexpected and appreciated." It is both a seemingly silly and powerful statement to ponder. The façade of the Virgin and child, various saints carved into the stonework of the cloister and guest house, literal ruins of the past abbey, and the brothers coming and going across the grounds are inescapable, but they are all invitations rather than obligations.

The sanctuary itself continues this inviting nature despite its almost cavernous size. A contemplative chapel designed by Christian Jaccard greets visitors upon entry and continues Orval's storied past of working with famed artists, architects, and other renowned figures. Designed in 2020 to celebrate the 950th anniversary of the first monastic presence at Orval, the domed room has walls of white plaster into which Jaccard burned soot patterns using thermal convection. Chaotic at first glance, the precision and care in design becomes apparent when spending extended time in the room. A microcosm of the monastery grounds themselves.

The Jaccard Room gives way to an outer hallway surrounding the nave which is filled with sculptures of various saints and a unique take on the stations of the cross. Sketches of Christ's journey to Calvary are embedded into the very rock of the sanctuary, an amalgamation of the monastery's general purpose in pursuing devotion to God and its dedication to the locale of Orval. Though on a larger scale than the other sanctuaries I visited, simplicity is still a central motif in Orval's approach.

The only ornateness comes in the form of a single stained-glass window above the altar depicting the Virgin Mary holding a baby Jesus in her lap, surrounded by vignettes of her presence throughout the Biblical depictions of Christ's life. Vaes's declaration that he wanted to capture both the eight centuries of history at Orval and its vibrant contemporary life is not just seen in the sanctuary but felt.

With regards to the brewing operations, the oscillation between the past and the present is evident beyond just the museum displays of former equipment amidst digital displays testing your Orval trivia. The late 1990s saw an increase in production at Orval which necessitated the rebuilding of the current brewhouse. Working with both KU Leuven and a German engineering firm, a state of the art fully automated system was put in place in 2007 which took its annual output capacity to around 80,000 hectoliters. There are thirty-eight stainless-steel horizontal lagering tanks where the beer is conditioned before packaging. 30,000 units per hour are filled as the famed 330-ml bowling pin bottles whiz down the impressive modern bottling line. These bottles are the only format in which the beer is available, the classic brew is not kegged. The five-week bottle conditioning process takes place in a cellar room that is built into the hillside at the edge of the brewing facility.

Like with Chimay, the brewing operations are technically in the hands of a holding company, but one that is supervised by a board which includes four monks and three lay directors. Brother Xavier shares, "While we have leased the rights of Orval to the Orval Brewing company as a separate entity, that lease comes with the stipulation that a high percentage of their profits are returned to charitable causes that the Abbey is associated with. We are not here to generate profits; we are here to serve social causes." Brother Xavier is also given daily updates on the brewery (though this has likely changed since my visit and his elevation to abbot).

With this approach and output, Orval employs over thirty lay workers at its brewery and a dozen more across the distribution landscape. The team is headed by brewmaster Anne-Françoise Pypaert, the first ever woman to run a Trappist brewery. In 2013, after over twenty years of experience in the quality control department at Orval (including a stint as its director), Pypaert was handed the keys by former brewmaster Jean Marie Rock in the wake of his retirement. She is also in charge of the cheese production at Orval and between the two facilities there are ten female employees, barrier breaking in Belgium and beyond.[2] Naturally, she is part of numerous programs and boards that encourage the growth of women's place in the

---

2. Lee-Weitz, "Meet Orval's Anne-Françoise Pypaert."

industry. Ultimately, Pypaert serves as a testament to the historical reality that women have always been central actors in the beer realm.

This brings us to the brewing process itself and the ingredients that make Orval a standout among wild yeasted beers, Trappist made beers, and Belgian styles alike. Beginning with the water provided from Matilda's famous spring, each of the resources undergoes rigorous lab work. The water table amidst Orval's yellow sandstone deposits is high in calcium and other alkaline materials. This hard water naturally lends itself to the elevated perceived-bitterness of the final product and is left largely unaltered by the brewers. Brother Xavier reiterates the importance that water has throughout our dialogue and this emphasis sticks with me for the duration of my stay.

The specific malt brought in by Orval varies from season to season depending on availability and harvest details but always involves two pale malt varietals, one caramel malt varietal, and a small amount of dark malt mostly for color attenuation—all grown in France and malted in Belgium to Orval's specifications. The brewery employs a wet milling method as the malt is prepared for brewing.[3] Hot water is added to the mill which makes the husks more malleable but keeps them intact during milling, resulting in higher mash efficiency, clearer wort, and a lower level of astringent tannins. The single infusion method sees the wort complete the mash-in and lautering processes in just a few hours before being pumped to the kettle for boil.

The boil lasts for sixty minutes and includes the addition of bittering hops via both pellets and hop extracts. The hop profile is made up predominantly of German grown Hallertau with Styrian Golding from Slovenia and French Alsace Strisselspalt taking a back seat. There is also a small addition of Tomahawk hops from the Yakima valley, a slight tweak that took place under Pypaert. The Pacific Northwest varietal has a high alpha acid count but mirrors the spicy and earthy profile of its continental European counterparts. The overall ratio and amount of the additions is a trade secret, but the hop addition in the boil pales in comparison to what is added later in the dry hopping process.

The wort makes one final stop before the fermentation tanks as a plate chiller cools down the liquid so that it can reach the optimal temperature for Orval's yeast. Pitched around fifty-five degrees Fahrenheit and never reaching above sixty-seven, it is the lowest fermentation temperature of any of the Trappist made beers covered here—partially responsible for the

---

3. Orval Brewery, "Brewery in the History of Orval."

cleaner flavor profile devoid of extensive ester presence. It is at this stage that Belgian candi sugar (in liquid form) is added to the wort as it is carried off to primary fermentation in stainless-steel tanks—this provides more fermentables to raise the alcohol content and to thin out the beer's body.

Once the yeast is pitched—for now it is the house yeast strain that is Brettanomyces free—primary fermentation takes four to five days to complete. Pypaert moved brewing days to Thursday in order to facilitate work free weekends for her staff, a move that arguably aligned closer with the Trappist ethos than was previously the case. Once this initial fermentation is complete, the beer makes its way into lagering tanks for two to three weeks where the true character of Orval comes out.

Each batch is doused with a second yeast pitch, this time with the proprietary blend of three yeasts that include Brettanomyces. The "wild" variant of yeast consumes sugars that the cultivated ale yeasts do not, creating the funky flavors, fruity esters, and dry finish so closely associated with Orval. These yeasts will also be added again for refermentation in the bottle, allowing Orval to develop for years to come and sparking the common occurrence of consumers cellaring the beer to taste its development. Secondary fermentation is also where the dry hopping aspect introduced all those years ago by Van Huele comes to the fore.

Whole cone hops rather than pellets or extract are introduced in a quantity much higher than in the boil. Hallertau and Alsace are loaded into mesh bags and placed directly into the fermenters, allowing the beer to develop resinous aromatics for the entire three-week lagering period. The beer is then filtered and centrifuged before making its way to the bottling line, a process that ensures an aesthetically pleasing final product free of both residue from the whole cone hops and extensive cloudiness from dead yeast cells. After the addition of fresh yeast, a small dousing of candi sugar, and the extensive cellaring process mentioned above, the beer is ready to be shipped off by those electric powered trucks I encountered on my first walk up the driveway. Which brings me to the profile of Orval itself.

> *Orval Classique:* Unlike any of the other Trappist made beers, Orval cannot be pigeonholed into a style. Its uniqueness is unfettered in every aspect including category. My best attempt would be to declare it a mixed fermentation Belgian pale ale, but this only scratches the surface. Though it has some characteristics reminiscent of Saison, this can be misleading given its malt complexity and hop profile. Similarly, its extensive lagering and the bottle conditioning make it cleaner than

any other pale ale, but its funk and yeast profile are nowhere near reminiscent of lagers themselves. Quite simply, it is Orval.

Anywhere between 6.2 percent and 6.9 percent ABV (depending on how much refermentation has taken place in the bottle), it pours a light amber in color with a highly carbonated white head that retains a decent amount of lacing throughout drinking. A flowery bouquet of spicy hop aromatics—a result of the dry-hopping—is evident on the nose and continues through to a distinctly bitter finish. Caramel sweetness and apricot jam are present in the body. The barnyard funk lingers long after the initial sip to round out the taste profile.

Consuming Orval can come with added nuance given its propensity for changing dramatically as it ages, so drinkers should be aware of its bottling date. The brewery itself notes that bottle conditioning changes the flavor profile and À *l'Ange Gardien* serves both a *jeune* (young) and a *vieux* (aged) version of the bottles depending on preference. The older the bottle, the more of the hop profile dies away in favor of the Brettanomyces character coming to the fore and the oxidation that comes with age allows the fruity character of the body to shine. Though Orval does not recommend holding on to bottles past the five-year mark, I have had a ten-year version on several occasions that is still exquisite despite being bone dry. Orval states that the flavor profile is also impacted by the temperature the beer is served at which is why the café also offers the bottles cold or cellar temperature—Orval branded fridges I have seen in the US have two differing compartments to mirror this choice. Whatever the vintage, whatever the chosen temperature, you are in for a treat.

> *Orval Vert:* The Trappist tradition of making a refectory beer is alive and well at Orval, so I apologize if declaring that they make only one beer was misleading. The Orval enjoyed around the world is technically the only product made available for the wider consumer market while *Orval Vert*, sometimes affectionately known as *Petite Orval*, can be tasted solely at the *Ange Gardien*. Not bottled, it is a draft offering that uses the same base wort as its bigger sibling but does not include the addition of Brettanomyces or any other supplementary yeast strains. It finishes at 4.5 percent, has a different hop profile (including American grown Mosaic),[4] and its current iteration was created to celebrate the café's re-opening. It is exceptionally refreshing, a good entry point for

---

4. Lee-Weitz, "Meet Orval's Anne-Françoise Pypaert."

palates that might not be used to Brettanomyces, and well worth a visit to the only place it is available. One of my favorite memories from the trip was ordering the full lineup (*jeune*, *vieux*, and *vert*) accompanied by three cheeses also made at the abbey.

With regards to the commercialization and marketing of Orval, in many ways it sells itself. Matilda's legend, its distinctive taste and inability to be categorized, impeccable quality, approachable price (in Belgium at least), the sleek bottles and architect designed chalice, the whole package is alluring. Orval does of course participate in the typical merchandising of coasters, bottle openers, tin tackers, cheeseboards, knives, glassware, etc. (a visit to the giftshop is a must), but the majority of Orval's outward-facing promotions deal with quality and presentation rather than sales.

For example, the Ambassador Orval program rewards around four hundred establishments around the world each year for extensive knowledge of Orval, technical quality in service, and growing what the brewery describes as the "art of Orval." The majority of these certificates are handed out within Belgium (mirroring the fact that 85 percent of Orval is sold there), but there are several in the United States. Interestingly, the program was created under Former Commercial Director, François de Harenne, a descendent of the family that first donated the abbey grounds back to the Trappists!

With regards to the American market, Orval's presence and influence is of astronomical proportions. Though the beer itself is readily available in any beer shop worth its salt, the sheer number of American craft breweries that tie their lineage distinctly to Orval is astounding. Goose Island's Matilda is not only an Orval clone, but founder John Hall has talked about how trips to Belgium were part of the inspiration for what is one of America's most recognizable brands. Years later, Goose even produced a limited release of Petit Matilda as another nod to this heritage.

Vinnie Cilurzo of the famed Russian River Brewing Company is consistently on record saying that Orval is one of his favorite beers and their Sanctification (along with arguably all of its Brett fermented cousins) is inspired by Orval. Steven Pauwels, the former brewmaster at Boulevard Brewing, hails from Belgium and their Saison Brett carved a path for mixed fermentation beers in a competitive market after Orval blazed the trial before it. It was a no-brainer for Pauwels to work with Jean-Marie Rock to kick off Boulevard's Collaboration Series. New Belgium (the name says it all) similarly partnered with Anne-Françoise Pypaert on their Lips of Faith wild series. The American beer scene would not be what it is today without these breweries and, by extension, without Orval's inspiration.

This influence is perhaps most noticeable in the creation of Orval's very own beer holiday in the US, "Orval Day." Merchant du Vin, Orval's American importer, came up with the idea in 2016 to celebrate the shining star of its portfolio. The idea was to have beer shops carrying Orval promote it on that particular day (March 26, 2016) with a portion of the proceeds from its sales nationwide going to a charitable cause (this year's was the National Forest Foundation). Since then, usually in the last week of March, the tradition has continued and includes taste testing various vintages, friendly competitions on which bar can sell the most Orval that day, raffles to win magnums or oversized Orval chalices, and of course, education on how to properly pour and enjoy the beer. I have enjoyed many an Orval on this day at Beer Temple, expertly poured by my favorite bartender who also happens to have the Orval trout logo tattooed on his arm—a phenomenon that Brother Xavier tells me he doesn't quite understand.

In many ways, this is the perfect encapsulation of Orval, fame they did not want from a process that is only a small part of their vocation. Nevertheless, it is acclaim they deserve and that will long continue even if the monks themselves are focused on their true contemplative calling. This fine balance between legend and simplicity surrounded me for the duration of my stay as I wrestled with both the storied grandeur of Orval and the day-to-day beauty of the liturgical offices.

My final morning at the abbey sees me strolling through the gardens, sitting by the fountain, and attending morning services. I grab a whole brick of cheese which will serve as lunch for weeks to come—a welcome continuation of meals served at the abbey—and make my way through the parking lots towards the bus stop. There are already hikers, bird watchers, cyclists, a few retreat guests with their bags, and of course cars with their hazards on eagerly loading crates of Orval into their trunks. A repetitive methodical pattern much like the one found inside the cloister.

Chapter 9

Abdij Onze Lieve Vrouw van Koningshoeven

A MASSIVE BRICK GATEHOUSE at the edge of a moat topped with a marble statue of the Virgin Mary stands before me in the pouring rain. The fact that I had just gotten off a bus after a short ride from Tilburg precluded any fantasies about being magically transported in time. However, the aura of rich history remained as the automated gate opened upon my approach. Gorgeous grounds complete with contemplative gardens, a pond with a fountain, prayer shrines, and a massive cloister attached to an even more impressive sanctuary were the backdrop for my walk up the gravel path to the historic Koningshoeven abbey in the Brabant region of the Netherlands.

Automated electric powered mowers glided around the wet lawn and fully electric vehicles were parked in an adjacent lot beyond the cloister gate. Solar panels adorned the roofs of several buildings off in the distance of the property as an analog clock tower began to chime. The contrast between modernity and the past was something that I was used to at this point of my trip, but Koningshoeven took this dichotomy to another level. With a distinct eye to the future, the Abdij Onze Lieve Vrouw van Koningshoeven brings Trappist values to a breadth of people.

Housing the La Trappe brewery, formerly known as Bierbrouwerij De Schaapskooi along with a cheese factory, a bakery, a jam making shop, an apiary, and even a small chocolatery, Koningshoeven's need for adaptation amidst an ancient ethos stretches across its programs and modes of sustaining the community. It navigates a multiplicity of partnerships with secular and religious communities alike while bucking trends and typical associations of what the monastic life "should be." Or, as guest master brother Jakobus would later tell me, "Our lives are better understood as a healthy struggle between tradition and progress." An air of openness even behind closed walls allows the monks to encounter God wherever God might meet them and bring the essence of the Gospel to the wider world. This is their story, one that proves a fitting end to my monastery profiles.

Historical Overview

Though its beginnings were briefly shared when discussing the formation of its daughter house at Zundert, I will provide a refresher here. Koningshoeven's story started in 1880 and as with most of the Dutch and Belgian Trappist communities, cannot be told without contextualizing anticlerical sentiment in France. The French Abbaye Sainte-Marie aux Monts-des-Cats and its abbot—Dominique Lacaes—preemptively began seeking refuge amidst a slew of secularization policies (the Jules Ferry Laws, expulsion of religious communities from France, targeted attacks on religious education, etc.). Lacaes sent brother Sébastien Wyart to Tilburg to work with the Brothers of Our Lady Mother of Mercy (an order focused on charitable outreach and preaching) on securing land for a potential site of refuge.

Franciscus Salesius de Beer, the superior of the Brothers of Tilburg, was able to work with a local landowner, Caspar Houben, to secure a site in Berkel-Enschot just east of the town. Initially a three-year rental, three tracts of farmland and a sheepfold were secured with an option for purchase at the end of the contract. Formerly the land of King Willem II, Koningshoeven quite literally means "the king's sheepfold." In 1881 a group of monks joined Wyart from Mont-des-Cats to work the land as they hoped for a swift resolution to the dire religious situation in France. On March 5, the first Mass was celebrated in a sheep barn on the property and construction of a monastery began in earnest. By 1883, with fully livable quarters, a functioning sanctuary, and no end to French religious strife in sight, Koningshoeven was raised to the position of priory with brother Nivard Schweykart elected as its first prior. They took on debt to purchase the property from Houben.

As the community grew and Schweykart pushed towards self-sufficiency, an alternative to farming and sheep herding was needed. Unfortunately, it was not an ideal parcel for feeding the monks, fulfilling charitable functions, and raising enough income to make payments on the land. As the son of a German brewer, Schweykart knew the potential that beer had for generating income and had enough experience with the processes to pursue its production. He made the decision to build a brewhouse at the monastery and modest amounts of beer began to flow from Koningshoeven in 1884 under the watchful eye of brother Isidorus Laaber—after a training stint with Schweykart's acquaintances in Bavaria.

Although the transition to brewing was logical at the time amidst an explosion of industrial technologies that made it more feasible, there were also several missteps taken in this early period. First, brother Isidorus's internship in Germany had made him familiar with lager brewing rather than the ale brewing of both other Trappist communities and the wider brewing scene of Belgium and the Netherlands. Isidorus brought in German engineers to reconfigure the brewhouse which had been initially built for ales, switched to refrigerated lagering tanks, and had to wait several weeks for each batch to finish its fermentation—time was money even back then.

The brothers themselves described this period of carving out their place in the market as a "beer war," a moniker that came about as local breweries in Tilburg banded together to set up a committee in 1891 to protest the monastery's beer production.[1] They thought that the religious nature of the brewery offered it an unfair marketing advantage and wanted the monks to cease their operations. The plan backfired as the controversy surrounding the Trappist-made beer only catapulted the brewery's status. A series of local sermons delivered from pulpits around the region saw priests offer support for the brothers' beer endeavor. Bierbrouwerij De Schaapskooi was there to stay.

1891 would prove to be a monumental year for Koningshoeven beyond the beer war as the priory was granted the status of abbey and Dom Willibrord Verbruggen was elected its first abbot. A magnanimous figure, Verbruggen completed his novitiate and took his vows at Westmalle before joining the community at Koningshoeven. He was the first ever Trappist to be granted entrance into the Pontifical University to pursue his degree in philosophy and when he rose to the rank of abbot, he had grandiose plans for the monastery. He wanted to grow the community not just in number but also wanted to reconstruct the abbey to mirror the prestige he thought it deserved. He was emboldened by the papacy's own wishes for a premier monastic presence in Holland.

1. La Trappe Trappist, "Rich History."

This required an expansion of the brewery to increase income and saw the implementation of a modernized brewhouse, steam-powered equipment, a bottling line, a massive malt silo—a looming tower that has become synonymous with the monastery's architecture—delivery trucks to fill lucrative distribution contracts, and a switch to running solely on electricity (a feat the city Tilburg itself would not achieve until 1910). The buildout of the abbey was equally as impressive and drew ire for both its grandeur and its modernized approach—something other Trappist abbots saw as a distraction and perhaps even a step away from the Rule. The sanctuary was re-consecrated on September 17 of 1894 and Koningshoeven spent the next few years paying for Verbruggen's ambition in more ways than one.

He consolidated the original debt owed to Houben through a series of loans with a banking institution in Antwerp and levied additional loans to cover the construction projects, all in his own name. It created a vicious cycle of financial precarity that is all too familiar in the modern craft beer world and took a toll on Verbruggen, the brewery, and the abbey. Amidst heightened tensions, he fired brewmaster Karl Frech. The mess had reached such heights by 1895 that Verbruggen took a sabbatical while brother Leon van Hoorne was sent to Koningshoeven from Monts-des-Cats to see if he could stabilize the situation.

With a background in finance, van Hoorne set the books straight at the brewery, supplemented income by bringing in weaving looms for textile production, and expanded distribution of Koningshoeven's beers via exclusivity rights and the hiring of a beer agency in Brussels. The stability did not last long as Verbruggen returned to the abbey less than a year later and continued to run things as he had before. To make matters worse, former brewmaster Frech made formal accusations of financial impropriety, favoritism, and outed Verbruggen's "sexual escapades" during his travels on monastic business (a fact that was never verified) to the Abbot General of the Order. Luckily for Verbruggen, at the time this was Dom Sebastian Wyart (the very same one involved in Koningshoeven's founding). Their close friendship along with the complicated fact that the holdings were in Verbruggen's name meant that the accusations entered the official record but did not come with consequences until after Dom Sebastian Wyart passed in 1904.

Augustin Marre was elected as the Abbot General and immediately began investigating Koningshoeven's finances as did Dom Bernard Richebé from Koningshoeven's mother house. These internal probes were coupled with a lawsuit filed by the brewery's distribution agent in Brussels, which was settled in the agent's favor. Things came to a head in 1908 as the Order, the Archdiocese, and even the Papacy pressured Verbruggen to step down and turnover ownership. He declined and held onto power for another year as his monks rallied behind him.[2]

Fed up, Pope Leo XIII issued a papal decree in May of 1909 which ousted Verbruggen as abbot and called for the monks to leave the property for other monasteries. A standoff ensued for two months, and ultimately, Verbruggen relented and departed Koningshoeven while the last of the monks loyal to him went to other houses. The monastery and brewery were both shuttered as a legal battle over the ownership rights of the property dragged on. In November, Verbruggen acquiesced to the Order's demands, handed over the rights to the property, left behind the contemplative life, and his place in the story of Koningshoeven ended in deflated fashion.

Brother Simon Dubuisson from Scourmont Abbey was elected first as Superior to oversee a transition to functionality and then as abbot. He got accounts back on track, reopened the brewery, and the community began producing a new low-ABV blond ale in 1928 that would change the trajectory of their product portfolio. The output at the brewery grew to the point that an automated bottling line was introduced in 1936 to keep up with demand and success continued until the outbreak of the Second World War. Though the community at Koningshoeven would continue to function throughout the conflict, even producing beer in a limited capacity for distribution and for the occupying German forces, it would be directly impacted by the Nazis in a way that most other Trappist abbeys were not.

In 1942, an SS investigation discovered that three of the brothers at Koningshoeven were of Jewish descent. Ignatius, Linus, and Nivardus Löb along with two of their sisters living at Koningshoeven's Daughter House—Hedwigis and Theresia—were all arrested and shipped off to Auschwitz. The brothers volunteered for the arrest order upon hearing that priests would be shot at random until the brothers identified themselves, a surreal moment of both bravery and a testament to the length that their fellow monks would go to protect them in the first place. None of the five survived the death camp but their memories remain honored at the abbey and the convent.[3]

2. Van de Wiel, "Trappist Question."
3. Ann, "Heroes of the Holocaust."

The period following WWII saw a mixture of prosperity for the growth of the community as well as precarity with regards to the brewery. Newly elected abbot Dom Willibrord van Dijk saw an increase in vocations in the wake of the spiritually devastating conflict and Koningshoeven's population grew to over one-hundred and fifty brothers. Van Dijk sent monks to both Java and Kenya to start daughter houses to further pursue the virtue of solidarity and consciously wrestle with the ills that Dutch colonialism had left in its wake. To continue this type of work, van Dijk also needed to rethink the status of the brewery.

The war had devastated the raw material chain needed to supply the brewery and its pre-war output was no longer feasible. Rather than close down entirely, Koningshoeven supplemented brewing with the production of soft drinks under the label "Ariston and Whist." The move got Koningshoeven through a period of difficulty before the 1950s saw them ramp up beer production once materials were available. Unfortunately, the 1960s was a trying decade for the monks at Koningshoeven as the sex, drugs, and rock'n'roll ethos leapt over the Atlantic and limited vocational growth.

Even amidst a laxing of the rules on silence, how individual reading time could be utilized, a shift towards individual rooms for brothers rather than a communal dormitory—adoptions of the wider air of freedom of the decade—the abbey stagnated. There was a virtual standstill in new arrivals, several monks left the monastery to return to secular life, and many of the older monks retired to nursing homes. It meant that a more tenable situation for operating the brewery needed to be found. Most employees were lay workers at this point and production was taking place at an industrial commercialized level, so van Dijk made the decision to partner with Leuven-based Stella Artois to manage the brewing assets.

Production was licensed to Stella in 1969, and several new brands were launched amidst an initial expansion. Pils, Dortmunder, Bock, and Dark joined the initial Superbier and Wheat as beer flowed to taverns across Belgium. However, the partnership soon became a cautionary tale for macro-breweries acquiring or working with smaller producers (truly there is nothing new under the sun). With Stella prioritizing their own brand, the brewery at Koningshoeven took a backseat and its production dropped in the mid-1970s. In 1979 the brothers rescinded the lease amidst what the abbey described as negligence. By that point, irreparable damage had been done to the brand and the abbey had to seriously consider the financial viability of reviving the brewery.

In the end, the decision was made to rebrand Bierbrouwerij De Schaapskooi as La Trappe in 1980—a nod to the Order's roots. "Trappisten Bier" was affixed to labels as they shifted to production of the more recognizable Trappist affiliated styles of Dubbel and Tripel. The change was well received—partially due to the success of their Trappist cousins—and necessitated an update to the brewing facility to match demand. In 1989, the century-old open fermentation vessels and lager tanks were replaced and a new brewhouse was installed. With production back in the hands of the monks and a renewed vision for how the brewery could support the abbey, La Trappe began its modern journey.

Contemporary Facets of the Community and Brewery

On the first day of my visit, as I made my way to the small chapel used daily by the brothers for the liturgy of the hours, I passed down a long corridor which also included the entrance to a much larger sanctuary. Though used for high holiday services, the vibrant stained-glass windows are now seldom admired by more than the occasional curious guest. I was entirely undisturbed as I walked its perimeter, seeing if I could guess the names of the Saints sculpted out of the same dark wood without looking at the placards. I hurried to morning service as the bells signaled its start—I would not have guessed Saint Joseph Labre anyway.

Grabbing my psalter, I found not just two dozen or so brothers at the service, but a handful of guests and locals participating as well. It was by far the busiest morning prayer I had attended at any of the abbeys thus far. The makeup of the room was truly inspirational. Koningshoeven is not only cross-generational but their work around the globe has led to the abbey having an international flair as well. Guest Master Jakobus would later give me precise details.

> We are a community of twenty-three people, twenty-three monks, and one monk is outside of the abbey, that is our Father General Dom Bernardus, he was the former Abbot here, until two years ago. Right now, we have seven Dutch monks, one German, two Belgian, but we also have brothers from Indonesia and Uganda. We have a former Abbot from Indonesia, and an Abbot on sabbatical from Nigeria. We have two novices, two postulates, one from Ghana and one from Bangladesh, so we're truly an international community.

The growth was initially sparked in the early 2000s because of conscious efforts on the part of Dom Bernardus to make accessibility and solidarity with younger generations priorities for Koningshoeven. Over the years this included founding a digital novitiate, creating e-newsletters, undertaking what he has called on several occasions a "dissenting voice" within the church, a true heart for eco-theology, a practical presence in the surrounding Tilburg community, and an overall air of openness to progress categorized his time as abbot. This ultimately led to his elevation as Father General. His influence continues at Koningshoeven, and abbot Dom Isaac has followed closely in his footsteps with regards to such engagement and initiatives.

My conversation with brother Jakobus shifted to beer as I pursued these intersections. "Well, for me as a guest master, I'm not very into the beer factory, and that's important to say, because none of the brothers, except for Father Abbot, are involved in beer. But that doesn't mean that we don't know what we sell or what we produce. We even drink it when one of the brothers is having his birthday or some other occasion, for example." One such occurrence was the 2013 celebration of Dom Bernardus's 25th anniversary of taking vows. A special beer, "Jubilarus," was brewed for the occasion. But again, this was a rarity and like with several other Trappist communities, the monks no longer follow the tradition of drinking the local beverage with their meal. Many choose to live a sober life entirely.

This does not apply to me as a guest and brother Jakobus kindly shares a Puur, their 4.5 percent organic blond, the first ever Trappist made beer with this designation. This is not just a nod to the ingredients, but to the purpose of the beer itself, proceeds from which go to the BuyWorld Foundation—a secular non-profit which founder Gerard van Dorth says he created to save the earth from humans.[4] The collectivist organization buys up plots of land in various Dutch micro-climates and simply allows nature to live in peace, a sentiment that the Trappists can fully get behind. Beyond this, brother Jakobus can also explain the taste profile and ingredients perfectly—he was not kidding about knowing his products.

This depth of knowledge was something that was almost made impossible by a controversy surrounding La Trappe in the early 2000s. In the wake of modernizing the facilities and the brewing operations, Koningshoeven made the bold choice to try another commercial partnership. The hangover from their relationship with Stella still loomed heavy but the growth that

---

4. BuyWorld, "BuyWorld, Save the Earth by Buying It."

Dom Korneel Vermeiren anticipated could not be matched solely by the community and their lay workers. A limited liability company was set up as a subsidiary of the Koningshoeven abbey to run operations and in 1999 brewing operations at La Trappe were leased to the Bavaria Brewing company. A staple in Brabant since 1719, the brewery owned by the Swinkels family had produced macro lager for generations and understood the scale at which La Trappe wanted to operate.

The newly formed ITA took exception to the hands-off approach implemented by the monks at Koningshoeven and demanded that they remove the Trappist logo and wording from the label. La Trappe complied somewhat, removing the ITA certification but keeping the "Trappist" moniker. A back-and-forth conversation ensued but ultimately resulted in both sides relenting and compromising through dialogue (another Cistercian value!). The monks heightened their oversight and involvement in the brewing and the ITA loosened its understanding of what "made by monks" meant. I am glad they found a resolution, as is brother Jakobus: "We have a very good partner in Bavaria Beers, the Swinkels Family Brewery, we would not change this or what it allows us to do."

With production totaling nearly 150k hectoliters annually, the state-of-the-art facility has its hands full and during its busy season hosts thousands of visitors every week for tours or a quick stop at the tasting room. Built in 2008 after the previous facility could no longer accommodate the sheer number of visitors, the tasting room architecture is a nod to Koningshoeven's original sheep barn and offers each of the La Trappe's draft offerings as well as vintage bottles. It is worth a trip even if you do not stay for a retreat. The monks operate the adjacent shop as well, so there are opportunities to grab the Trappist made products that Koningshoeven is involved in—beer, cheese, bread, chocolate, jams, glassware, gift sets, clothing, etc., and I even found fair trade coffee produced by La Trappe in conjunction with their African sister communities. This plethora and diversity are also present in La Trappe's beer offerings.

Below are descriptions of their core brands which I sampled during my stay. Each offering utilizes locally grown barley as much as possible, features organically grown hops in pellet and extract form, and draws water directly from the well on the property—it has a neutral profile and is adjusted according to each differing style. The yeast strain dominant at La Trappe is far more subdued than the other breweries profiled here, and although its origins are a closely guarded secret, has a profile similar to English ale yeast. Bottle conditioning with sugar and yeast additions is also present throughout the portfolio. Having discussed the commercial production process elsewhere, I will save space to highlight the beers themselves and the initiatives that La Trappe is involved in.

> *Witte Trappist*: An unfiltered wit beer first released in 2003, it pours a hazy golden straw color with a light and vigorously carbonated head. Its predominant nose profile is one of wheat and the flowery aromatics added by the Saphir hops. Low in alpha acids and bitterness, the hops do not linger long. It is crisp, refreshing, tart on the finish and a favorite of the multitude of cyclists that visit the taproom. At just 5.5 percent ABV, they usually have more than one. Like with all La Trappe core offerings, it is available on draft, in 750-ml corked bottles, and in 330-ml capped bottles, and it occasionally makes its way to the States as well—La Trappe's largest non-Dutch/Belgian market.
>
> *Blond*: An exceptional example of a traditional Belgian Blond, it pours golden in color with a beautiful frothy heady. Extremely approachable, it has a balance of malty sweetness (a mixture of pale malt and Munich malt), spiciness from the hops, and the most pronounced white pepper, lemon zest, and apricot yeast aromatics of any of the La Trappe offerings. At 6.5 percent ABV, it still goes down easily and serves as a conduit to contemplative thought.
>
> *Dubbel*: Representative of the style that has become synonymous with Trappist made beer, La Trappe's take allows the malt profile (caramel, Munich, and pale) to shine while the yeast takes a back seat. A viscous ruby hue, the beer gives of aromatics of molasses and subtle hop spice as its beige head beautifully laces the glass. Its 7 percent ABV is hidden behind a well-balanced beer.
>
> *Bockbier*: First released in October of 2004, this nod to the German inspired brews of La Trappe's past is built off of a recipe revived from the 1950s. It continues to make its appearance each fall, though it is top fermented rather than lagered like most bocks. An addition of roasted malt provides a smokey backbone to the prominent flavors of licorice, caramel malt, and dry herbaceous hops—traditional German hop varietals add a pronounced bitterness to this 7 percent ABV offering.
>
> *Isid'or*: First brewed in 2009 for the 125th anniversary of Koningshoeven Abbey and named after the same Isidor that brewed the community's

first batch of beer, this Belgian amber ale is worthy of celebrating occasions big and small. A malty richness with a surprisingly light body (likely due to the addition of wheat into the malt bill) is dominated by caramel sweetness and dried fruits esters. The candi sugar comes through exceptionally well but is balanced by a slight bitterness. At 7.5 percent ABV, it is far too drinkable for its alcohol content. It was the last beer I had before leaving the abbey, a fitting memento of La Trappe's story.

Tripel: A common place style in the Trappist realm, La Trappe's is significantly different than its relatives. Peach, apricot, hop spiciness, and a hint of white pepper follow the typical Tripel pattern, but its effervescence quickly dissipates into a malty sweetness. There is far less of a boozy presence than with other examples of the style. However, it comes in at 8 percent ABV, so be careful.

Quadrupel: Introduced for the Christmas season in 1991, it quickly became a fan favorite which necessitated its inclusion in the year-round portfolio. Big, bold, and 10 percent ABV, this beer is full of dates, caramel, warm booziness, and a kiss of herbal tones. A nose of clove comes from the yeast consuming copious amounts of malt (rather than any spice additions), and as your glass warms and the caramel-colored head dissipates, you really slip into tasting the silence.

Oak Aged: A barrel aged version of the Quadrupel, this project started in 2009 to tap into La Trappe's roots but also with a nod to the future of the market. A mixture of new French oak barrels and a collection of port, whisky, wine, and cognac barrels, this vintage changes slightly year to year. Soaking up barrel contents and refermentation leaves this above the 11 percent ABV mark. A true treat if you can find it.

Lest it seem like this extended catalogue of beer and wide range of other products is pure commercialization, Brother Jakobus clarifies the purpose behind each of these products. "What we try to produce with the beer or any of our products are the values of the monastic life. A good product, attention to the environment, charitable giving, etc." This subtlety in care for creation is fundamental to the Cistercian ethos of eco-consciousness, and brother Jakobus continued unprompted by further questioning.

> For us monks, we think that it is a Christian responsibility to take responsibility for the Earth and so that's what we do. Our Father Abbot, Dom Isaac, he is very far in this [mentality] together with

a lot of the brothers like the former Abbot who left two years ago for Rome. We have a stamp of *Groene Kerk*, a "green church". It's a Dutch initiative for Churches and our monastic communities to have an official signature that this is who we are and what we like to do.

The costs associated with such work is a huge turn-off for most commercially oriented breweries (though there are exceptions in the States like Allagash, Maine Beer Company, Russian River, Sierra Nevada etc.), but this reality dissipates when you have a higher purpose beyond profit generation.

Additional initiatives aimed at such sustainable measures have also included the following: A partnership with G-Star, the chic Dutch denim designer, to create 100 percent organic and hazard-free habits for the monks while also raising awareness of the fashion industry's propensity for environmental degradation. A honey infused Quadrupel made with famed brewery BrewDog called "Practice What You Preach" which donated the equivalent cost of 1,000 glasses of fresh drinking water per bottle sold to the Made Blue Foundation (another long-term partner of La Trappe). La Trappe then teamed up with Zundert and Tynt Meadow (a Trappist brewery in England) to produce "Three Rules," a special style Dubbel that features elements important to each of the collaborators' beers—organic hops, toasted malt, and peated botanicals respectively. The goal was not just to reiterate the three requirements for receiving ITA certification—though vignettes representing each of the three facets and each of the three breweries adorned the bottles—but to raise funds for Trees for All, a Dutch organization which focuses on re-planting forests and general tree conservation. Lastly (for now) 2025 will see the release of "Blond Special Edition," a grain forward version of their year-round blond containing barley, wheat, oats, and rye. Proceeds from this release will help supply water to orphanages in Kyotera, Uganda.

Not all of the commitments to eco-sustainability are as simple as these collaborations, with some projects at Koningshoeven taking on significant labor, planning, and careful execution. The most impressive of these is the Biopolus BioMakery water treatment system built at the abbey in conjunction with the regional water board Waterschap de Dommel.[5] Brother Jakobus explained that "in 2017 we built a water purification system for the brewery and the wastewater from the monastery. It is now fully working and a lot of people come to visit, those whose jobs are connected to wastewater

---

5. Biopolus, "First Biomakery of the Netherlands."

purification. So that's very good." His Cistercian modesty is apparent in his response because I had already seen the treatment plant earlier in the day and gotten a rundown from one of the brewery employees. It was the first ever such plant in Holland and the visitors he is talking about are climate scientists, conservation big-wigs, EU and UN representatives, university researchers, etc.; all analyzing and admiring the system's potential.

The treatment process itself relies on tropical water plants—with an enclosed greenhouse eco-system created to ensure their survival—filtering wastewater from the abbey, the brewery, the tasting room/restaurant, and the gift shop. The water passes through various chambers in which microorganisms (3,000 differing varieties!) growing on the plant roots feed off of contaminants. Once they pass through this stage further filtration is necessary to make the water potable and reusable in the brewery (via reverse osmosis) but it can be immediately utilized for irrigation and agricultural purposes. The leftover sludge that is created in the filtration process makes excellent fertilizer, which the monks graciously give away to surrounding farmers. The process is as close to net neutral water usage as any brewery can hope to get and makes the abbey itself a fully enclosed cycle of self-sufficiency as far as water is concerned.[6]

The work does not stop there as brother Jakobus begins to describe how the abbey is powered.

> We are using solar panels here as well. There are over 500 because there are flat roofs around the grounds that are also covered with solar panels. That is very important for us. All of the electricity from the monastery, including the bakery, because that's on our property as well, but not the brewery, all the electricity we used in the monastery for lighting, cooking, for the electric oven in the bakery, and for the machines in the laundry service, we provide all of it for ourselves. All by solar panels.

The whole system was such a refreshing reminder of what is possible when contemplation, intentionality, and faith are combined to pursue better living. An example by which we can all live by.

But of course, the monks are not insular. Hospitality also comes to the fore with regards to this energy usage. "The excess energy which is created by our solar panels, that's sold to the brewery. So, they have to buy much less from another provider. We try to save as much as possible, we try to fundraise for good organizations which do work on that, and we try to

6. NextGen Water, "La Trappe Brewery."

make sure our newsletters show people what is possible." In the month that I visited, the monks actually put more electricity back onto the local grid than they had used. This care extends to a multiplicity of communities, even ones that might seem counterintuitive on the surface. Brother Jakobus clues me in on one such initiative,

> Also, we have our non-alcoholic beers which we think are important to sell. Someone might like to drink with his friends but maybe he cannot have alcohol, maybe he has to drive home after a party, or an evening at the café, or for whatever reason. So that's what we try to experiment with.

La Trappe did more than experiment with non-alcoholic beers, they brought them into their permanent rotation. *Nillis*, a play on Latin for zero and also a nod to the Nile which provides water to Koningshoeven's daughter house in Uganda, is an amber ale that is completely alcohol free and organic. Their support of this community has also included the installation of a similar water filtration plant to the one described above at the African abbey. Released in 2021, *Nillis* celebrates the 140th anniversary of the community and its focus on contemplation being accessible to all.

This was followed up with *Epos*, an alcohol-free blond beer. Not only do proceeds from these brews go back to the African abbey, they are geared towards eco-initiatives explicitly. Brother Jakobus proudly states, "we try to do what we can also by supplying water systems for our partner communities in the developing World." The beers themselves provide an important alternative to those who choose a sober lifestyle. As reality shifts even among brewing industry workers in the States, I had several friends that greatly appreciated me bringing back a few 0.0 percent bottles of Trappist made brew. The quality associated with Trappist products was in no way lessened by the lack of alcohol, but the opportunity for conversation remained.

The list goes on and on as brother Jakobus continues to describe their work amidst my furious note taking. The abbey partners with the Prins Heerlijk Foundation[7] and the Diamant Groep[8] which support young adults with learning disabilities and neurodivergences by providing specialized job training along with continued education diplomas in hopes of growing

---

7. Prins Heerlijk, "Home."
8. Diamant Groep, "About."

their independence. Aside from monetary donations, La Trappe hires Heerlijk foundation graduates throughout their connected enterprises.

Such rootedness in Tilburg and the surrounding region re-emphasizes the Rule's focus on stability. The sheer amount of good that flows into the community is humbling as brother Jakobus finishes with another slew of partnerships and initiatives aimed at changing the world around the abbey.

> We have a small race that we do every year, a 5k, for a special purpose. One year we host it abroad and the next we do it here in Tilburg. This year the income from all of the participants, three hundred runners, went to buy musical instruments here for a primary school in Tilburg-Noord which is a quite poor area. Those are the things we find important. We also bake bread once a week, about one hundred loaves, for the bread shop there, where people can get free bread. That's the way we are. We are happy to share with others. That's what Benedict taught us.

I can think of no better way to end than that. From Isidor to Dom Bernardus and Dom Isaac, the beer has only been a vehicle for wider goals. Not just the inner-cloister goals of contemplation, community growth, and stability but the outward facing goals of sustainability, sparking conversation, care for others, shaping society, and protecting the world. That is what awaits in every glass of La Trappe brewed beer, but the brothers and I hope that it does not stop there.

Conclusion: Only the Beginning of Perfection
A Word of Hope

As I sit to reflect on this project, I am once again guided by St. Benedict. In the last chapter of the Rule, he reminds his audience that the seventy-two preceding chapters are not a road map to perfection for monastic communities but should be seen merely as an entry point for individual and communal growth. He praises the church fathers generally and points to St. Basil specifically as vital reading for all who wish to continue towards something greater. Additionally, he reminds his fellow monks that the Hebrew Bible and the New Testament should be valued above all else in one's search for perfection. Pursuing unity with Christ and cultivating the virtues of the Spirit are the ultimate goals. They extend to all, within the cloister and beyond. His Rule is for beginners on this journey and is meant to guide, not overwhelm.

When my students discuss this final chapter in class, without fail, there is always at least one comment about Benedict's own humility in ending with this sentiment. Not only was he asked to provide guidance via the creation of a Rule, but his extensive experience with living in community and founding monasteries could certainly have led him to believe that the preceding instructions were of ultimate importance. Instead, he builds off chapters discussing mutual obedience within the cloister, patience with your fellow brothers, respect towards differing personalities, and unfeigned care for others. A final nod to the approach present all along—concern for the well-being of his monks and a look at what it might mean to love ourselves, love others, and love God.

Conclusion: Only the Beginning of Perfection

This naturally leads to a reintroduction of a question from the beginning of the unit on the Rule—why is it that we are still reading this guidebook in a classroom more than fifteen hundred years later? Gone now are responses like "because we are at a Christian institution," or "because you have a degree in Patristics and choose the readings." Having gotten past Benedict's writing style, the structure of the Rule, and instances of perceived harshness, students come to realize that like with the other theologians covered in introductory courses, he is offering answers to big picture questions that all humans face. Questions of identity, purpose, meaning, relationality, interaction with the world around us, and cultivation of virtue go beyond Benedict's own context and offer everyone a chance for reflection. But most importantly, the parameters for love are not abstract thought exercises. Students realize the importance of how theory and praxis intersect within the Rule.

Everyday mundane tasks and manual labor are just as important for individual formation as moments of intentional contemplation and can serve as occasions for loving others. They are struck by how extraordinary the ordinary can be if we allow it to. Students start to think about the ways in which liturgy can offer both structure and a sense of freedom within their own lives (both the Liturgy of the Word but also intentional moments for work and prayer). They reflect on how the rejection of materialism and the constant cycle of consumption and production can be liberating even when practiced in the smallest ways. The volunteer hours associated with the course take on a different meaning with the backdrop of Benedict's emphasis on serving others as a virtue. Religious or not, they indicate that they have gained an appreciation for what it might mean to construct a worldview based on humility and selflessness. They begin to express the need to radically alter how we view the Other. Ultimately, many students come to treat the Rule as a living document—a moment of success that goes far beyond any learning outcomes listed in the syllabus. These are important lessons for not just the classroom but for readers here as well, I hope.

The final question on the reading guide then brings a bit of tension to the conversation, "What is stopping you from pursuing the monastic vocation?" I include this in the prompt not because I think that religious orders are an option for all, or even because I think any of my students will seriously consider the prospect (though there is always a sense of hope that they might). I do it for two reasons. First, it forces students to wrestle with just how ingrained an individualistic and materialistic mindset is in our society. They quickly start to backpedal about what it might look like to give up their possessions. Even the very idea of pursuing such a lifestyle within a structured thought exercise introduces panic. It truly allows them an opportunity to question what they value and why. Though they often find themselves advocating for a happy medium of materialism, individuality, and outreach to the Other, the difficulty of undertaking even this approach becomes all too apparent.

Second, the question reiterates that religious vocations are indeed alive and well in our own context and that the stories of these individuals and communities are worth uplifting. The Rule is certainly useful for those outside of monasteries, as Benedict says, but it is first and foremost a guide for those called to communal living of a particular sort. Its relevancy as a document in this sense cannot be forgotten. The vibrancy of these communities is an important reminder of the wide range of Christian callings and gifts. Cataloging these individuals, providing stories of the work that various monasteries do, and tying their ethos directly to the types of labor that Catholic Social Teaching strives for are refreshing anecdotes for what praxis can look like. I also tell students that one does not need to take vows to participate in these communities. Retreats, attendance at services, even just correspondence or conversation with monks and nuns allows for an exchange of ideas, two-way growth, and creates the potential for friendships and mentoring in a world that desperately needs them. These facets continued to reinforce my decision to undertake this project.

Ultimately, these communities open the door to take to heart what it means to slow down, take a breath, and listen to the potential present in other ways of pursuing a faithful life. Lest I seem like I am dispensing answers rather than fostering conversation, this last conclusion is one that is important not just for college students, but for everyone, and myself especially. In fact, it was what planted the seeds for this project to begin with. The Rule's requirement of hospitality then served as the soil for them to grow, facilitating stays at each of the communities described above. It was a much-needed vocational refresher for me, but ultimately it served as much more than that as I was continually surprised by the beauty, wisdom, space for growth, and love I was offered over the course of the four months I spent as a guest. I realized I never fully grasped the conclusions that I hope my students reach in discussing the Rule. I had forgotten Gregory's description of Benedict as a humble example of living out our virtues, someone that "could not live otherwise than he taught." First and foremost, I began to learn what it means to truly listen as I surrounded myself with those dedicated to such a pursuit. What I heard left me changed forever.

Though I have provided quotations and analysis from my interviews about what it means to listen with the ear of your heart, it behooves reiteration here as I came to live this reality. Participation in the liturgy, intentional moments of personal contemplation, *Lectio Divina*, conversation with the monks, and reflection on how the Trappist tradition addresses social ills, personal plights, and the climate crisis only scratch the surface of how this listening manifested itself throughout my stays.

Yes, I was able to learn about each community, its history, and especially its approach to the labor of brewing, but the internalization of *Obsculta* went beyond the research material I was able to garner through conversation. It was personally formative as I shifted towards a mentality of allowing the needs of others to come to the fore of my interactions. This led to the realization that there were far more important stories to tell beyond those of the beers that I had been so enamored with. The guests that I interacted with throughout my stays, the monks and their uniqueness both individually and collectively, strangers in the towns I passed through, and my family and students when I returned—each dictating a different type of humility and hospitality in response to their presence. In turn, the noise of the outside world as well as my own internal chaos were suspended.

Much like with the Rule itself, the beer became a vehicle for something greater, merely an entry point. I was in awe of the meticulous, innovative, and responsible approaches that I witnessed in the brewhouses. Care for laborers, care for creation, efficiency, quality, and living up to the values literally imprinted on the labels, these were reinforced in every bottle that I was graciously gifted in the monasteries. Little did I know, these were not instances of the completion of perfection but merely byproducts of its pursuit. The *Ora* of these communities (both in the mystical, spiritual, and liturgical senses but also in their pursuit of social praxis, hospitality, and charity) was subsumed in their *Labora* but also founded it, set its boundaries, and went beyond it. It overflowed the bounds of even the most exquisitely designed Trappist chalices in my guestrooms. It was infectious, it was inspiring, it was humbling.

Alternatives to greed, destructive consumption/production, unfettered individualism, hopelessness, and malaise were as lively in these abbeys as the yeast added to their bottles and equally as encouraging of further development. It is impossible to spend time with these communities without catalyzing change—internally or on a wider scale. I hope to have shown that this type of growth is not just inherent in the monasteries themselves or in the Rule that they follow, but in the endeavors that the brothers undertake. This includes the endeavor most extensively catalogued here, the brewing of beer.

I want to reiterate the number of times that the brothers at various abbeys insisted that the brewing of beer is not a spiritual calling and must be separated from their monastic vocation in the mystical sense. However, I also must be honest in saying that my experiences in retreat, conversation, and observation, such a separation is not entirely possible. Benedict declared that the tools of manual labor in the monasteries are God's very own possessions and thus the outcomes of their use must seem to be endowed with at least a bit of that character.

I fully acknowledge that the oft repeated ethos of "we brew to live not live to brew" is noticeable immediately in these communities, but I for one am glad that this is still their chosen means of supporting themselves. The bread, chocolate, jams, soaps, and even coffins made by Trappists are equally exquisite, but those are discussions for different audiences. This project promised a different type of satiation, one which I hope goes beyond the glass, one which allows me to issue a plea to those that enjoy these beers. Do not miss the opportunity to understand, appreciate, reflect on, and give thanks for the rich heritage that has allowed you that enjoyment. Moreover, as you flip back through these pages, remember that these are not abstract realities, they are living people and vivacious communities that are welcoming and will surprise you in ways you could never imagine. May each pour open you up to contemplation, conversation, and joy. May the beauty in each glass give you hope for living otherwise. And may we dream up and then practice different ways of being in our homes, in our classrooms, in our beer spaces, and in the wider world.

Bibliography

Abbaye Notre-Dame de Saint-Remy. "Home." https://www.abbaye-rochefort.be/fr/
Abbaye Notre-Dame de Scourmont. "Histoire de L'Abbaye." https://www.scourmont.be/vie-de-la-communaute/histoire-de-l-abbaye.html
Abdij Koningshoeven. "Home." https://www.koningshoeven.nl/
Abdij Maria Toevlucht. "History of Our Lady of Refuge." https://abdijmariatoevlucht.nl/en/history/
Ann, Elizabeth, SJW. "Heroes of the Holocaust." *Catholic Heritage Curricula*, August 1st, 2023. https://chcweb.com/wp-content/uploads/2023/09/hhholland.pdf.
Barbry, Eddy. *Van den Grooten Oorlog*. Belgium: Malegijs, 1978.
Bell, David. "'A Holy Familiarity': Prayer and Praying According to Armand-Jean de Rance." *Cistercian Studies Quarterly* 51 (2016) 343–72.
———. "On a Rough Road, Drive Fast: De Rance's Advice to Religious." *Cistercian Studies Quarterly* 56 (2021) 3–21.
Benedict of Nursia. *The Rule of St. Benedict*. Translated by Timothy Fry. Collegeville, MN: Liturgical, 1981.
Bernard of Clairvaux. *Bernard of Clairvaux: Selected Works*. Mahwah, NJ: Paulist, 1987.
Biopolus. "The First Biomakery of the Netherlands is Opened at Koningshoeven Abbey." October 15, 2018. https://www.biopolus.net/2018/10/287/.
Bomans, Godfried. "Bomans in Triplo." https://www.youtube.com/watch?v=3VZVYZabwYk.
———. *Trappistenleven*. Amsterdam: Elseiver, 1976.
Bruner, James, et al. "Brewing Efficacy of Non-Conventional Saccharomyces Non-cerevisiae Yeasts." *Beverages* 7 (2021) 1–15.
Bruun, Mette Birkedal. *The Cambridge Companion to the Cistercian Order*. Cambridge: Cambridge University Press, 2012.
Butler, Jay. "Monastic Revival in France 1815–1848: The Trappistines of Notre-Dame des Gardes and the Trappists of Melleray." Thesis, North Carolina State University, 2020.
BuyWorld. "BuyWorld, Save the Earth by Buying It." https://collectiefeigendom.nl/en/agriculture-nature/buyworld.
Casey, Michael. *Strangers to the City Reflections on the Beliefs and Values of the Rule of Saint Benedict*. Brewster, MA: Paraclete, 2013.
Chappell, Bill. "From Belgium to Piggly Wiggly: U.S. Beer Fans Snatch Up Elusive Ale." *NPR: Food, History, and Culture*, December 12, 2012. https://www.npr.org/sections/thesalt/2012/12/12/167084488/from-belgium-to-piggly-wiggly-u-s-beer-fans-snatch-up-elusive-ale.

Bibliography

Chimay Beer. "@1862 Chimay YouTube Channel." https://www.youtube.com/channel/UCT3MCw_KO4toeo7zwjpNpiQ.

———. "Since 1850." https://chimay.com/us/discover-chimay/.

Chimay-Wartoise Foundation. "Home." https://www.chimaywartoise.be/.

Collins, John. "Michael Carlier: A Contemplative in the Trenches." *The Merton Seasonal* 35 (2010) 24–36.

Darchambeau, Niole. *Les Trappistes de Rochefort: Une Cuisine de Terroir.* Sucy-en-Brie, France: Les Capucines, 2006.

De Achelse Kluis. "Brasserie." https://achelsekluis.be/.

De Clerck, Jean. *A Textbook of Brewing.* London: Chapman & Hall, 1957.

Diamant Groep. "About." https://diamant-groep.nl/.

Fletcher, Janet. *Cheese and Beer.* Kansas City, MO: McMeel Publishing, 2013.

Forman, Janet. "Abbey Roads." *National Geographic Traveler* 30 (2013) 72–78.

———. "A Glorious Secret." *World and I* 10 (2000) 174–84.

Garrett, Jonny. "West is Best—How Westvleteren 12 Accidentally Became the Best Beer in the World." *Belgian Smaak*, November 28, 2024.

Gregg, Stephen A. "Beginning with the *Carta Caritas*." *Cistercian Studies Quarterly* 55 (2020) 409–16.

Grün, Anselm. *Benedict of Nursia: His Message for Today.* Liturgical, 2006.

Hieronymus, Stan. *Brew Like a Monk: Trappist, Abbey and Strong Belgian Ales and How to Brew Them.* Boulder, CO: Brewers Publications, 2005.

Hope, Alan. "The World Is One Trappist Beer Poorer as Abbey Loses Last Monk." *Brussels Times*, January 23, 2021. https://www.brusselstimes.com/150901/the-world-is-one-trappist-beer-poorer-as-abbey-loses-last-monk.

International Trappist Association. "About." https://www.trappist.be/en/about-ita/.

James, Bruno Scott. *Letters of St. Bernard of Clairvaux.* Collegeville, MN: Liturgical, 2003.

Jonveaux, Isabelle. "Monasticism and Ecologism: Between Economic Opportunity and Religious Convictions?" *Religions* 14 (2023) 575–89.

Kardong, Terrence. *Benedict's Rule: A Translation and Commentary.* Collegeville, MN: Liturgical, 2016.

———. *Day by Day with St. Benedict.* Collegeville, MN: Liturgical, 2005.

———. *The Life of St. Benedict by Gregory the Great: Translation and Commentary.* Collegeville, MN: Liturgical, 2009.

Kearney, Breandan. "My First Belgian." *Belgian Smaak*, May 9, 2014. https://www.belgiansmaak.com/westmalle-tripel/.

———. "Once a Trappist—St. Bernardus Brewery in Watou, Belgium." *Good Beer Hunting*, November 30, 2016. https://www.goodbeerhunting.com/blog/2016/11/7/once-a-trappist-st-bernardus-brewery-in-watou-belgium.

———. "One Shareholder—The Trappist Brewery of Westmalle, Belgium." *Good Beer Hunting*, July 12, 2017. https://www.goodbeerhunting.com/blog/2017/6/6/one-shareholder-the-trappist-brewery-of-westmalle-belgium.

Knox, Noelle. "Monks Who Make World's Best Beer Have a Message for USA: Drinking Illegally Imported Brew is Very Un-Trappist." *USA Today*, October 3, 2005.

Krailsheimer, Alban J. "Armand-Jean de Rance: Convert and Reformer." *Cistercian Studies Quarterly* 60 (2025) 23–43.

Laffay, Augustin. "Dom Augustin de Lestrange (1754–1827): The Saga and the Man." *Cistercian Studies Quarterly* 40 (2005) 173–89.

Bibliography

La Trappe Trappist. "Rich History." https://uk.latrappetrappist.com/gb/en/la-trappe-trappist/history.html.

Lauwers, Michel. "Orval, une Bière Unique aux Confins de Trois Cultures." *L'Echo*, May 13, 2006.

Leclercq, Jean. *Bernard of Clairvaux and the Cistercian Spirit*. Kalamazoo, MI: Cistercian Publications, 1976.

———. "Introduction to the Sentences of Bernard of Clairvaux." *Cistercian Studies Quarterly* 46 (2011) 277–304.

Lee-Weitz, Grace. "Meet Orval's Anne-Françoise Pypaert, the First Female Trappist Brewmaster." *Hopculture*, November 29, 2023. https://www.hopculture.com/orval-brewmaster-anne-francoise-pypaert/.

L'Espace Chimay. "Museum Tour." https://chimay.com/espace-chimay/.

Linman, Jonathan. *Holy Conversation: Spirituality for Worship*. Minneapolis: Augsburg Fortress, 2010.

McColman, Carl. *Befriending Silence: Discovering the Gifts of Cistercian Spirituality*. Notre Dame, IN: Ave Maria, 2015.

Merton, Thomas. *The Waters of Siloe*. New York: Houghton Mifflin, 1949.

Miller, John W. "The Only Trappist Brewery in the US is Closing (And IPAs are to Blame)." *America Magazine: The Jesuit Review of Faith and Culture*, May 23, 2022. https://www.americamagazine.org/politics-society/2022/05/23/spencer-trappist-brewery-closes-243040.

———. "The Secret Business Life of Monks." *America Magazine: The Jesuit Review of Faith and Culture* 221 (2019) 40–46.

Mosher, Randy. *Tasting Beer: An Insider's Guide to the World's Greatest Drink*. North Adams, MA: Storey Publishing, 2009.

Musschoot, Dirk. *Belgie Bevrijd: Verteld door Wie er toen Bij Was*. Belgium: Lannoo, 2004.

NextGen Water. "La Trappe Brewery." https://nextgenwater.eu/demonstration-cases/la-trappe/.

Oliver, Garrett. *The Oxford Companion to Beer*. Oxford: Oxford Reference, 2011.

Order of Cistercians of the Strict Observance. *The Cistercian Order of the Strict Observance in the Twentieth Century Vol. 1: From 1892 to the Close of the Second Vatican Council*. Rome: Curia Generalis, 2008.

———. "Who We Are." https://ocso.org/who-we-are/our-structure/.

Orval Brewery. "The Brewery in the History of Orval." https://www.orval.be/en/page/481-the-brewery-in-the-history-of-orval.

Poelmans, Eline, and Jason E. Taylor. "Belgium's Historic Beer Diversity: Should We Raise a Pint to Institutions?" *Journal of Institutional Economics* 15 (2019) 695–713.

Prins Heerlijk. "Home." https://prinsheerlijk.nl/.

Sint Sixtus Abdij. *Golden Book of Signatures of St Sixtus Abbey, Belgium, 1914–1918*. Guestbook.

———. "Home." https://www.koningshoeven.nl/.

Slade, Stephanie. "Booze, Profit, and Prayer: When Europe's Beer-Brewing, Liquor-Distilling Monks Combine Catholicism and Capitalism, The Results are Delicious." *Reason* 50 (2019) 28–35.

Spapens, Paul, et al. *Bier in Alle Eeuwigheid: 125 Jaar Trappistenbrouwerij De Koningshoeven 1884–2009*. Dongen, Netherlands: Stads Foto & Ontwerp, 2009.

Trappistenbrouwerij de Kievit. "Our History." https://zunderttrappist.nl/en/history/.

Bibliography

Trappistes Rochefort. "The Brewery." https://www.trappistes-rochefort.com/en/the-brewery/.

Trappist Westmalle. "Get to Know Our Abbey." https://www.trappistwestmalle.be/en/abbey/.

———. "History of Our Brewery." https://www.trappistwestmalle.be/en/trappist-beer/.

Trappist Westvleteren. "The History of the Brewery." https://www.trappistwestvleteren.be/en/history.

Van Damme, J. B. *Geschiedenis van de Trappistenabdij te Westmalle: 1794–1956*. Antwerp: De Nederlandsche Boekhandel, 1978.

Van de Steen, Jef. *Belgian Trappist and Abbey Beers: Truly Divine*. Tielt, Belgium: Lannoo Publishers, 2018.

Van de Wiel, Anton. "The Trappist Question." *Memory of Tilburg*, February 12, 2011. https://www.geheugenvantilburg.nl/page/13767/de-trappistenkwestie-1.

Van Hecke, Manu. *Geschiedenis Spiritualiteit Bouwen aan de Toekomst*. N.d.: Clauwaert, 2012.

Van Reeth, Bob. "Bob Van Reeth about the Saint-Sixtus Abbey in Westvleteren." *Architectura*. https://architectura.be/nl/nieuws/bob-van-reeth-over-de-sint-sixtusabdij-in-westvleteren/.

Varneux, Jean. "Our Lady of Orval Abbey and Philately." *The Marian Philatelist* 1 (1965) 23–28.

Veilleux, Armand. "A Great Monastic Formator: Dom Anselme Le Bail." *Cistercian Studies Quarterly* 38 (2003) 27–34.

Verstl, Ina. "Trappist Monks Beat Quarry Owner in Water Battle." *Brauwelt International*, May 27, 2021. https://brauwelt.com/en/international-report/europe-russia/643077-trappist-monks-beat-quarry-owner-in-water-battle.

Vincent van Gogh Huis. "History and Building." https://www.vangoghhuis.com/en/historie-gebouw/.

Vollebregt, Rens. "New Problems in the History and Historiography of the Trappist Tradition." Thesis, University College Roosevelt, 2022.

Waddell, Chrysogonus. "Rance and His *Declarationes in Regulam Beati Benedicti*." *Cistercian Studies Quarterly* 44 (2009) 322–66.

Wallace, Caroline, et al. *Trappist Beer Travels, Second Edition: Inside the Breweries of the Monasteries*. Atglen, PA: Schiffer Publishing, 2017.

Westmalle Abbey. "Our History." https://www.trappistwestmalle.be/en/trappist-beer/.

William of Saint-Thierry. *Vita Prima of Bernard of Clairvaux*. Collegeville, MN: Liturgical, 2015.

Index

Abbaye d'Orval, xvi, 31, 123–38
Abbaye Notre-Dame de Scourmont, xvi, 57–76, 98, 108, 143
Abbaye Notre-Dame de Saint-Remy, xvi, 94–104
Abdij Onze Lieve Vrouw van Koningshoeven, xvi, 2, 18–20, 36, 128
Abdij Maria Toevlucht, xvi, 22, 28, 77–93
Abdij van de Trappisten van Westmalle, xvi, 30, 36–56
AB InBev. *See* Stella Artois
Achel, 46, 97
Adriaensens, Jan, 42
A l'Ange Gardien, 124, 136
Alberic, Abbot, 13
Alchemist Brewing, 105
Allagash Brewing, 150
Alsace Strisselspalt hops, 134–35
Amsterdam, 115
Antwerp, 36–37, 41, 110, 115, 121, 126, 142
Ardennes, 94, 98, 124
Arnold of Bonneval, 14
Ariston and Whist Soda Company, 144
Auberge de Poteaupré, 65, 70
Augustine of Hippo, 20, 107
Authentic Trappist Product. *See* International Trappist Association

Basil of Caesarea, XV, 3, 8, 154
Baileux, 66, 70
Bavaria, 59, 141
Bavaria Beers. *See* Swinkels Family Brewery

BeerAdvocate, 114
Beer Temple, xi, 120, 138
Belgian Army, 41, 60, 109, 128
Belgian Independence, 41
Benedictine Order, xv, 1, 5–6, 9, 10, 12–13, 19, 38, 125–26
Benedictine University, xiii, xv
Benedict, Rule of, xv, xvii, 7–12, 22–23, 26, 85, 107, 125
Benedict, Saint, xv, xvii, 1–13, 17–20, 23, 28, 45, 70, 153–58
Berkel-Enschot, 140
Bernard of Clairvaux, xvii, 1–2, 12–18, 20, 27, 60, 95, 127
Bernardus, Dom, 145–46, 153
Bierbrouwerij De Schaapskooi, 139, 141, 145
Bière Forte, 59, 62, 97
Bière Goudronné, 59
Biopolus BioMakery, 150
Blanche, 65, 67
Bleue, xiii–xiv, 65, 68, 74
Bock, 144, 148
Bomans, Godfried, 80
Bottle conditioning, 53, 54, 103, 117, 131, 133, 135, 148
Bottling, 41, 44, 48, 54, 60, 64, 66, 70, 83–84, 90, 99, 103, 112, 116–17, 130, 133, 135, 136, 142–43
Bouteca, Hyacinthe, 58–60
Brabant, 91, 139, 147
Breda, 22, 77
Brettanomyces, 130–31, 135–37

Index

Brewhouse, xvi, 39–43, 48–49, 53, 59–62, 67, 82–83, 94, 99, 107, 112–13, 116, 129, 133, 141–42, 145
Brother Benedikt, 30, 34, 40, 43–56
Brother Christiaan, 28, 33, 81–90
Brother Daniel, 122
Brother Jakobus, 140, 145–53
Brother Joris, 113, 116, 120–21
Brother Jos, 106–7, 116, 121
Brother Theodore, 63–65, 72, 99, 131
Brother Xavier, 31, 123–24, 128–34, 138
Brouwerij Westvleteren. See Westvleteren, brewery
Brussels, 39, 73, 99, 115, 130, 131, 142–43
BuyWorld Foundation, 156

Calvinism, 95
Candi sugar, xiv, 41, 50–51, 54, 65, 71, 74, 103, 135, 149
Carlier, Maxime, 61
Carta Caritatis, 13
Cascade hops, 91, 118
Catholic Social Teaching (CST), 156
Catholic Worker, xv, 121–22
Cellaring, 41, 54, 66, 73, 103, 117, 133, 135
Cent Cinquante (Cinq Cent), 67–68, 75
Centrifuge, 54, 72, 117
Cheese, 32, 58–62, 65–67, 70, 100, 104, 107, 109, 111–12, 129, 133, 138–39, 147
Chocolate, 32, 64, 74, 103, 119, 147, 158
Cilurzo, Vinnie, 137
Citeaux, 2, 13–15
Clerc, Dom, 128
Cluny Abbey, 13
Challenger hops, 118
Chimay brewery, ix, xii, 48, 58–75, 84, 90, 97–99, 101, 130, 133
Chimay, town of, 57, 67, 76,
Collectanea, 61
Craft brewing, xiii, 47–48, 63, 68–69, 89, 99, 116, 137, 142

Dairy, 40, 43, 58–60, 66–67, 79, 108
Dairy cows, 40, 58, 71

Day, Dorothy, xv, 121–22
de Chiny, Arnould, 125
Debaisieux, Dom, 70
De Clerck, Jean, 63–64, 72, 99, 131
Deconinck, Evariste, 111
Decoction mash, 118, 130
de Beer, Franciscus, 140
De Groote, Dom.108
de Harrene, family, 127–28
Deleye, Dom, 110–11
de Lestrang, Augustin, 36–37
de Nelis, Cornelius Franciscus, 37
de Rancé, Armand-Jean, xvii, 1–2, 18–20, 127
de Riquet, Joseph, 58
Dialogues, 3, 6, 9, 12
Diamant Groep, 152
Dingemans malt, 118
Divine Office. *See* Liturgy of the Hours
Dorée, 68, 75
Dry hopping, 130, 134–36
Dubbel, 73, 103, 110, 113, 119, 148, 150
Dubuisson, Dom, 143
Dutch Army, 39, 95

Eighty Year's War, 95–96
Eugenius III, Pope, 14

Fabry, Dom, 96
Fermentation temperature, 64, 66, 119
Flanders, 36–39, 51, 61, 105, 110, 114, 121
Flemish culture, 45, 57, 106, 110, 127, 131
Fondation Chimay-Wartoise, 67, 70,
Francis, Pope, 7, 55
Frech, Karl, 142
French Army, 37, 60, 96–97
French barley, 51,
French Revolution, 37, 96, 127
Foignay, 17
Fontenay, 17
Forges, 59

Gale, 88–92
General Chapter, 13, 16, 20, 93, 95
Geoffrey of Auxerre, 14
German Army, 60, 62, 80, 98, 109, 143,
German hop varietals, 134, 148

Index

Ghent, 128–29
Godfrey IV, 125–26
Golding hops, 102, 118, 134
Goose Island, xiii-xiv, 69, 137
Gospel, 6, 140
Grande Réserve, 65, 69, 74, 90
Gregory the Great, xv, 3, 12
Gregory VII, Pope, 125
Gregory XVI, Pope, 39
Guest House, 56, 94, 106, 108, 123–24, 132

Hainaut, 57–58, 62, 66, 71
Hallertau Mittelfrüh hops, 72, 74, 91, 102, 118, 134–35
Hall, John, xiv, 137
Harding, Abbot, 13–15
Henry IV, Emperor, 125
Heyse, Dom, 112
Hieronymus, Stan, x, 81, 100, 102, 118,
Houben, Caspar, 140–42
Holy Mass, 106, 132, 140
Hombergen, Dom, 82
Hop extract, 72, 135, 147
Hopleaf, xi, 50
Hop pellets, 51–5, 72, 118, 134–35
Hops, 48, 50, 51–52, 56, 72, 74–75, 85, 89, 92, 96, 104, 118–19, 130, 134–35, 147–50
Hops, whole cone, 51, 72, 118, 135
Hospitality, xv–xviii, 2, 11–12, 31, 37, 40, 44, 48, 52–54, 55, 62–63, 80, 86, 107, 113. 120–25, 131–32, 151, 156–57
Humility, xv, 2, 4, 11, 13–16, 19, 26, 105, 122, 154–57

In de Vrede, 108, 110, 113–16
International Trappist Association (ITA), 31–32, 36, 46, 48, 55, 57, 68, 84, 88, 90, 112, 115, 117, 147, 150
Investiture Contest, 125–26
Issac, Dom, 146, 149, 153

Jaccard Room, 132
James, Bruno Scott, 17
Jan Linders grocery, 115
Jansen, Cornelius, 20

Jesus Christ, 4, 6, 11–12, 16, 154, 129, 132
Jordan, Kim, xiv
Jourdain, Jean-Baptiste, 58, 108
Judong, Anselme, 97
Jules Ferry Laws, 78, 140

Katholieke Universiteit Leuven (KU Leuven), xvi, 63, 70, 72, 97, 99, 105, 117, 131, 133, 144
Kegging, 53–54, 73, 90, 133
Keinemans, Constant, 33, 82, 88–92
Kempeneers, Dositheus, 108
Kievet, 92
Knights Templar, 14
Koningshoeven, town of, 78, 139–40,
Kuypers, Dom, 97

Laaber, Isidorus, 141
Labels, 62, 64–65, 83, 87, 92, 112, 117, 145, 157
Lacaes, Dom, 78, 140
Laffler, John, x
Lager, 26, 59, 141, 145, 147
Lagering, 33–34, 72, 83, 90, 102, 116–17, 135, 141
La Trappe abbey. *See* Abdij Onze Lieve Vrouw van Koningshoeven
La Trappe Blond, 143, 146, 148, 150
La Trappe Bockbier, 148
La Trappe Brewery, xvi, 35, 78, 84, 139–53
La Trappe Dubbel, 148
La Trappe Epos, 152
La Trappe Isid'or, 148
La Trappe Nillis, 148
La Trappe Oak Aged, 149
La Trappe Puur, 146
La Trappe Quadrupel, 149, 150
La Trappe Tripel, 149
La Trappe Witte Trappist, 148
La Valle-Sainte, 37
Le Bail, Dom, 60–63
Lebesch, Jeff, xiv
Lectio Divina, 10, 19, 31, 121, 157
Le Moine Soldat, 60, 62
Leo XIII, Pope, 20, 143
Leopold I, 39, 59, 108
L'Espace Chimay, 70

Index

Lhoist Mining Company, 101
Liturgy of the Hours, xiii–xvi, 9, 19, 28, 34, 56, 80, 84–85, 100–101, 111, 120, 124, 145, 155–57
Löb siblings, 143
Lorraine, 125–26

Mabillon, Jean, 19
Made Blue Foundation, 150
Maine Beer Company, 150
Maisonneuve, Dom, 95
Malle, 36–37, 41
Malt, 41, 48–51, 60, 64–65, 74–75, 85, 89, 91–92, 102–3, 112, 118–19, 134–35, 142, 148–50
Map Room, xi, 68
Marre, Dom, 142
Martinus, Dom, 39, 58
Mary the Mother of Jesus, 16, 22, 78, 126, 129, 132, 139
Matilda beer, xiv, 137
Matilda of Tuscany, 125–26
Merchant du Vin, 138
Merton, Thomas, 7, 61–62
Merveille, 99
Metropolitan Brewing, xiii, xv, 25–26
Molesme Abbey, 13
Mosaic hops, 136
Monte Casino, 3, 5–6, 11
Monts-des-Cats, 78, 140, 142

Namur, 94, 98, 129
Napoleon, 38
Nazis, 62, 110, 143
New Belgium, xiii–xiv, 137
Non-alcoholic, 152
Nooit Rust, 37–38, 40, 43
Northern Brewer hops, 118
Nursia, 1–4

Obedience, 11–12, 22, 27, 154
Obsculta, 23, 157
Off Color Brewing, xi
Omega Yeast Labs, 99
Ooms, Edmond, 41
Ora et Labora, xviii, 9, 58, 108, 129, 157
Orval ambassador program, 137
Orval brewery, xiv, 123–24, 129–38
Orval *Classique*, xiv, 129–30, 133–36
Orval Day, 138

Orval, town of, 123–28
Orval *Vert*, 136–37

Palais de l'Agriculture, 129
Pappenheimer, Martin, 130
Part-Gyle method, 117
Pater bier, 46, 60, 68, 75, 91
Pauwels, Manu, 31, 34, 43–44, 47–55
Pères Trappistes, 62, 100
Pitch rate, 90, 119, 131, 135
Poperinge, 105–7, 110, 117–18
Primary fermentation, 33, 41, 53–54, 59, 71–73, 83, 90, 110–12, 116–19, 130–31, 134–35, 141–45
Prins Heerlijk Foundation, 152–53
Procopius Abbey, xv
Prayer, xi, 1–10, 14–15, 37, 44, 56, 93, 126, 128, 139, 145, 155
Première, 59, 64–65, 73, 98
Psalms, 4, 8–10, 45
Primary fermentation. *See* fermentation
Pypaert, Anne-François, 133–37

Quadrupel (Quadruple, Quad), xiv, 47, 74, 114, 92, 119, 149–50

RateBeer, 114
Refectory beer, 48, 91, 97, 100, 110, 136
Richebé, Dom, 142
Robert, Dom, 13
Rochefort 6 beer, 100, 103
Rochefort 8 beer, 100, 103
Rochefort 10 beer, 100, 103
Rochefort brewery, 94, 98–104
Rochefort, town of, 94–98
Rochefort Triple Extra, 103–4
Rock, Jean Marie, 133, 137
Rome, 3–5, 11, 150
Rouge, 64–65, 68, 74
Rule. *See* Benedict, Rule of
Russian River Brewing, 105, 114, 137, 150

Saaz hops, 91
Saccharomyces, 131
Sas, Thomas, 42
Scholastica, Saint, 2
Schuurmans, Dom, 81
Schweykart, Dom, 140–41

Index

Secondary fermentation, 69, 102, 130–31, 135, 137
Selves, Sandrine, 72
Seny, Victor, 97
Seynaeve, Dom, 111
Sierra Nevada Brewing Company, xiii, 150
Silence, xv–xviii, 2, 8–11, 24–35, 66, 111, 114, 144, 149
Sint-Sixtusabdij, xvi, 34, 58, 105–20
Slaghmuylder, brewery, 42
Solar panels, 55, 139, 151
Spécial Noël, 64
Spencer Brewing, 46–47, 108
Stability, 6, 11, 50, 63, 67, 71, 82, 85, 88, 108, 115, 125, 153
St. Bernardus, brewery, 111–13
StellaArtois, 44, 63, 144, 146
Step infusion mashing, 71, 102, 117, 130
St. Joseph's Abbey, 46, 108
Subiaco, 4–5
Superbier, 42, 144
Sustainability, xv, xviii, 9, 18–21, 32, 40, 43, 46–47, 55, 95, 98, 115, 127, 150, 153
Swinkels Family Brewery, 147
Szafranski, Mathieu, 111

Thirty Year's War, 96
Three Floyds Brewing, 105
Tilburg, 78, 139–42, 146, 153
Tomahawk hops, 134
Trappisten Brouwerij De Kievit. See Zundert Brewery
Treehouse Brewing, 105
Tres-Fontaines, 17
Trois-Fontaines, 127
Trillium Brewing, 47
Tripel, 34, 42, 49–54, 65, 68, 75, 88, 105, 145, 149
Two Brothers Brewing, xiii
Tynt Meadow, 150

Untappd, 26, 51, 114

Vaes, Henri, 128–30
Van der Cruyssen, Albert, 128–29
van Dijk, Dom, 144
van Dorth, Gerard, 146

Van Hoorne, Leon, 142
Van Langendonck, Franciscus, 107
Van Gogh, Vincent, 77
Van Hecke, Dom, 120–22
Van Hofstraeten, Lieven, 42, 52
Van Huele, John, 130, 135
Van Kalken, Dom, 81
Van Reeth, Bob, 121
Van Zande, Honoré, 130
Veilleux, Dom, 61, 69
Verbruggen, Dom, 79, 141–43
Verhelle, Dom, 108
Verlinden, Hendrick, 42
Vermeiren, Dom, 147
Virgin Mary. *See* Mary the mother of Jesus
Vita Prima, 14–15

Water, 43, 50, 55–56, 59, 65, 71, 84, 89–91, 101–2, 117–18, 126–27, 134, 147, 150–52
Watou, 111
Westmalle abbey. *See* Abdij van de Trappisten van Westmalle
Westmalle brewery, 31, 33–34, 39–56
Westmalle Dubbel, 34, 41, 49–54, 68
Westmalle Duo, 49–50.
Westmalle Extra, 34, 48–49, 54
Westmalle Tripel, 34, 42, 49–54
Westmalle Trip-Trap, 50
Westvleteren abbey. *See* Sint-Sixtusabdij
Westvleteren, town of, 105–7
Westvleteren 8 beer, 117, 119
Westvleteren 12 beer, 114, 117, 119, 121
Westvleteren Blond, 113, 119
Westvleteren brewery, 48, 52, 59, 105–21
William of St. Thierry, 14
Witkam, Dom, 81
World War I, 40, 60, 98, 128
World War II, 62, 80, 98, 143
Wuyts, Dom, 108
Wyart, Dom, 140–42

Yakima Valley, 72, 118, 134

Index

Yeast, xiv, 32–34, 42, 48–54, 63–66, 72–75, 89–90, 99, 102–4, 111, 117–21, 130–31, 134–36, 147–49, 157

Zundert 4 beer, 91

Zundert 8 beer, 86, 88, 90–91

Zundert 10 beer, 92

Zundert abbey. *See* Abdij Maria Toevlucht

Zundert, brewery, 77–86, 88–93, 102, 116, 150

Zundert, town of, 22, 77

www.ingramcontent.com/pod-product-compliance
Lightning Source LLC
Chambersburg PA
CBHW020849160426
43192CB00007B/851